The Supreme Court

Fourteenth Edition

To my students

The Supreme Court

Fourteenth Edition

Lawrence Baum

Ohio State University

FOR INFORMATION:

CQ Press

An imprint of SAGE Publications, Inc.

2455 Teller Road

Thousand Oaks, California 91320

E-mail: order@sagepub.com

SAGE Publications Ltd.

1 Oliver's Yard

55 City Road

London EC1Y 1SP

United Kingdom

SAGE Publications India Pvt. Ltd.

B 1/I 1 Mohan Cooperative Industrial Area

Mathura Road, New Delhi 110 044

India

SAGE Publications Asia-Pacific Pte. Ltd.

18 Cross Street #10-10/11/12

China Square Central

Singapore 048423

Library of Congress Cataloging-in-Publication Data

Names: Baum, Lawrence, author.

Title: The Supreme Court / Lawrence Baum, Ohio State University.

Description: Fourteenth edition. | Washington, D.C. : CQ Press, a division of Sage, [2021] | Includes bibliographical references and index.

Identifiers: LCCN 2020040305 | ISBN 9781544390109 (paperback) | ISBN 9781544390123 (epub) | ISBN 9781544390130 (epub) | ISBN 9781544390147 (pdf)

Subjects: LCSH: United States. Supreme Court. | Constitutional law—United States. | Courts of last resort—United States. | Judicial review—United States.

Classification: LCC KF8742 .B35 2021 | DDC 347.73/26—dc23 LC record available at https://lccn.loc.gov/2020040305

Acquisitions Editor: Scott Greenan

Editorial Assistant: Tiara Beatty

Production Editor: Bennie Clark Allen

Copy Editor: Christina West

Typesetter: C&M Digitals (P) Ltd.

Proofreader: Sue Schon

Indexer: Integra

Cover Designer: Glenn Vogel

Marketing Manager: Erica DeLuca

BRIEF CONTENTS

DETAILED CONTENTS

TABLES, FIGURES, AND BOXES

TABLES

FIGURES

BOXES

PREFACE

The United States Supreme Court is not the most powerful institution in American government. But the first two decades of this century underline the Court's considerable impact on politics, public policy, and society. Its rulings on issues such as immigration policy and same-sex marriage have made a substantial difference for many people's lives. Its decisions have affected the continuation and functioning of the health care system that President Obama proposed and Congress enacted in 2010. A series of undramatic decisions has shaped the balance of power between businesses and the people who work for them or buy products and services from them. The Court resolved a contested presidential election at the beginning of the century, and its decisions since then have helped to determine whether Republicans or Democrats win elections for state and national office.

The Supreme Court's impact has hardly gone unnoticed. Indeed, we are in an era of extraordinary attention to the Court. News media of all types cover the Court, collectively putting out a great deal of information about both the Court's decisions and the justices who make them. As a result, the justices have all gained a degree of celebrity. And when the Court allowed people to listen live to its oral arguments for the first time in May 2020, the arguments attracted a sizeable audience even though most arguments are considerably more technical than exciting.

Because the membership of the Court has so much effect on its decisions, the selection of justices is a major focus for both participants in the selection process and observers of the Court. In this century presidents and their advisors have expended considerable energy on their choices of nominees, and every nominee's confirmation has been the subject of a heated battle within and outside the Senate. For their part, people who care about the Court look for hints about possible retirements of justices and closely follow the process of nominating and confirming candidates for the Court. In 2018 the confirmation of Brett Kavanaugh became a national spectacle.

The death of Justice Ruth Bader Ginsburg in September 2020 marked the beginning of another battle. President Trump quickly nominated Amy Coney Barrett to succeed Ginsburg, and the Republican leadership in the Senate set out to secure Barrett's confirmation before the November election. Animosities between the parties over the selection of justices were renewed and intensified, and the nomination and confirmation processes were closely watched by the news media and a good share of the public.

The strong expectation that Barrett would win confirmation, albeit by a close vote, intensified interest in the future of the Court. Throughout the time since the early 1970s, with the exception of one short period, a majority of the justices were best labeled as conservatives. But that majority was slim, and the Court's decisions on some major issues favored liberal policies. Barrett's confirmation would create a 6-3 conservative (and Republican) majority on the Court, likely giving it a stronger leaning in one ideological direction than it had had for more than half a century. As a result, its decisions on issues such as abortion, affirmative action, and regulation of the economy might turn more sharply to the right. That prospect, hailed by some observers and condemned by others, seemed certain to focus even greater attention on the Court and its work in the years to come.

The attention that the Supreme Court receives in the current era has done much to improve understanding of the Court. Yet that understanding remains quite incomplete. The Court is a complicated institution, one that is more difficult to comprehend than the other branches of government. As a result, many people with great interest in American politics—even some who are experts in most aspects of that field—have only limited knowledge of the Court.

I have written this book to provide a better understanding of the Supreme Court. The book is intended to serve as a short but comprehensive guide to the Court, both for readers who already know much about the Court and for those who have a more limited sense of it. I discuss how the Court functions, the work that it does, and the effects of its rulings on politics, government, and the lives of people in the United States. And I probe explanations of the decisions that the Court and its justices make, of actions by other people and groups that affect what the Court does, and of the Court's impact on government and society.

The book discusses several elements of the Court's history, but it focuses primarily on the current era. One key concern is the impact of the most promi- nent attribute of government and politics today, the high level of political polariza- tion in its various forms. I have been struck more and more by how pervasive that impact is, and that realization is reflected in the frequency with which this edition discusses the ways that polarization affects the Court and its members. At the same time, I give considerable attention to other developments that shape the Court in the current era.

The book's first chapter introduces the Court. In this chapter, I discuss the Court's role in general terms, examine its place in the judicial system, analyze the Court as an institution and its personnel, and present a brief summary of its history.

Each of the other chapters deals with an important aspect of the Court. Chapter 2 focuses on the justices: their selection, their backgrounds and careers, and the circumstances under which they leave the Court. Chapter 3 discusses how cases reach the Court through the actions of parties to cases, the lawyers who represent them, interest groups, and the special role of the federal government. The chapter then considers how and why the Court selects the small number of cases that it will fully consider and decide.

Chapter 4 examines decision making in the cases that the Court accepts for full consideration. After outlining the Court's decision-making procedures, I turn to the chapter's primary concern, the factors that influence the Court's choices among alternative decisions and policies. Chapter 5 describes and explains the kinds of issues on which the Court concentrates, the policies it supports, and the extent of its activism in the making of public policy. I give special attention to changes in the Court's role as a policy maker and the sources of those changes. The final chapter examines the ways in which other government policy makers respond to the Court's decisions, as well as the Court's impact on American society as a whole.

The book reflects the very considerable help that many people gave me with earlier editions. This edition was strengthened by suggestions for revision from the reviewers for the Press: Michelle Belco, University of Houston Honors College; Ericka Christensen, Southern Utah University; Hans J. Hacker, Arkansas State University, Jonesboro; and Julie A. Keil, Saginaw Valley State University. In updating information for this edition, I received valuable help from Saul Brenner, Jake Horton, Simon Tam, and Matthew Weisberg. I owe a special debt to Neal Devins, because of all that I have learned about the Court and especially about the impact of political polarization from our collaborations on research.

As always, the professionals at CQ Press and SAGE did much to make my life easier and, more important, to make the book better. I am pleased to thank Scott Greenan, Christina West, Bennie Clark Allen, and Tiara Beatty.

I benefit a great deal from the professional community of scholars who study the courts and American politics. The ideas and findings of their research are incorporated throughout this book, and I learn directly from them as well. Traditional news media and online media such as blogs have both become increasingly valuable sources of information and ideas on the Court, and I have used these sources a great deal. I owe more specific thanks to the talented group of people who have made *SCOTUSblog* an enormously useful place to find information about the Court and to Howard Bashman, whose *How Appealing* blog provides links to a wide array of current sources on the Court. The Supreme Court's staff has made the Court's own website an excellent source of information on cases and decisions, and in doing so it has made the process of gathering material for the book considerably easier.

Throughout the life of this book in its various editions, I have received a great deal of support for my work from Ohio State University and particularly from the political science department at OSU. I am grateful for that support, and I also appreciate all that I have learned from colleagues at the university.

I owe the greatest debt to the students in my classes. The material in this book reflects my experience working with them to help them gain a thorough understanding of the Supreme Court. For their part, my students have added to my own understanding of the Court with the questions they raise and the ideas they offer. In this and other ways, they make teaching a great pleasure.

ABOUT THE AUTHOR

Lawrence Baum is professor emeritus of political science at Ohio State University and holds a doctorate from the University of Wisconsin. A widely recognized authority on the court system, Baum is the author of *The Company They Keep: How Partisan Divisions Came to the Supreme Court* (2019) (with Neal Devins), *Ideology in the Supreme Court* (2017), *The Battle for the Court* (2017) (with David Klein and Matthew Streb), *Specializing the Courts* (2011), *Judges and Their Audiences: A Perspective on Judicial Behavior* (2006), and *The Puzzle of Judicial Behavior* (1997), as well as articles on a range of topics related to the courts. He has received the Alumni Award for Distinguished Teaching and the University Distinguished Scholar Award at Ohio State University, as well as the Lifetime Achievement Award from the Law and Courts Section of the American Political Science Association.

CHAPTER ONE

THE COURT

I n the current era, the Supreme Court reaches full decisions in an average of fewer than eighty cases a year. But in those cases, the Court addresses some of the most important and controversial issues in the United States. The decisions it reaches on those issues sometimes have a powerful impact on government, politics, and society. Thus the enormous attention that the Court receives is fully justified, and there is good reason to gain an understanding of the Court.

In this book, I try to contribute to that understanding. Who serves on the Court, and how do they get there? What determines which cases and issues the Court decides? In resolving the cases before it, how does the Court choose between alternative decisions? In what policy areas does the Court play an active role, and what kinds of policies does it make? Finally, what happens to the Court's decisions after they are handed down, and what impact do those decisions have?

Each of these sets of questions is the subject of a chapter in the book. As I focus on each question, I seek to show not only what happens in and around the Court but also why things work the way they do. This first chapter is an introduction to the Court, providing background for the chapters that follow.

A PERSPECTIVE ON THE COURT

The Supreme Court is a complicated institution in some important ways, so it is useful to begin by considering some important attributes of the Court.

The Court and the World Around It

The Supreme Court has considerable insulation from the rest of government and society. The key source of that insulation is the justices' life terms, which give them some freedom to chart their own course without concern about the potential reactions of political leaders and voters.

Individually and collectively, the justices have adopted other practices that help them to maintain distance from the outside world. Litigants and their lawyers cannot make arguments to individual justices in person; rather, they are limited to written briefs and formal oral presentations to the Court as a whole. In contrast with Congress, the Court's collective deliberations over cases are held in private. There are relatively few leaks of information about the Court's decision-making process, though leaks about the positions of key justices in some major decisions have occurred in recent years.[1] The justices have not allowed their oral arguments to be televised despite pressure from members of Congress and others to do so. Indeed, in response to the coronavirus pandemic in 2020, the justices chose to hear arguments by telephone rather than through video links.

But the Court's insulation is far from total. One reason is that people in government, politics, and society as a whole have a strong interest in what the Court decides. This interest underlies the political battles that arise when a new justice is to be appointed. It is also reflected in the efforts of interest groups to bring cases to the Court and to make convincing arguments for their positions in those and other cases. An array of people lobby the Court indirectly with statements and commentaries about pending cases. Presidents and members of Congress sometimes try to put direct pressure on the justices by threatening adverse action such as eliminating the Court's power to hear certain kinds of cases.

The justices might simply shut out the world around them when they decide cases, but in practice that is impossible. For one thing, they may worry about negative reactions to their decisions. Justices frequently refer to the need to maintain the Court's "legitimacy" with the general public in order to gain acceptance of their decisions. And because justices are human beings, they care about how they are viewed by people outside the Court, especially the sets of people who are most important to them.

More fundamentally, justices' own views are shaped by what is going on in the outside world. For instance, justices could hardly be immune to the heightened concern about terrorism that developed in 2001. And social movements, such as the ongoing campaigns for racial equality and women's rights, change opinion in the Court just as they do in other segments of society.

Even if the justices were completely insulated from the rest of government and society when they made decisions, the outside world would still have a very substantial influence on what the Court does and what impact it has. The power of presidents to select justices fundamentally shapes the Court, and the set of cases brought to the Court determines what kinds of issues the justices can address. After the Court reaches its decisions, the consequences of those decisions depend heavily on the reactions of other policy makers and sometimes the reactions of people outside government.

The Court still stands out for its autonomy: far more than most other people in government, the justices are free to take the actions that they want to take. But one central theme of this book is that a full understanding of the Court requires close attention to the activities and impact of people and institutions outside the Court.

Law, Policy, and Politics

The Supreme Court, of course, is a court—the highest court in the federal judicial system. Like other courts, it has jurisdiction to hear and decide certain kinds of cases. And like other courts, it can decide legal issues only in cases that are brought to it.

As a court, the Supreme Court makes decisions within a legal framework. Congress writes new law, but the Court interprets existing law. The Court justifies its rulings on the basis of its reading of the law, usually a provision of the Constitution or a statute enacted by Congress.

In interpreting the law, however, the Court inevitably makes public policy as well. In *Apple Inc. v. Pepper* (2019), the Court ruled that iPhone owners who bought apps through Apple's App Store could sue the company by alleging that it engaged in monopolistic practices. In reaching this decision, the Court was choosing one interpretation of Section 4 of the Clayton Antitrust Act, enacted by Congress in 1914. But it was also choosing a position on antitrust policy, a position that favored consumers over businesses on one issue in that field. Taken together, the Court's decisions in antitrust law powerfully shape antitrust policy. The same is true of its decisions in other fields such as civil rights, environmental protection, and criminal procedure.

Some of the Court's decisions have a direct impact on electoral politics. Its 2019 rulings on partisan gerrymandering of legislative seats and on inclusion of a question about a person's citizenship in the national census had potentially significant effects on the electoral success of the Republican and Democratic parties.[2] One of its decisions ensured that President Richard Nixon would leave office in 1974, and another ensured that George W. Bush would become president in 2001.[3] Other decisions have indirect but powerful effects on politics. *Roe v. Wade* (1973) has spurred political action and shaped partisan politics for half a century. The series of Supreme Court decisions on the health care law sponsored by President Barack Obama has helped set the terms of debates between the parties.[4]

For some people in the legal community, the most important aspect of Supreme Court decisions is how, and how well, they interpret the law. On the whole, however, the Court's audiences care about its decisions because of their impact on policy and politics. Presidents and senators sometimes talk about nominees to the Court in terms of their legal philosophies, but their primary concern is whether their votes and opinions are likely to favor liberal policies and Democrats or conservative policies and Republicans.

What about the justices themselves? When justices talk about their work, especially when they testify at their Senate confirmation hearings, they usually emphasize that their job is simply to interpret the law. The opinions they write analyze cases primarily in terms of their legal merits. Indeed, the goal of reaching good interpretations of the law almost surely is an important element in their decision making.

But even more surely, the justices' views about what constitutes good policy strongly affect their choices. That effect is unavoidable for two reasons. First, in the cases that the Court decides, it is often quite uncertain which of the alternative decisions that are available to the justices constitutes the best interpretation of the law. As a result, other considerations must come into play. Second, people who become justices have developed strong views about an array of policy questions: they are unlikely to be neutral on issues such as government regulation of abortion or protection of the environment. Because of those conditions, it is not surprising that justices' disagreements in cases often mirror differences in their ideological positions.

Like other people who are interested in politics and government, most if not all justices have partisan loyalties and feelings. Those feelings may be especially strong in an era of bitter rivalry between Republicans and Democrats. And it might be that justices' partisan views affect their positions in certain cases alongside their concerns with making good law and good policy. This motivation and others that may shape the justices' votes and opinions are another central concern of this book.

THE COURT IN THE JUDICIAL SYSTEM

Because the Supreme Court is part of a court system, its place in that system structures its role by determining what cases it can hear and the routes those cases take.

State and Federal Court Systems

The United States has a federal court system and a separate court system for each state. Federal courts can hear only those cases that Congress has put under their jurisdiction. Nearly all of the federal courts' jurisdiction falls into three categories.

First are the criminal and civil cases that arise under federal laws, including the Constitution. All prosecutions for federal crimes are brought to federal court. Some types of civil cases based on federal law, such as those involving antitrust and bankruptcy, must go to federal court. Other types can go to either federal or state court, but most are brought to federal court.

Second are cases to which the U.S. government is a party. When the federal government brings a lawsuit, it nearly always does so in federal court. When someone sues the federal government, the case must go to federal court.

Third are civil cases involving citizens of different states in which the amount of money in question is more than $75,000. If this condition is met, either party may bring the case to federal court. If a citizen of New Jersey sues a citizen of Texas for $100,000 for injuries from an auto accident, the plaintiff (the New Jersey resident) might bring the case to federal court, or the defendant (the Texan) might have the case "removed" from state court to federal court. If neither does so, the case will be heard in state court—generally in the state where the accident occurred or the defendant lives.

Only a small proportion of all court cases fit in any of those categories. The most common kinds of cases—criminal prosecutions, personal injury suits, divorces, actions to collect debts—typically are heard in state court. The courts of a single populous state such as Illinois or Florida hear far more cases than the federal courts across the country. However, federal cases are more likely than state cases to raise major issues of public policy.

State court systems vary considerably in their structure, but some general patterns exist (see Figure 1-1). Each state system has courts that are primarily trial courts, which hear cases initially as they enter the court system, and courts that are primarily appellate courts, which review lower-court decisions that are appealed to them. Most

Figure 1-1 The Most Common State Court Structures

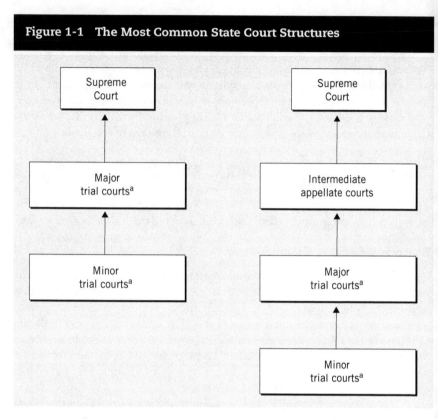

Note: Arrows indicate the most common routes of appeals.

a. In many states, major trial courts or minor trial courts (or both) are composed of two or more different sets of courts. For instance, New York has several types of minor trial courts.

states have two sets of trial courts, one to handle major cases and the other to deal with minor cases. Major criminal cases usually concern what the law defines as felonies. Major civil cases are generally those involving large sums of money. Most often, appeals from decisions of minor trial courts are heard by major trial courts.

Appellate courts are structured in two ways. Ten states, mostly with small populations, have a single appellate court—usually called the state supreme court. All appeals from major trial courts go to this supreme court. The other forty states have intermediate appellate courts below the state supreme court. These intermediate courts initially hear most appeals from major trial courts. In those states, supreme courts have discretionary jurisdiction over most challenges to the decisions of intermediate courts. Discretionary jurisdiction means that a court can choose which cases to hear; cases that a court is required to hear fall under its mandatory jurisdiction.

The structure of federal courts is shown in Figure 1-2. At the base of the federal court system are the federal district courts. The United States has ninety-four

Figure 1-2 Basic Structure of the Federal Court System

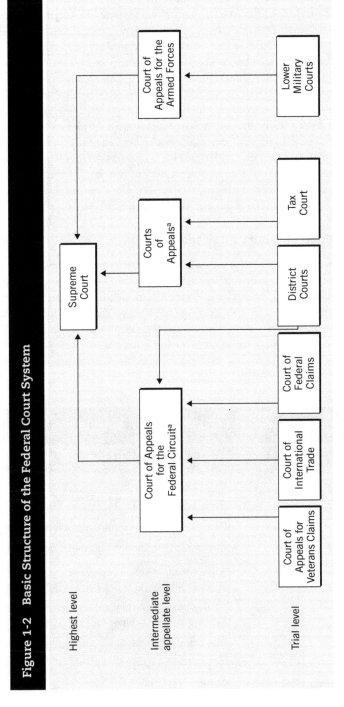

Note: Arrows indicate the most common routes of appeals. Some specialized courts of minor importance are excluded.

a. These courts also hear appeals from administrative agencies.

district courts. Each state has between one and four district courts, and there is a district court in the District of Columbia and in some U.S. territories such as Puerto Rico and Guam. District courts hear all federal cases at the trial level, with the exception of a few types of cases that are heard in specialized courts.

Above the district courts are the twelve courts of appeals, each of which hears appeals in one of the federal judicial circuits. The District of Columbia constitutes one circuit; each of the other eleven circuits covers three or more states. The Second Circuit, for example, includes Connecticut, New York, and Vermont. Appeals from the district courts in one circuit generally go to the court of appeals for that circuit, along with appeals from the Tax Court and from some administrative agencies. Patent cases and some claims against the federal government go from the district courts to the specialized Court of Appeals for the Federal Circuit, as do appeals from three specialized trial courts. The Court of Appeals for the Armed Forces hears cases from lower courts in the military system.

The Supreme Court's Jurisdiction

The Supreme Court stands at the top of the federal judicial system. The Court has two types of jurisdiction, summarized in Table 1-1. First is the Court's original jurisdiction: the Constitution gives the Court jurisdiction over a few categories of cases as a trial court, so these cases may be brought directly to the Court without going through lower courts. The Court's original jurisdiction includes some cases to which a state is a party and cases involving foreign diplomatic personnel.

Under federal statutes, most cases within the Court's original jurisdiction can be heard alternatively by a district court. The exception is lawsuits between two

Table 1-1 Summary of Supreme Court Jurisdiction	
Types of jurisdiction	**Categories of cases**
Original	Disputes between states
	Some types of cases brought by a state
	Disputes between a state and the federal government
	Cases involving foreign diplomatic personnel
Appellate[a]	All decisions of federal courts of appeals and specialized federal appellate courts
	All decisions of the highest state court with jurisdiction over a case, concerning issues of federal law
	Decisions of special three-judge federal district courts (mandatory)

a. Some minor categories are not listed.

states, which can be heard only by the Supreme Court, and this category accounts for the preponderance of cases that the Court decides under its original jurisdiction. Some disputes between states have involved disagreements about state borders, and water rights have become a common issue in recent decades. The Court frequently refuses to hear cases that are brought under its original jurisdiction. In *Arizona v. California* (2020), Justices Clarence Thomas and Samuel Alito questioned that practice as it applies to the lawsuits between states that only the Court can hear. Altogether, the Court has decided fewer than 200 original jurisdiction cases in its history. When the Court does accept a case under its original jurisdiction, it ordinarily appoints a "special master" to gather facts and propose a decision to the Court.

The disputes that produce original cases can take a long time to resolve. The Court heard oral argument in a conflict over water rights between New Mexico and Texas in 2020. An earlier version of that conflict in the same case was brought to the Court in 1974.[5]

All the other cases that come to the Court are based on its appellate jurisdiction. Under its appellate jurisdiction, the Court hears cases brought by parties that are dissatisfied with the lower-court decisions in their cases. Within the federal court system such cases can come from the federal courts of appeals and from the two specialized appellate courts. The Court can hear a case before a court of appeals has reached judgment in the case. It seldom does so. But in *Department of Commerce v. New York* (2019), a case about the addition of a citizenship question to

▶ **Photo 1-1** The Pecos River. Lawsuits between states fall under the Supreme Court's original jurisdiction, and the Court has dealt with a suit between New Mexico and Texas over use of water from the Pecos for several decades.

the 2020 Census, the Court accepted the federal government's argument that the Court should hear the case before the court of appeals acted in order to resolve the issue before census forms had to be printed. Cases also come to the Court directly from special three-judge district courts that are set up to decide specific cases. Most of these cases involve voting and election issues.

State cases can come to the Supreme Court after decisions by state supreme courts if they involve claims based on federal law, including the Constitution. If a state supreme court chooses not to hear a case, the losing party can then go to the Supreme Court. As shown in Table 1-2, a substantial proportion of both the cases brought to the Court and the cases it hears came from state courts, but most originated in federal courts.

The rule under which state cases come to the Supreme Court may be confusing, because cases based on federal law ordinarily start in federal court. But cases brought to state courts on the basis of state law sometimes contain issues of federal law as well. This situation is common in criminal cases. A person accused of burglary under state law will be tried in a state court. During the state court proceedings, the defendant may argue that the police violated rights protected by the U.S. Constitution during a search. The case eventually can be brought to the Supreme Court on that issue. If it is, the Court will have the power to rule only on the federal issue, not on the issues of state law involved in the case. Thus, the Court cannot rule on whether the defendant actually committed the burglary.

Table 1-2 Sources of Supreme Court Cases in Recent Periods (in percentages)

	Federal courts			State courts
	Courts of appeals	District courts	Specialized courts	State courts
Cases brought to the Court[a]	73	0	2	25
Cases decided on the merits[b]	77	2	6	15

Source: Data on cases decided on the merits are from SCOTUSblog, http://www.scotusblog.com/reference/stat-pack.

Note: Original jurisdiction cases are not included. Non-federal courts of the District of Columbia and of U.S. territories are treated as state courts. For cases heard by the Court, the rules for inclusion of cases are described in the source cited above.

a. Cases in which the Court issued rulings on petitions for hearings, October 7, 2019 (1,445 cases).

b. Cases that the Court decided on the merits, ruling on the issue or issues in the case, including summary reversals, 2018 and 2019 terms (142 cases).

Nearly all cases brought to the Court under its appellate jurisdiction also are under its discretionary jurisdiction, so it can choose whether or not to hear them. With occasional exceptions discretionary cases come to the Court in the form of petitions for a writ of certiorari, a writ through which the Court calls up a case from a lower court for a decision "on the merits"—that is, ruling on the legal issue or issues in the case. The cases that the Court is required to hear are called appeals. In a series of steps culminating in 1988, Congress converted the Court's jurisdiction from mostly mandatory to almost entirely discretionary. Today, appeals can be brought to the Court in only the few cases that come directly from three-judge district courts.

The Supreme Court hears only a tiny fraction of the cases brought to federal and state courts. As a result, courts other than the Supreme Court have ample opportunities to make law and policy on their own. Moreover, their decisions help determine the ultimate impact of the Court's policies. Important though it is, the Supreme Court certainly is not the only court that matters.

THE COURT AS AN INSTITUTION

Several attributes of the Supreme Court shape the Court as an institution. Especially important are the activities of justices and the people who help them do their work.

The Court's Building and Grounds

The Supreme Court did not move into its own building until 1935. In its first decade, the Court met first in New York and then in Philadelphia. The Court moved to Washington, D.C., with the rest of the federal government at the beginning of the nineteenth century. For the next 130 years, it sat in the Capitol, a tenant of Congress. In 1808, during renovation work in the Capitol, the Court's hearings were moved temporarily to a nearby tavern.[6]

The Court's accommodations in the Capitol were not entirely adequate. Among other things, the lack of office space meant that justices did most of their work at home. After an intensive lobbying effort by Chief Justice William Howard Taft, Congress appropriated money for the Supreme Court building in 1929. The five-story structure occupies a full square block across the street from the Capitol. Because the primary material in the impressive building is marble, it has been called a "marble palace."

The building houses all the Court's facilities. Formal sessions are held in the courtroom on the first floor. Behind the courtroom is the conference room, where the justices meet to discuss cases. Also near the courtroom are the chambers that contain offices for the associate justices and their staffs. The chief justice's chambers are attached to the conference room. On the top floor is a basketball court, "the highest court in the land," that law clerks and some justices use during breaks from their official duties.[7]

Parts of the building are open to the general public. The building has been closed to the public twice, after anthrax spores were discovered in the Court's mail warehouse at another site in 2001 and during the coronavirus pandemic beginning in March 2020. During that second period, the justices and many other court personnel worked at other locations. Meanwhile, Justice Ruth Bader Ginsburg regularly came to the "largely empty courthouse" for her widely publicized workouts with her personal trainer.[8]

People who want to attract attention to their causes sometimes use the area around the Court building to publicize those causes. In 1983 the Court struck down the part of a federal statute that prohibited an array of such activities on the sidewalks around the building. But in 2015 a federal court of appeals upheld the provision of the statute that prohibited the same activities in the building and on the Court grounds, and the Court made that decision final by choosing not to hear the case.[9] Occasionally people are arrested for violating that statute, and protesters who disrupted two proceedings in the courtroom in 2015 were also arrested.

Personnel: The Justices

Under the Constitution, Supreme Court justices are nominated by the president and confirmed by the Senate. If a nominee is confirmed, the president then appoints the successful nominee to the Court. When the chief justice leaves the Court, the president can elevate an associate justice to chief and also appoint a new associate justice (as President Ronald Reagan did in 1986 when he named William Rehnquist as chief justice) or appoint a chief justice from outside the Court (as President George W. Bush did in 2005 when he chose John Roberts).

By long-established Senate practice, a simple majority is required for confirmation. But a supermajority was required to end a filibuster and thus allow a vote on a nomination until Senate rules were changed in 2017. The Constitution says that justices will hold office "during good behavior"—that is, for life unless they relinquish their posts voluntarily or they are removed through impeachment proceedings. Beyond these basic rules, questions such as the number of justices, their qualifications, and their duties have been settled by federal statutes and by tradition.

Congress has imposed some ethical rules such as financial reporting requirements on federal judges other than Supreme Court justices. One unresolved question is whether Congress has power to impose those rules on the justices. In any event, justices are not required to adhere to the Code of Conduct that the federal Judicial Conference has established for lower-court judges. But justices adhere to the financial reporting requirements voluntarily, and they have said that they also follow the Code of Conduct.

The Court's exemption from ethical rules mandated by Congress played the central role in the resolution of complaints of misconduct brought against Justice Brett Kavanaugh in 2018, complaints that were based on his testimony at his confirmation hearings for the Supreme Court and at earlier confirmation hearings for the court of appeals. A committee of the federal Judicial Conference ruled that once

Kavanaugh had joined the Supreme Court, he was no longer subject to the federal statute governing judicial conduct.[10]

The Constitution says nothing about the number of justices. The Judiciary Act of 1789 provided for six justices. Later statutes changed the number successively to five, six, seven, nine, ten, seven, and nine. The changes were made in part to accommodate the justices' duties in the lower federal courts and in part to serve partisan and policy goals of the president and Congress. The most recent change to nine members was made in 1869, and that number has become firmly established. The most serious effort to change that number, President Franklin Roosevelt's proposal to increase the number of justices, failed in 1937.

In 2020, each associate justice received an annual salary of $265,600, and the chief justice received $277,700. There are limits on the amount of outside income that justices can receive from activities such as teaching (about $29,600 in 2020), but there are no limits on income from books. Clarence Thomas earned about $1.5 million from his memoir and Sonia Sotomayor more than $3 million from hers. Some of the current justices, including John Roberts and Stephen Breyer, were wealthy when they came to the Court. Thomas and Sotomayor were far from wealthy, and their book earnings improved their financial status enormously.[11]

Personnel: Law Clerks and Other Support Staff

A staff of about 500 people, serving in several units, supports the justices. Most of the staff members carry out custodial and police functions under the supervision of the marshal of the Court. The clerk of the Court handles the clerical processing of all the cases that come to the Court. The reporter of decisions supervises preparation of the official record of the Court's decisions, the *United States Reports*. The librarian is in charge of the libraries in the Supreme Court building. The Court's public information office responds to inquiries and distributes information about the Court.

Of all the members of the support staff, the law clerks have the most direct effect on the Court's decisions.[12] Associate justices may employ four clerks each, the chief justice five (though the chief almost always hires only four). A retired justice has one clerk, who often works primarily with one of the sitting justices. Clerks almost always serve for only one year. The typical clerk is a high-ranked graduate of a prestigious law school. The clerks who were hired to serve sitting justices in the 2016–2020 terms came from two dozen law schools, but more than half had gone to Harvard or Yale.[13] Typically, clerks come to the Supreme Court after clerkships with one or two lower-court judges, most often on the federal courts of appeals. Some clerks in the Court also have experience in law firms, academia, or government. In an era of political polarization there has come to be a strong ideological element in hiring: as a group, law clerks selected by conservative justices are considerably more conservative than those selected by liberal justices. And with the exception of John Roberts, the sets of clerks that each justice chose for the 2018–2020 terms had their prior clerkships overwhelmingly with judges who had been appointed by a president of the same party as the justice's appointing president.[14]

Clerks typically spend much of their time on the petitions for certiorari, reading the case materials and summarizing them for the justices. Clerks also work on cases that have been accepted for decisions on the merits. They analyze case materials and issues, discuss cases with their justices, and sometimes consult with clerks for other justices to help in the process of winning support for opinions and reaching consensus. It appears that all the current justices have their clerks write the first drafts of their opinions.

The extent of law clerks' influence over the Court's decisions is a matter of considerable interest and wide disagreement.[15] Observers who depict the clerks as quite powerful probably underestimate the justices' ability to maintain control over their decisions. Still, the jobs that justices give to their clerks ensure significant influence. Drafting opinions, for instance, allows clerks to shape the content of those opinions, whether or not they seek to do so. The same is true of the other work that clerks do.

After law clerks leave the Court, they are in great demand among law firms that do Supreme Court litigation. Some former law clerks receive a "signing bonus" of as much as $400,000 in addition to substantial salaries. They take a variety of career paths, and many have had distinguished careers as practicing lawyers, law professors, and government officials. Among President Trump's first forty-one nominees to the federal appellate courts, 44 percent had been Supreme Court clerks—including his Supreme Court nominees Neil Gorsuch and Brett Kavanaugh.[16] Alongside John Roberts, Stephen Breyer, and Elena Kagan, Gorsuch and Kavanaugh created a majority of justices who had served as clerks on the Court.

The Court's Schedule

The Court has a regular annual schedule.[17] It holds one term each year, lasting from the first Monday in October until the beginning of the succeeding term a year later. (However, the clerk's office treats terms as starting and ending earlier, when the Court announces its final decisions for a term.) Ordinarily, the Court does nearly all its collective work from late September to late June. This work begins when the justices meet to act on the petitions for hearings that have accumulated during the summer and ends when the Court has issued decisions in all the cases it heard during the term.

Most of the term is divided into sittings of about two weeks, when the Court holds sessions to hear oral arguments in cases and to announce decisions in cases that were argued earlier in the term, and recesses of two weeks or longer. In May and June, the Court ordinarily hears no arguments but holds one or more sessions nearly every week to announce decisions. It issues few decisions early in the term because of the time required after oral arguments to write opinions and reach final positions, and a large minority of all decisions—about 40 percent in the 2018 term—are issued in June. The justices scramble to meet the internal deadline of June 1 to circulate drafts of all majority opinions to their colleagues and to reach final decisions by the end of June. The scramble is especially frenetic for cases argued in April and for the most consequential and controversial cases. It is not surprising that a high proportion of the Court's major decisions are announced in the last few days of the Court's term.

When the Court has reached and announced decisions in all the cases it heard during the term, the summer recess begins. Cases that the Court accepted for hearing but that were not argued during the term are carried over to the next term. In summer, the justices generally spend time away from Washington but continue their work on the petitions for hearings that arrive at the Court. During that time, the Court and individual justices respond to applications for special action. When the justices meet at the end of summer to dispose of the accumulated petitions, the annual cycle begins again.

The pandemic that began in early 2020 led to an extraordinary change in the Court's schedule. The Court postponed the oral arguments it had scheduled for the last two sittings of the 2019 term. It later rescheduled a subset of those arguments for May, setting aside the others for the 2020 term. The May arguments were made by telephone, with live audio available to the public for the first time. The justices also met remotely for their conferences. And the Court departed from its usual practice of holding public sessions to announce decisions, instead simply issuing them in written form. The Court did not finish issuing decisions until July 9, 2020, going past the informal deadline of late June that it almost always meets.

The schedule of weekly activities, like the annual schedule, is fairly regular. During sittings, the Court generally holds sessions on Monday through Wednesday for two weeks and on Monday of the next week. The sessions begin at ten o'clock in the morning. Oral arguments usually are held during each session except on the last Monday of the sitting. They may be preceded by several types of business. On Mondays, the Court announces the filing of its order list, which reports the Court's decisions on petitions for hearing and other actions that were taken at its conference the preceding Friday. On Tuesdays, as well as the last Monday of a sitting, justices announce their opinions in any cases the Court has resolved. In May and June, however, opinions may be announced on any day of the week.

The oral arguments consume most of the time during sessions. The usual practice is to allot one hour for arguments in a case. On most argument days, the Court hears two cases.

During sittings, the Court holds two conferences each week. At the Wednesday afternoon conference, justices discuss the cases that were argued on Monday. In a longer conference on Friday, the justices discuss the cases argued on Tuesday and Wednesday, along with petitions for certiorari and other matters the Court must address. In May and June, after oral arguments have ended for the term, the Court has weekly conferences on Thursdays.

The Court also holds a conference on the last Friday of each recess to deal with the continuing flow of business. The remainder of the justices' time during recess periods is devoted to their individual work: study of petitions for hearing and cases scheduled for argument, writing of opinions, and reaction to other justices' opinions. This work continues during the sittings.

WHAT THE JUSTICES DO

Supreme Court justices carry out an array of tasks on the job. Many of them also have busy professional lives outside the Court.

Work in the Court

On a day-to-day basis, the justices do most of their work separately from each other even in ordinary times. But the Court makes its decisions as a collective body. The most visible decisions are rulings on petitions for certiorari and on the merits of cases that the Court accepts. Both types of decisions will be discussed extensively in later chapters. A third type of decision involves responses to applications for various forms of preliminary action in cases. The most important form is a request for the Court to issue or vacate (remove) a stay of action by a lower court or another government body that prevents this action from going into effect.

The justices' work on applications for preliminary action is a partial exception to the rule that the Court acts collectively, an exception that has historical roots. Originally, each justice had the duty of sitting alongside lower-court judges to decide appeals within a federal circuit. This "circuit-riding" duty was arduous, especially in an era when travel was difficult. This duty was gradually cut down and then eliminated in 1891. One vestige remains: an application for preliminary action ordinarily goes first to the justice assigned to the relevant circuit. If the circuit justice rejects an application, it can then be made to a second justice. That justice ordinarily refers it to the whole Court, with five votes required to issue or vacate a stay. With occasional exceptions, stays on important matters are decided by the full Court, usually after referral by the circuit justice (who may issue a temporary stay until the full Court acts).

One common subject of stay requests is the death penalty. The Court is confronted with numerous requests to stay executions or vacate stays of execution, many of which come near the scheduled execution time. The Court grants only a small proportion of requests to stay executions.

Since 2017 the Court has addressed many stay requests that involve issues of significance for politics or policy. Some of these requests have concerned the drawing of legislative districts and other election matters, and the Court ruled on several of these requests in connection with the 2020 elections. Others have concerned abortion, gun regulation, the census, the DACA immigration program (Deferred Action for Childhood Arrivals), building of walls along the Mexican border, military service by transgender individuals, and release of the full report by special counsel Robert Mueller about Russian involvement in the 2016 presidential election. The growth in this kind of stay request has come in part from challenges by the Trump administration to lower-court rulings that blocked administration policies. The Court's grants of a majority of the administration's stay requests have allowed some significant programs to continue.[18]

Justices can dissent from decisions on stays, just as they can from decisions on the merits and on certiorari, and dissents by either liberal or conservative justices are common. The DACA, border wall, and military service cases split the Court along ideological lines, with the Court's four liberals dissenting from the grants of stays that the Trump administration sought.[19] The same lineup appeared in two 2020 decisions that stayed lower-court orders to facilitate absentee voting in Wisconsin and Alabama during the coronavirus pandemic.[20]

Liberal justices have also dissented from denials of stays of execution in several cases. In one 2019 case, Justice Breyer wrote a six-page opinion for the four liberal justices arguing that the Court should not have vacated the stay of execution granted by the lower courts. In a further stage of the same case a month later, Justice Thomas wrote a thirteen-page opinion (joined by Justices Alito and Gorsuch) to refute Breyer's earlier opinion.[21]

In collective decision making, typically every justice participates in every case— nine justices unless there is a vacancy on the Court, as there was in the first week of the 2018 term before Justice Kavanaugh was confirmed. Occasionally a justice's poor health leaves the Court temporarily shorthanded. (But a justice who misses oral argument in a case can still participate in that case, as Justice Ginsburg did in a set of cases in 2019 while she was recovering from surgery.) More often, a justice does not participate in a case because of a perceived conflict of interest. As with financial reporting requirements, it has never been determined whether the federal statute that lists circumstances under which judges should withdraw from cases—recuse themselves—applies to the Court. In any event, the Court leaves this decision to the individual justice.

Across all the cases that are brought to the Court for consideration, recusals are common. In the 2015–2019 terms, the average number of recusals per term was a little under 200. Only a few of those recusals, about four per term, were in cases that the Court accepted for decisions on the merits. Justices seldom explain why they recused in a case, though Justice Sotomayor did so in 2020 when she cited her friendship with one of the litigants.[22] But those reasons usually can be discerned. Most recusals—about three-quarters in the 2019 term—result from a justice's prior involvement in a case as a lower-court judge or in another capacity.[23] The frequency of such recusals declines with justices' tenure on the Court. But Anthony Kennedy recused from a case in 2018 because he had participated in an earlier phase of the case as a court of appeals judge in 1985.[24] Financial conflicts of interest have become relatively uncommon because the justices collectively own fewer stocks in individual companies than they once did. Justice Alito has "unrecused" several times by selling a stock holding after the Court accepted a case.[25]

Controversies about justices' recusal decisions have arisen in recent years, spurred primarily by public statements by justices about matters related to pending or future cases and by interactions between justices and people who have an interest in the outcome of a case.[26] Litigants and others who care about particular cases have sought recusals on those grounds, sometimes in formal requests. In 2020 President Trump said that Justices Ginsburg and Sotomayor "should recuse themselves on all Trump, or Trump related, matters" because, he said, they were biased against him.[27] Justices seldom recuse themselves in response to these initiatives.

The Court may have a tie vote when only eight justices participate in a decision. A tie vote affirms the lower-court decision. If the tie applies to the whole decision, the votes of individual justices are not disclosed and no opinions are written. The justices seek to avoid that result: they may work to achieve a compromise outcome that a majority of the eight justices can accept, and they may set a case for rehearing at a time when a full complement of nine justices becomes available. When the Court was shorthanded for an extended period of time in 2016–2017 because the Senate did not act on President Obama's nomination of Merrick Garland, it appears that the justices tried to avoid tie votes by turning down some cases in which a 4–4 split seemed likely and postponing arguments in others.

Similarly, the lower-court decision in a case is affirmed if the Court cannot reach a quorum of six members. This situation is uncommon. When it occurs, it is usually because a litigant named at least four justices as defendants in a lawsuit, as litigants did in two 2017 cases.[28]

The eight associate justices are equal in formal power. The chief justice is the formal leader of the Court. The chief presides over the Court's conferences and public sessions and assigns the Court's opinion whenever the chief voted with the majority. The chief also supervises administration of the Court with the assistance of committees.

One justice—by tradition, the most junior in seniority—sits with other Court employees on the cafeteria committee. It is a thankless task, because the cafeteria has long been viewed as substandard (a 2010 review in the *Washington Post* said that "this food should be unconstitutional") and colleagues are happy to complain to the junior justice about deficiencies in the cafeteria. After he joined the cafeteria committee in 2018, Justice Kavanaugh succeeded in getting pizza added to the menu. He said that "my legacy is secure. It's fine by me if I'm ever known as the pizza justice." But his initiative went unrewarded: two reviews of the new pizza offering in the news media were decidedly negative.[29]

The chief justice has additional administrative responsibilities as head of the federal court system, a role reflected in the official title of Chief Justice of the United States. In that role, the chief justice appoints judges to administrative committees and some specialized courts. Since 1975, the chief has issued a "Year-End Report on the Federal Judiciary," which usually includes recommendations to Congress about matters such as court budgets and the creation of additional judgeships.[30] Chief Justice Roberts presided over the Senate impeachment trial of President Trump in 2020, as his predecessor William Rehnquist had done in the trial of President Clinton in 1999.

Roberts has served as an advocate for federal judges. In 2007 he met with President George W. Bush and won his support for a bill that would raise judges' salaries.[31] In 2018, after President Trump referred to a district judge who had ruled against one of his administration's immigration policies as an "Obama judge," Roberts issued a statement arguing that federal judges should not be seen as partisans.[32] In 2020, after Senate minority leader Chuck Schumer threatened retaliation against Justices Gorsuch and Kavanaugh for their prospective positions in an abortion case, Roberts condemned Schumer's remarks as "inappropriate" and "dangerous."[33]

▶ **Photo 1-2** Chief Justice John Roberts, presiding over the Senate impeachment trial of President Trump in 2020. The chief justice has administrative duties both within and outside the Court.

Like any other job, the position of Supreme Court justice has both positive and negative elements. There are some major positive elements, including the prestige and status of the position and the satisfaction of shaping legal policy in important ways. Those attractions explain why so many people want to serve on the Court.

The respect that justices receive may be all the more attractive because it is combined with considerable anonymity. One commentator said that justices are in an enviable position: "Almost nobody knows what you look like, but you always get the reservation you want."[34] The desire to maintain that enviable position probably helps to explain justices' aversion to televising of their public sessions. Yet the justices are not immune to the dangers that go along with celebrity: some receive death threats, and they sometimes request protection by security personnel when they travel or make public appearances.

The tasks and responsibilities that go with the job may weigh heavily on justices. That is especially true of new justices, whether or not they have extensive experience on lower courts. Justice Thomas said that "by the end of my first Term, I was very ill," and Justice Breyer said that "I was frightened to death for the first three years."[35]

As some observers of the Court see it, once justices become acclimated their workload is relatively light. These observers point to the relatively small number of cases that the Court now hears and the excellent support that the justices get from their law clerks. One law professor, exaggerating for emphasis, said that in many ways "it's the cushiest job in the world."[36] In contrast, justices often refer to the time their work requires, especially the volume of material they must read in the cases that come to the Court. At least some justices spend very long hours on the job.

In the current era, it seems clear that the satisfactions of serving as a justice out-weigh the burdens of the job. That is clear from the justices' tenure on the Court: in the past half century, no justice has resigned to take another position and only two justices have retired before age seventy.

Activities Outside the Court

Supreme Court justices attract wide interest from lawyers and from other peo-ple who are interested in government and politics. That interest has grown in the current era, in part because of the new media that provide more information about the Court's work and about the justices.

The extent of this interest is striking. Some of the Court's decisions receive extensive coverage in newspapers, television broadcasts, and blogs. Justices are sati-rized in stories and cartoons, and their activities are extensively chronicled. Beyond the news media, individual justices and the Court as a whole have been the topics of many books for a general audience over the years, as well as plays, movies, and even an opera. Antonin Scalia, who sat on the Court from 1986 to 2016, was a folk hero among conservatives. Ruth Bader Ginsburg achieved a similar status among liberals. She is the subject of several books, a widely seen documentary movie, and a theatrical movie in which she was played by Felicity Jones. Justice Ginsburg was also a recurring character on *Saturday Night Live*, played by Kate McKinnon. Merchandise portraying her included several T-shirts, an action figure, and Halloween costumes. Her public appearances often drew large audiences—more than 10,000 people for her 2019 con-versation with a reporter in the Little Rock area.[37] Not surprisingly, late in her career Ginsburg ranked well ahead of any colleague in the numbers of people who could name her as a justice and who chose her as their favorite justice.[38]

Because of this widespread interest in the justices, they have ample opportuni-ties to interact and communicate with people outside the Court. Law schools and an array of groups within and outside the legal profession vie with each other to attract visits from justices. Reporters would be delighted to gain an interview with a justice. Any book by a justice attracts wide attention. According to one legal scholar, "individual Justices have become celebrities akin to the Kardashians."[39]

Justices differ in their use of their opportunities for attention and adulation. David Souter, who served from 1990 to 2009, kept his distance from the news media and sel-dom made public appearances. Most other justices in this century have been more active than Souter but in limited ways, such as speaking with reporters from time to time, making occasional visits to law schools and other legal groups, and participating in other public events and in Washington social life. Justices who write books often make appear-ances and grant interviews to promote those books, as Neil Gorsuch did in 2019.

Some justices have been even more active, embracing their celebrity status and the opportunities it provides. Sandra Day O'Connor and her husband engaged in so much social activity that they hired a person to serve as assistant and social secretary. The assistant reported that "they were out more nights than they were in." Sixteen years after her 1981 appointment, O'Connor achieved her goal of speaking

▶ **Photo 1-3** Felicity Jones as Ruth Bader Ginsburg in the movie "On the Basis of Sex," about Ginsburg's work litigating sex discrimination cases. Ginsburg's celebrity is one indication of the widespread interest in the Court and its members.

in all fifty states.[40] Among the current justices, Sonia Sotomayor makes the most public appearances.[41] Ginsburg visibly enjoyed her folk hero status.[42] She cooperated in creation of the movies about her and some of the books about her. She sometimes spoke out on public issues and talked about cases and issues that the Court addressed.

A year after she joined the Court in 2009, Justice Sotomayor estimated that what a friend called "her celebrity" took up about 40 percent of her time.[43] Sotomayor has written several books, including a best-selling memoir about her life before she became a judge. Many of her personal appearances outside the Court are related to her books. She gives talks that focus primarily on her personal story and efforts to inspire young people in her audiences, rather than the Court and legal issues. Her commitment to encouraging children is reflected in her two appearances on the television show *Sesame Street* in 2012.

In the aggregate, the justices make a great many public appearances—by one incomplete count, a total of 112 appearances in 2019.[44] These appearances are not limited to the summers, when the Court is out of session; justices find time for activities away from the Court throughout the year. Indeed, justices are occasionally absent from the sessions at which decisions are announced because of other activities. At one such session in 2018, only five of the nine justices were present.

Justices often receive awards at their public appearances. Perhaps the most unusual of these awards was for "Small Town Lawyer Made Good," presented to both John Paul Stevens and Antonin Scalia in the 1980s by the lawyers in Poulsbo,

Washington. Neither justice had been a lawyer in anything like a small town. When Stevens was invited to come to Poulsbo to receive his award, he pointed out that he had practiced antitrust law in Chicago. The lawyer who invited him responded, "Justice Stevens, more than most people, you should understand that words have many interpretations. We define a 'small town lawyer' as anyone who practices in a town under 50,000 or any US Supreme Court Justice we can get here."[45]

Box 1-1 illustrates the array of public activities in which justices participate.

BOX 1-1

Examples of Public Activities by Justices in 2019

Participating in the Winter Mock Trial of the Shakespeare Theater Company (Stephen Breyer and Samuel Alito)

Hosting a reception of the Horatio Alger Association (Clarence Thomas)

Speaking at a conference on comparative constitutional approaches to civil liberties (Stephen Breyer)

Participating in a preshow conversation on the musical West Side Story and music, culture, and identity at the Kennedy Center in Washington, D.C. (Sonia Sotomayor)

Delivering the Anderson Lecture at Yale Law School (Elena Kagan)

Receiving an honorary doctorate from Lund University in Sweden (Ruth Bader Ginsburg)

Presiding at the installation of a new Secretary of the Smithsonian Institution (John Roberts)

Co-teaching a study-abroad class of the Antonin Scalia Law School of George Mason University (Brett Kavanaugh)

Speaking at the Federal Bar Association Civics Essay Award Reception (Neil Gorsuch)

Source: Information about justices' appearances was obtained from SCOTUS Map, https://www.scotusmap.com/, and descriptions of the events in the Box are taken or adapted from that site.

HISTORICAL DEVELOPMENTS

This book is concerned primarily with the Supreme Court at present and in the recent past, but I frequently refer to the Court's history in order to provide perspective on the current Court. A brief examination of some major developments in that history will provide background for later chapters.

One key development was a strengthening of the Court as an institution. In its first decade, the Court was not viewed as an important body. Several people rejected offers to serve on the Court, and two justices—one of them Chief Justice John Jay—resigned to take more attractive positions in state government. But John Marshall, chief justice from 1801 to 1835, sought to strengthen the Court's standing. Marshall asserted the Court's power to rule that federal statutes are unconstitutional in his opinion for the Court in *Marbury v. Madison* (1803). A few years later, the Court claimed the same power of judicial review over state acts.

Some of the Marshall Court's actions led to denunciations and threats, including an effort by President Thomas Jefferson to have Congress remove at least one justice through impeachment. Marshall's skill in minimizing confrontations helped to prevent a successful attack on the Court. The other branches of government and the general public gradually accepted the powers that he claimed for the Court. Those powers are challenged from time to time, and the Court is frequently denounced for decisions that critics see as overstepping its proper role. But the Court's position as the ultimate interpreter of federal law, with the power to strike down actions by other government institutions, is firmly established.

The Court has been strengthened in other respects as well.[46] The elimination of the justices' circuit-riding duties in 1891 allowed them to focus on their duties in the Court, and the shift in the Court's jurisdiction from mostly mandatory to nearly all discretionary gave it control over its agenda. The Court's move from the Capitol to its own building in 1935 was an important symbolic step that also improved the justices' working conditions. The gradual growth in the size of the Court's staff, especially the law clerks, has also enhanced the justices' ability to do their work.

A second development has been evolution in the subjects of the Court's work.[47] In the period when the Court had little control over its agenda, the subject matter of its work reflected the cases that came to it. But even then, the justices could emphasize some types of cases over others, especially in their interpretations of the Constitution. After 1925, when the Court gained substantial control over its agenda, the justices had even greater ability to determine what kinds of issues they would address.

In the nineteenth century, up to the Civil War, the primary emphasis was federalism, the division of power between the federal government and the states. That emphasis reflected the heated battles in government and politics over federalism and the justices' efforts to develop constitutional principles relating to the federal–state balance. In the late nineteenth and early twentieth centuries, as government increasingly enacted legislation to regulate economic activity, constitutional challenges to that regulation became the most prominent element of the Court's agenda.

After a confrontation between the Court and President Franklin Roosevelt over decisions that struck down several of Roosevelt's New Deal programs, the Court in 1937 retreated from the limits that it had put on government power to regulate the economy. Beginning in the 1940s, the Court gave greater attention to civil liberties. Since the 1960s, that has been the most prominent area of the Court's work. Its decisions address a wide range of civil liberties issues, among them freedom of expression, privacy, equality, and the procedural rights of criminal defendants.

The Court also plays a significant role in other fields, including government regulation of business and other economic issues.

A third development is change in the legal policies that the Court makes on the issues it addresses. In the eras when the Court focused on federalism and economic regulation, its policies shifted over time. The same has been true of the Court in the second half of the twentieth century and the early twenty-first century.

In the 1960s, the Court became highly liberal, by the usual meaning of that term, in both economic policy and civil liberties. Its civil liberties policies were especially noteworthy, with major rulings expanding defendants' rights, supporting freedom of expression, and favoring racial equality.

A series of appointments by Republican presidents beginning in 1969 shifted the Court's ideological balance. Since the early 1970s, the Court has almost always had a conservative majority, although usually by a small margin. With some major exceptions, the Court's policies have become more conservative on both economic and civil liberties issues. The close balance between liberals and conservatives has raised the stakes in the selection of new justices, and those high stakes have been reflected in battles over Supreme Court appointments.

One constant in the Court's history is that the Court is shaped in powerful ways by events and trends elsewhere in government and society. The most important change in American politics over the last few decades has been a growth in polarization: the views of people in politics have moved toward more extreme positions, the ideological distance between the Republican and Democratic parties has grown considerably, and there is greater hostility between partisan and ideological camps.[48] Polarization has affected the Court in powerful ways, ways that are discussed later in the book. Its most direct effect has been on the nomination and confirmation of justices, which I discuss in the next chapter.

NOTES

1. See Joan Biskupic, "Behind Closed Doors During One of John Roberts' Most Surprising Years on the Supreme Court," *CNN*, July 27, 2020.
2. *Rucho v. Common Cause* (2019); *Department of Commerce v. New York* (2019).
3. These decisions were *United States v. Nixon* (1974) and *Bush v. Gore* (2000).
4. The decisions were *National Federation of Independent Business v. Sebelius* (2012), *King v. Burwell* (2015), and *Zubik v. Burwell* (2016).
5. The history of the case is reflected in its docket sheet, *Texas v. New Mexico*, 22O65. Docket sheets for cases are available at https://www.supremecourt.gov/docket/docket.aspx.
6. Adam Winkler, *We the Corporations: How American Businesses Won Their Civil Rights* (New York: W. W. Norton, 2018), 57.
7. Stanley Kay, "The Highest Court in the Land," *Sports Illustrated*, July 25, 2018, 66–71.
8. Adam Liptak, "With the Supreme Court Sequestered, a Docket of Major Cases Sits Idle," *New York Times*, April 10, 2020, A23.

9. The decisions were *United States v. Grace* (1983) and *Hodge v. Talkin* (2015).

10. *In re: Complaints Under the Judicial Conduct and Disability Act*, Committee on Judicial Conduct and Disability of the Judicial Conference of the United States, C.C.D. No. 19-01 (August 1, 2019).

11. The justices' annual financial disclosure reports list the (very) approximate values of their financial assets at the end of each calendar year. They also list the justices' outside income, including book royalties. The reports for the justices since 2002 are posted at https://www.opensecrets.org/pfds.

12. On law clerks and justices, see Todd C. Peppers and Artemus Ward, eds., *In Chambers: Stories of Supreme Court Law Clerks and Their Justices* (Charlottesville: University of Virginia Press, 2012); and Todd C. Peppers and Clare Cushman, eds., *Of Courtiers and Kings: More Stories of Supreme Court Law Clerks and Their Justices* (Charlottesville: University of Virginia Press, 2015).

13. This figure was calculated from information sheets provided by the Supreme Court and from postings at the blog *Above the Law*, https://abovethelaw.com.

14. The clerks' own ideological positions are analyzed in Adam Bonica, Adam S. Chilton, Jacob Goldin, Kyle Rozema, and Maya Sen, "Measuring Judicial Ideology Using Law Clerk Hiring," *American Law and Economics Review* 19 (April 2017): 143. The party affiliations of lower-court judges for whom the clerks had served were taken from David Lat, "Supreme Court Clerk Hiring Watch: The Complete Clerk Roster for October Term 2018," *Above the Law*, August 2, 2018; and David Lat, "Supreme Court Hiring Watch: The Return of the Tiger Cub," *Above the Law*, June 18, 2019.

15. See Christopher D. Kromphardt, "US Supreme Court Law Clerks as Information Sources," *Journal of Law and Courts* 3 (Fall 2015): 277–304.

16. Tony Mauro, "Former SCOTUS Clerks Dominate the Ranks of Trump's Judicial Nominees," *National Law Journal*, November 21, 2018.

17. The Court's schedule is described in Stephen M. Shapiro, Kenneth S. Geller, Timothy S. Bishop, Edward A. Hartnett, and Dan Himmelfarb, *Supreme Court Practice*, 10th ed. (Arlington, Va.: Bloomberg BNA, 2013), 11–16.

18. Stephen I. Vladeck, "The Solicitor General and the Shadow Docket," *Harvard Law Review* 133 (November 2019): 123–163.

19. These cases were, in order, *In Re United States* (2017), *Trump v. Sierra Club* (2020), and *Trump v. Karnoski* (2019).

20. *Republican National Committee v. Democratic National Committee* (2020); *Merrill v. People First of Alabama* (2020).

21. *Dunn v. Price* (2019); *Price v. Dunn* (2019).

22. Letter from Clerk of Court to Counsel of Record, *Colorado Department of State v. Baca*, 19-518, March 20, 2020, available in the docket sheet for this case.

23. Information on the frequency and sources of recusals was obtained from Fix the Court, "OT19 Recusal Report," July 21, 2020, https://fixthecourt.com/2020/07/ftc-uncovers-reasons-justices-ot19-recusals/.

24. Letter from Clerk of Court to Counsel of Record, *Washington v. United States*, 17-269, available in the docket sheet for this case.

25. Tony Mauro, "Justice Alito 'Unrecuses' for 9th Time, Rejoining Oracle Copyright Case," *National Law Journal*, January 3, 2019.

26. James M. Sample, "Supreme Court Recusal: From Marbury to the Modern Day," *Georgetown Journal of Legal Ethics* 95 (Winter 2013): 95–151.

27. Peter Baker, "Trump Assails Supreme Court in a Startling Turn," *New York Times*, February 26, 2020, A1.

28. *Arunga v. Obama* (2017); *Jaffe v. Roberts* (2017).

29. Becky Krystal, "Supreme Court Cafeteria," *Washington Post*, July 14, 2010, E2; Tim Carman, "Brett Kavanaugh Added Pizza to the Supreme Court Cafeteria, But These Don't Pass the Bar," *Washington Post*, January 30, 2020; Clyde McGrady, "Brett Kavanaugh Brings Pizza to the Supreme Court and It Is Not Good," *Roll Call*, January 14, 2020. The Kavanaugh quotation is from the Carman article.

30. Richard L. Vining Jr. and Teena Wilhelm, "The Chief Justice as Administrative Leader: Explaining Agenda Size," in *The Chief Justice: Appointment and Influence*, ed. David J. Danelski and Artemus Ward (Ann Arbor: University of Michigan Press, 2016), 360.

31. Joan Biskupic, *The Chief: The Life and Turbulent Times of Chief Justice John Roberts* (New York: Basic Books, 2019), 195.

32. Adam Liptak, "Roberts Rebukes Trump for Swipe at 'Obama Judge," *New York Times*, November 22, 2018, A1.

33. Adam Liptak, "Roberts Condemns Schumer's Remarks," *New York Times*, March 5, 2020, A19.

34. Patrick Radden Keefe, "Journeyman: Anthony Bourdain's Moveable Feast," *The New Yorker*, February 13–20, 2017, 62.

35. David Lat, "'The White Man's Burden': A Frank and Funny Interview with Justice Clarence Thomas," *Above the Law*, May 16, 2016; Adam Liptak, "Confident and Assertive, a New Justice in a Hurry," *New York Times*, July 4, 2017, A13.

36. Devin Dwyer, "'Cushy' Job, or 'Isolated' Hell? Life as a Supreme Court Justice," *ABC News*, April 23, 2010, http://abcnews.go.com/Politics/Supreme_Court/life-supreme-court-cushy-job-justice/story?id=10449434.

37. David Lippman, "Supreme Court Justice Ruth Bader Ginsburg Tells NLR Crowd She Feels 'Very Well' as New Term Nears," THV 11 (CBS), September 3, 2019, https://www.thv11.com/article/news/ruth-bader-ginsburg-in-little-rock/91-83567be5-783c-4d7e-ae15-d0dab4b7be3e.

38. "C-Span PSB Supreme Court Survey: Agenda of Key Findings," August 2018, 7; "Fox News Poll," January 2019, archived at Roper Center for Public Opinion Research.

39. Suzanna Sherry, "Our Kardashian Court (and How to Fix It)," Vanderbilt Law Research Paper No. 19-30, July 24, 2019.

40. Evan Thomas, *First: Sandra Day O'Connor* (New York: Random House, 2019), 185–188, 238. The quotation is from page 185.

41. Information on the justices' public appearances is drawn from the compilation at *SCOTUSMap*, https://www.scotusmap.com.

42. See Jane Sherron De Hart, *Ruth Bader Ginsburg: A Life* (New York: Alfred A. Knopf, 2018), 475, 530–531.

43. Frederic Block, *Disrobed: An Inside Look at the Life and Work of a Federal Trial Judge* (Eagan, Minn.: West Publishing, 2012), 186.

44. This figure was computed from lists of appearances at *SCOTUSMap*.

45. Jeff Tolman, "Faces on the Wall," *Kitsap Bar Report*, Summer 2019, 4.

46. See Kevin T. McGuire, "The Institutionalization of the U.S. Supreme Court," *Political Analysis* 12 (2004): 128–142.

47. This evolution is discussed in Robert McCloskey, rev. Sanford Levinson, *The American Supreme Court*, 6th ed. (Chicago: University of Chicago Press, 2016).

48. James A. Thurber and Antoine Yoshinaka, eds., *American Gridlock: The Sources, Character, and Impact of Political Polarization* (New York: Cambridge University Press, 2015).

CHAPTER TWO

THE JUSTICES

In recent years, the selection of Supreme Court justices has been a highly visible battleground. After Justice Antonin Scalia died in February 2016, the Republican majority in the Senate refused to consider President Obama's nomination of Merrick Garland for Scalia's seat, saying the seat should be saved for the new president in 2017. In the next two years, President Trump's nominations of Neil Gorsuch and Brett Kavanaugh to the Court led to bitter conflicts between the two parties, and both nominees were confirmed by votes that followed party lines almost perfectly. After Justice Ruth Bader Ginsburg died in September 2020, President Trump and Senate Republicans moved quickly to fill her seat over heated complaints from Democrats. And there were no signs that this partisan strife would abate.

These battles reflect the importance of the Court's membership: what the Court does is determined to a considerable degree by who the justices are, so people who care about the Court's decisions also care about the selection of justices. The battles also reflect two key developments over the past several decades. One is a growing recognition of the Court's substantial role in shaping public policy, which has brought increased attention to the selection of justices. The other is the high level of polarization that has developed in the world of government and politics, especially in the form of increased hostility between Republicans and Democrats.

The first and longest section of this chapter examines the process by which justices are nominated and confirmed to fill vacancies on the Court. The second section turns to the outcomes of that process in terms of the attributes of the people who win seats on the Court. The final section deals with the process by which vacancies are created in the first place. Throughout the chapter, I give particular attention to the changes that have occurred in both the processes that determine the Court's membership and the kinds of people who become justices.

THE SELECTION OF JUSTICES

As of mid-2020, presidents had made 163 nominations to the Supreme Court, and 114 people had served as justices. The difference between those two numbers has several sources, including nominees who declined appointments and those who were appointed as associate justice and then as chief justice. But the most common source was a failure to win Senate confirmation. Table 2-1 lists the thirty-six nominations to the Court and the twenty-eight justices chosen between 1953 and 2019.

The Constitution gives formal roles in the selection of justices only to the president (for nomination, and then appointment if a nominee is confirmed) and the Senate (for confirmation of nominees). But in addition to those who assist presidents and senators, a variety of other people and groups play significant unofficial roles. I will discuss those unofficial participants and then consider how the president and the Senate reach their decisions.

Table 2-1   Nominations to the Supreme Court since 1953

Name	Nominating president	Justice replaced	Years served
Earl Warren (CJ)	Eisenhower	Vinson	1953–1969
John Harlan	Eisenhower	Jackson	1955–1971
William Brennan	Eisenhower	Minton	1956–1990
Charles Whittaker	Eisenhower	Reed	1957–1962
Potter Stewart	Eisenhower	Burton	1958–1981
Byron White	Kennedy	Whittaker	1962–1993
Arthur Goldberg	Kennedy	Frankfurter	1962–1965
Abe Fortas	Johnson	Goldberg	1965–1969
Thurgood Marshall	Johnson	Clark	1967–1991
Abe Fortas (CJ)	Johnson	(Warren)	Withdrew, 1968
Homer Thornberry	Johnson	(Fortas)	Moot, 1968
Warren Burger (CJ)	Nixon	Warren	1969–1986
Clement Haynsworth	Nixon	(Fortas)	Defeated, 1969
G. Harrold Carswell	Nixon	(Fortas)	Defeated, 1970
Harry Blackmun	Nixon	Fortas	1970–1994
Lewis Powell	Nixon	Black	1971–1987
William Rehnquist	Nixon	Harlan	1971–2005

Name	Nominating president	Justice replaced	Years served
John Paul Stevens	Ford	Douglas	1975–2010
Sandra Day O'Connor	Reagan	Stewart	1981–2006
William Rehnquist (CJ)	Reagan	Burger	1986–2005
Antonin Scalia	Reagan	Rehnquist	1986–2016
Robert Bork	Reagan	(Powell)	Defeated, 1987
Douglas Ginsburg	Reagan	(Powell)	Withdrew, 1987
Anthony Kennedy	Reagan	Powell	1988–2018
David Souter	G. H. W. Bush	Brennan	1990–2009
Clarence Thomas	G. H. W. Bush	Marshall	1991–
Ruth Bader Ginsburg	Clinton	White	1993–2020
Stephen Breyer	Clinton	Blackmun	1994–
John Roberts (CJ)	G. W. Bush	Rehnquist	2005–
Harriet Miers	G. W. Bush	(O'Connor)	Withdrew, 2005
Samuel Alito	G. W. Bush	O'Connor	2006–
Sonia Sotomayor	Obama	Souter	2009–
Elena Kagan	Obama	Stevens	2010–
Merrick Garland	Obama	(Scalia)	Not considered, 2016
Neil Gorsuch	Trump	Scalia	2017–
Brett Kavanaugh	Trump	Kennedy	2018–

Note: CJ = chief justice. Fortas and Rehnquist were associate justices when nominated as chief justice. Roberts was originally nominated to replace O'Connor and then was nominated for chief justice after Rehnquist's death.

Withdrew = Nomination or planned nomination was withdrawn. The Fortas nomination was withdrawn after a vote to end a filibuster failed. Douglas Ginsburg withdrew before he was formally nominated.

Moot = When Fortas withdrew as nominee for chief justice, the Thornberry nomination to take Fortas's position as associate justice became moot.

Defeated = Senate voted against confirmation.

Not considered = Senate did not consider nomination.

Unofficial Participants

Because Supreme Court appointments are so important, many people seek to influence those appointments. When a vacancy occurs, and even before then, presidents and other administration officials may hear from a wide array of individuals and groups. So do senators who are deciding whether to vote to confirm a nominee. The most important of these individuals and groups fall into three categories: prospective justices, the legal community, and other interest groups.

Candidates for the Court

Some Supreme Court nominees had never thought of themselves as potential justices. Indeed, some prospective nominees withdraw from consideration, and some turn down nominations. Even those who accept nominations sometimes do so reluctantly, as Abe Fortas did in 1965 and Lewis Powell did in 1971.

But for many lawyers, the Supreme Court is a long-standing dream, so they would (and do) accept nominations readily. Indeed, people who hope for appointments to the Court sometimes make considerable effort to maximize their chances of success. William Howard Taft became chief justice in 1921 after years of efforts to position himself for that appointment. As an ex-president he had a great deal of influence, and one commentator described Taft as "virtually appointing himself" chief justice.[1]

One longtime acquaintance of Brett Kavanaugh said, perhaps in jest, that "he's been running for the Supreme Court since he's been 25 years old."[2] Some of Kavanaugh's activities off the bench may have reflected his interest in achieving a nomination to the Court. When he was a leading candidate for a nomination in 2018, his judicial chambers were the central location for work by his former law clerks to help secure the nomination for him. According to one account, "Nobody was working harder than Kavanaugh himself," because "he wouldn't be able to live with himself if he were not chosen because he had failed to prepare."[3]

There is circumstantial evidence that some judges on the federal courts of appeals campaign in a different way, taking positions in cases that they hope will enhance their chances of a Supreme Court nomination.[4] In 2019 and 2020 some judges on the federal courts of appeals wrote long concurring or dissenting opinions that were likely to appeal to President Trump and to those advising him on nominations to the Court. In doing so they may have been "auditioning," as some other judges have described such opinions.[5]

Nominees participate actively in the confirmation process. They typically meet with most senators before their confirmation hearings. Occasionally, what nominees say in those meetings has an impact. After conferring with his advisors, Neil Gorsuch replied to a Democratic senator's question by saying that he was unhappy about President Trump's criticisms of federal judges. After the senator reported Gorsuch's response, some administration officials feared that the president would want to withdraw the Gorsuch nomination, and by some accounts he did consider that step.[6]

Nominees also testify for many hours before the Senate Judiciary Committee at their hearings and provide voluminous written materials to the committee. Nominees go through elaborate preparations for their testimony. The Trump administration brought together advisors to help Gorsuch prepare, and he ultimately rebelled at their efforts to tell him how to respond to senators' questions. Gorsuch even suggested that he could withdraw his own nomination and continue to serve as a court of appeals judge.[7]

When nominees testify, senators who support confirmation typically use their questions to help the nominee make a favorable impression. Senators who are negatively inclined ask questions that raise criticisms of the nominee or that might elicit damaging answers. Questions often concern a nominee's views about past decisions or issues that the Court might address in the future.[8] Typically, nominees take positions on a few issues on which they know their answers will be popular or uncontroversial. With that exception, they turn back questions about judicial issues on the ground that they do not want to prejudge issues that might come before the Court. One commentator described the "key lessons" for nominees from recent confirmation hearings: "Say nothing, say it at great length, and then say it again."[9]

When senators are truly undecided about their confirmation votes, what a nominee says (or refuses to say) before the Judiciary Committee can affect the outcome. In 1987, for instance, Robert Bork's testimony increased some senators' concerns about his views on issues that the Court addresses. But today, in an era of

▶ **Photo 2-1** Judge Brett Kavanaugh testifying at the special confirmation hearing before the Senate Judiciary Committee on charges of sexual misconduct against him in 2018. Supreme Court nominees' testimony has become a key stage in the selection process for justices.

strong political polarization, senators generally make up their minds on a partisan basis quite early. For that reason, few votes on confirmation are affected by nominees' testimony.

Just as Brett Kavanaugh played an active role in the campaign to win President Trump's nomination in 2018, he played an unusually active role late in the confirmation process. After charges of sexual misconduct were raised against Kavanaugh, he worked to refute those charges. He gave an interview to Fox News before testifying at the special Judiciary Committee hearing on the charges. His combative testimony at that hearing helped to solidify support for him from Republican senators. It also raised questions about his "judicial temperament" for some people, and he responded with an op-ed in the *Wall Street Journal* in which he apologized for some of the things he had said.[10]

The Legal Community

Lawyers have a particular interest in the Supreme Court's membership, and their views about potential justices may carry special weight. As the largest and most prominent organization of lawyers, the American Bar Association (ABA) occupies an important position. An ABA committee investigates presidential nominees for federal judgeships, including the Supreme Court, and rates them as "well-qualified," "qualified," or "not qualified."

Ideally, from the ABA's perspective, it would make ratings of prospective nominees before they are selected, so the president's administration could take those ratings into account. But Republican presidents have become unwilling to give that role to the ABA committee, based on a perception that the committee is biased against conservative nominees. Even so, the ABA's unanimous ratings of nominees as "well-qualified," which every nominee since 1993 has received (Harriet Miers in 2005 withdrew before she was rated), strengthen their credentials. By the same token, if a nominee does not get such strong approval, that negative sign might affect the judgments of some senators.

Other legal groups and individual lawyers also participate in the selection process. The most important legal group for Republican presidents is the Federalist Society, the leading organization of conservative lawyers and law students. When then-candidate Donald Trump sought to assure conservatives that he would select conservative justices if he became president, the Federalist Society was one of two groups that played key roles in assembling a list of potential nominees that Trump announced in May 2016 and the revised lists that were issued later in 2016 and in 2017 and 2020. Trump said in June 2016 that "we're going to have great judges, conservative, all picked by the Federalist Society."[11] Leonard Leo, executive vice president of the Society, helped to coordinate the processes that culminated in the nominations of Neil Gorsuch and Brett Kavanaugh.

Supreme Court justices sometimes participate in the selection process, most often by recommending a potential nominee. Chief Justice Warren Burger, appointed by Richard Nixon in 1969, was active in suggesting names to fill other vacancies during the Nixon administration. He played a crucial role in the nomination of his longtime friend Harry Blackmun. Some years later, Burger lobbied the Reagan administration on behalf of Sandra Day O'Connor.[12] Anthony Kennedy's support for his former law clerk Brett Kavanaugh as a prospective justice helped to bring about President Trump's selection of Kavanaugh as Kennedy's successor.[13]

Other Interest Groups

Many interest groups have a stake in Supreme Court decisions, so groups often seek to influence the selection of justices. The level of group activity has grown substantially in the past half century, and it now pervades both the nomination and confirmation stages of the selection process.

Interest groups would most like to influence the president's nomination decision. The groups that actually exert influence at this stage typically are politically important to the president. Democratic presidents usually give some weight to the views of labor and civil rights groups. Republican presidents usually pay attention to groups that take conservative positions on social issues such as abortion. The Heritage Foundation, a conservative group with a broad agenda, worked alongside the Federalist Society in helping to build the lists of potential Trump nominees for the Court.

The influence of these core groups was underlined in 2005, after President George W. Bush nominated White House Counsel Harriet Miers to succeed Sandra Day O'Connor. Many conservatives were uncertain that Miers was strongly conservative, and some groups and individuals mounted a strong campaign against her. After their campaign secured Miers's withdrawal, President Bush chose Samuel Alito, who was popular with conservative groups.

Once a nomination is announced, groups often work for or against Senate confirmation. Significant interest group activity at this stage was limited and sporadic until the late 1960s.[14] Its higher level since then reflects growth in the intensity of interest group activity, greater awareness that nominations to the Court are important, and group leaders' increased understanding of how to influence the confirmation process. Leaders of some groups have also found that opposition to controversial nominees is a good way to generate interest in their causes and monetary contributions from their supporters.

Groups that opposed specific nominees achieved noteworthy successes between 1968 and 1970. Conservative groups helped to defeat Abe Fortas, nominated for elevation to chief justice by President Lyndon Johnson in 1968, and labor and civil rights groups helped to secure the defeats of Richard Nixon's nominees Clement Haynsworth and G. Harrold Carswell. President Reagan's nomination of Robert Bork in 1987 gave rise to an unprecedented level of group activity, and the strong mobilization by liberal groups was one key to Bork's defeat in the Senate.

Since the Bork nomination, interest groups have been involved in the confirmation process for every nominee. Group activity increases with perceptions that a nominee would shift the ideological balance in the Court substantially and that a nominee might be vulnerable to defeat. But even when these conditions are lacking, there are always some groups that mount campaigns for and against nominees.

Conservative groups were quite active in the battles over confirmation of Merrick Garland, Neil Gorsuch, and Brett Kavanaugh. The conservative Judicial Crisis Network spent at least $7 million in opposition to Garland, $10 million in support of Gorsuch, and $12 million on behalf of Kavanaugh.[15] These campaigns centered on advertising in states with potentially wavering senators, especially Democrats from strongly Republican states. For their part, liberal groups pushed Democratic senators to oppose Gorsuch and Kavanaugh vigorously. Their advertising campaigns against the two nominees were substantial but less extensive than the campaigns for the nominees.

The regular involvement of interest groups and their appeals to the general public underline how the process of selecting justices has opened up over time. Nomination and confirmation now include "a broad array of players—both internal and external—and are conducted much like other political processes in a democracy."[16]

The President's Decision

One key attribute of Supreme Court nominations is variation: the process of selecting nominees and the criteria for choosing those nominees differ from president to president and even among the nominations that one president makes. But there are also some general patterns in process and criteria that can be identified.[17]

Presidents vary in their personal involvement in the selection process. Bill Clinton, George W. Bush, and Barack Obama played a more active role in the process than did their predecessors Ronald Reagan and George H. W. Bush. Obama, a former constitutional law professor with a strong interest in the Court, was especially active. Still, all presidents delegate most of the search process to other officials in the executive branch. In recent administrations, the process has been centered in the Office of the White House Counsel.

Administrations in the current era typically do a good deal of preparatory work before a vacancy in the Court actually arises. In the George W. Bush administration, White House officials interviewed prospective nominees in 2001, four years before there was a vacancy to fill.[18] Once a vacancy occurs, occasionally a president fixes on a single candidate for nomination. More often, administrations create a short list and then work to identify the best candidate from that list. President Obama, for instance, chose Elena Kagan from a group of finalists that also included three judges on the federal courts of appeals.[19] This process allows presidents and other officials to work systematically through the advantages and disadvantages of choosing different names from the list. But uncertainties about potential nominees and shifting conditions often introduce an element of chaos to the process. That was true of the George W. Bush nominations and, even more, those made by President Clinton.

President Trump's nominations of Neil Gorsuch and Brett Kavanaugh were unusual in the announcement of prospective nominees before Trump was elected and in the integral roles played by two interest groups in identifying those candidates. In other respects, the process that culminated in those nominations was fairly typical for the current era. The lists of candidates were put together by Donald McGahn, who became White House Counsel after Trump was elected. McGahn also headed up the efforts to choose the actual nominees. Even before Trump took office, according to one report, McGahn had a clear vision of what was going to happen: Gorsuch would be nominated to fill the existing vacancy on the Court, the administration would encourage Anthony Kennedy to retire, and Kavanaugh would be nominated to fill his seat.[20]

Although that vision was fulfilled, President Trump and his advisors considered and interviewed several candidates from the list of prospective nominees for each vacancy. Gorsuch was one of three judges on the federal courts of appeals whom Trump interviewed in 2017. A fourth court of appeals judge reportedly was not interviewed because one advisor "thought him too impressive and was worried that Trump might favor him over Gorsuch, upending the underlying strategy."[21] When those interviews were completed, McGahn strongly recommended Gorsuch and Trump chose him.[22]

Before he nominated Kavanaugh in 2018, Trump met four prospective nominees and spoke on the phone with a fifth. The path to nomination was not as smooth for Kavanaugh as it was for Gorsuch, in part because some conservatives lobbied strongly against him. But after two interviews of Kavanaugh and a telephone conversation with him, as well as considerable input from an array of other people, the president offered him the nomination.[23]

Amy Coney Barrett was widely expected to win a nomination for Justice Ginsburg's seat if Ginsburg left the Court while Trump was president. Indeed, she was nominated with extraordinary speed. Two White House staff members contacted her the day after Ginsburg's death. After she had a series of meetings with members of the administration, two days later President Trump offered her the nomination and she accepted it, though the nomination was not announced until later that week.

The possible criteria for nominations fall into several categories: the "objective" qualifications of potential nominees, their policy preferences, rewards to political and personal associates, and building political support. Cutting across these criteria and helping to determine their use is the goal of securing Senate confirmation for a nominee.

"Objective" Qualifications

Presidents have strong incentives to select Supreme Court nominees who have demonstrated high levels of legal competence and adherence to ethical standards. For one thing, most presidents respect the Court. Further, highly competent justices are in the best position to influence their colleagues. Finally, serious questions about a candidate's competence or ethical behavior work against Senate confirmation.

Because presidents care about competence, only in a few cases has a nominee's capacity to serve on the Court been seriously questioned. One of those was Nixon's nominee G. Harrold Carswell, who was denied confirmation. Perceptions that Harriet Miers had only limited knowledge of constitutional law were one source of the opposition that led her to withdraw as a nominee in 2005.

The ethical behavior of several nominees has been questioned. Opponents of Abe Fortas (when nominated for promotion to chief justice), Clement Haynsworth, Stephen Breyer, and Samuel Alito pointed to what they saw as financial conflicts of interest. Fortas was also criticized for continuing to consult with President Johnson while serving as an associate justice. The charges against Fortas and Haynsworth helped prevent their confirmation. After Douglas Ginsburg was announced as a Reagan nominee, a disclosure about his past use of marijuana led to his withdrawal. Allegations of sexual misconduct by Clarence Thomas in 1991 and Brett Kavanaugh in 2018 resulted in special sets of Senate hearings on these allegations and potentially put their confirmation in jeopardy.

To minimize the possibility of such embarrassments, administrations today give close scrutiny to the competence and ethics of potential nominees. This does not necessarily mean that the people chosen to serve on the Court are the most qualified of all possible appointees. One highly respected federal judge expressed the view that the justices are probably not "nine of the best 100 or, for that matter, 1,000 American lawyers."[24] But presidents do seek to choose lawyers who have demonstrated a high level of skill as well as ethical conduct.

Policy Preferences

By policy preferences, I mean an individual's attitudes toward policy issues. These criteria have always been a consideration in the selection of Supreme Court justices. In the current era, every president pays considerable attention to the policy preferences of prospective nominees. This emphasis reflects the Court's increased prominence as a policy maker and the fact that interest groups associated with both parties care so much about the Court's direction. But presidents of the two parties have taken somewhat different approaches.

Republican presidents give special emphasis to policy considerations. In part, this is because Republican leaders, activists, and voters generally share strongly conservative views on issues that the Court addresses. Also important are past disappointments. Between 1969 and 1991, all ten appointments to the Court were made by Republican presidents. But the records of some of those justices were relatively moderate, and three—Harry Blackmun (appointed by Nixon), John Paul Stevens (Ford), and David Souter (George H. W. Bush)—were actually on the liberal side of the Court's ideological spectrum during much of their tenure. The same was true of two justices appointed by Republican President Eisenhower in the 1950s, Earl Warren and William Brennan.

In response to these disappointments, party activists have pushed Republican administrations to give strong weight to prospective nominees' policy preferences as a criterion and to probe carefully for evidence about those preferences. Their efforts were reflected in the nominations of John Roberts and Samuel Alito by George W. Bush and in the key roles that conservative groups played in the selection of potential Donald Trump nominees and Trump's choices of Gorsuch, Brett Kavanaugh, and Amy Coney Barrett from those candidates.

For recent Democratic presidents, it was important that their nominees be liberals, but not that they be strong liberals. On the whole, the Clinton and Obama nominees were relatively moderate. Memoranda by people helping Clinton in 1993 described Stephen Breyer as moderate or even moderately conservative on some issues, but Clinton nonetheless nominated Breyer to the Court a year later.[25]

Obama's 2016 nomination of the moderate liberal Merrick Garland was a special case, because Obama sought someone who might cause some senators in the Republican majority to break from their leadership's position that it would not consider any Obama nominee. The other four Clinton and Obama nominations came when Democrats held Senate majorities, yet none were perceived as highly liberal. For the two presidents, one motivation was to choose people who would not arouse strong opposition from Republicans, so that confirmation would be relatively easy.

Also relevant are differences between the parties in the current era. Most fundamentally, ideology is not the key unifying force in the Democratic Party that it is for Republicans; the Democrats are more "a coalition of social groups."[26] And in part for that reason, Supreme Court policy has not been as high a priority for Democrats. As a result, Democratic presidents have felt relatively little pressure to choose strong liberals. But because of widespread unhappiness among liberals about the Senate's refusal to consider Garland and President Trump's appointments to the Court, future Democratic presidents will feel much greater pressure to make ideology the key criterion for nominations.

Presidents of both parties seek to ascertain the views of prospective nominees on issues of legal policy. This is the primary reason why every nominee since 1986 except for Elena Kagan and Harriet Miers has come from a federal court of appeals. If a judge has a long record of judicial votes and opinions on issues of federal law, as Sonia Sotomayor, Neil Gorsuch, and Brett Kavanaugh did, presidents and their advisors can be fairly confident about the kinds of positions the judge would take on many issues as a justice.

Some nominees do not have these long records. Miers and Kagan had never served as judges. Sandra Day O'Connor had served only on state courts, and most kinds of issues that come to the Supreme Court are uncommon in state courts. John Roberts, Clarence Thomas, and David Souter had only short service on federal courts of appeals—for Souter, so short that he had written no opinions. For candidates such as these, other sources of information can be consulted.

Most justices do reflect the ideological leaning of the president's party at least fairly well. But the Republican appointees from the 1950s to 1990 who developed moderate or liberal records on the Court are a reminder that this is not always the case. These exceptions generally fall into two categories. First, some justices were chosen by presidents who did not have a strong interest in choosing ideologically compatible justices or who were not careful about doing so. For instance, policy considerations were not dominant in Gerald Ford's choice of John Paul Stevens or in Ronald Reagan's choice of Sandra Day O'Connor. President Eisenhower and his aides did not scrutinize Earl Warren and William Brennan as closely as they might have, and those two justices helped to establish a highly liberal Court majority in the 1960s.

Second, some justices shift their ideological positions after reaching the Court. Richard Nixon's one "failure" was Harry Blackmun, who had a distinctly conservative record in his early years on the Court but gradually adopted more liberal positions. Anthony Kennedy also may have shifted in a liberal direction after reaching the Court, although to a lesser degree. A conservative publication later referred to Kennedy as "surely Reagan's biggest disappointment."[27]

To the extent that presidents seek nominees who reflect their party's dominant ideological orientation, the increased "sorting" of conservatives into the Republican Party and liberals into the Democratic Party in the last few decades has made presidents' jobs easier. Because of sorting, fewer people with the credentials needed for a Supreme Court appointment deviate from their party's dominant orientation. The enhanced role of ideology in the selection of court of appeals judges in the past few decades has reinforced that development. A Republican president, for instance, can choose from a substantial pool of judges with strongly conservative backgrounds and judicial records. Because of those changes and the increasing care with which nominations are made, the overall records of justices on the Court are now unlikely to disappoint the presidents who chose them.

Political and Personal Reward

For most of the country's history, it was a standard practice for presidents to nominate friends and acquaintances to the Supreme Court. As of 1968, about 60 percent of nominees had known the nominating president personally.[28] Certainly this was true in the mid-twentieth century. With the exception of Dwight Eisenhower, all the presidents from Franklin Roosevelt through Lyndon Johnson selected mostly people whom they knew personally.

Rewarding personal and political associates seemed to be the main criterion for Harry Truman in choosing justices. Sherman Minton, a friend and former Senate colleague of Truman's, was serving as a federal judge in Indiana when he learned that one of the justices had died. Minton reportedly traveled to Washington, D.C. as quickly as he could, went to the White House, and asked Truman to nominate him for the vacancy. Truman immediately agreed, and Minton became a justice.[29]

Some appointments to the Court were direct rewards for political help. Eisenhower selected Earl Warren to serve as chief justice largely because of Warren's crucial support of Eisenhower at the 1952 Republican convention. As governor of California and leader of that state's delegation at the convention, Warren had provided Eisenhower the needed votes on a preliminary issue and thereby helped secure his nomination.

This pattern has changed fundamentally. Of the twenty-six nominees from Warren Burger in 1969 to Amy Coney Barrett in 2020, only Harriet Miers and

Elena Kagan were acquainted with the presidents who chose them. Indeed, few nominees in that period had any contact with the president before they were considered for the Court. For instance, after President Trump nominated Kavanaugh, Trump told an audience that "I don't even know him. I met him for the first time a few weeks ago."[30]

Perhaps the main reason for the decline in the selection of personal acquaintances is that such nominees are vulnerable to charges of cronyism. That charge was made in 1968 when President Johnson nominated Justice Abe Fortas for elevation to chief justice and nominated Judge Homer Thornberry to succeed Fortas as associate justice; both Fortas and Thornberry were personally close to Johnson. The charge played a small role in building opposition to Fortas and Thornberry in the Senate. Ultimately, Fortas's confirmation was blocked by a filibuster, and Thornberry's nomination thus became moot. Miers's nomination was also attacked as a case of cronyism, and that charge was one factor in the pressures that led to her withdrawal as a nominee.

One element of political reward has remained strong, however: about 90 percent of all nominees to the Court—and all those chosen since 1975—have been members of the president's party. One reason is that lawyers who share the president's policy views are more likely to come from the same party, especially in the current era of partisan sorting. There is also a widespread feeling that such an attractive prize should go to one of the party faithful.

Building Political Support

Nominations can be made to reward people who helped the president in the past, but they can also be used to seek political benefits in the future. Most often, presidents select justices with certain attributes in order to appeal to leaders and voters who share those attributes.

Geography and religion were important criteria for selecting justices in some past eras, but their role in nominations has nearly disappeared. The decline of interest in maintaining geographical diversity is symbolized by the fact that four of the nine justices who served between 2010 and 2016 had grown up in New York City. Similarly, the decline of religion as a consideration is symbolized by the fact that the 2010–2016 Court included no Protestants, even though Protestants constitute a clear majority of people in the country who have religious affiliations. (Neil Gorsuch, appointed in 2017, was raised Catholic but attended an Episcopal church in Colorado before he joined the Supreme Court. Brett Kavanaugh, like his predecessor Anthony Kennedy, is Catholic.)

In contrast, representation by race, gender, and ethnicity has become quite important. This is especially true of Democratic presidents because women and racial and ethnic minority groups are important to the Democratic political coalition. Lyndon Johnson chose the first African American justice (Thurgood Marshall), and Barack Obama chose the first Hispanic justice (Sonia Sotomayor). Three of the five Clinton and Obama nominees (Ruth Bader Ginsburg, Sotomayor, and Elena Kagan) were women.

To a lesser degree, these considerations affect Republican nominations as well. George H. W. Bush's nomination of Clarence Thomas to succeed Thurgood Marshall reflected the pressure he felt to maintain Black representation on the Court. President Reagan felt even greater pressure to choose the first female justice, and he responded by selecting Sandra Day O'Connor as his first nominee. When George W. Bush nominated Harriet Miers, all the finalists were female. But Bush's choice of Samuel Alito after Miers withdrew reflected the dominance of ideology as a criterion for Republican presidents, though gender may have been one consideration in Trump's selection of Amy Coney Barrett in 2020.

Senate Confirmation

A president's nomination to the Court goes to the Senate for confirmation. The nomination is referred to the Judiciary Committee, which gathers extensive information on the nominee, holds hearings at which the nominee and other witnesses testify, and then votes on its recommendation for Senate action. After this vote, the nomination is referred to the floor, where it is debated and a confirmation vote taken.

Although a simple majority is needed for confirmation, until 2017 a large minority of senators (from 1975 on, forty-one) could block confirmation through a filibuster that used extended debate to prevent a vote on the nominee. That was the fate of Abe Fortas's nomination for chief justice in 1968. In 2017, after forty-five senators voted against ending the debate on the Gorsuch nomination, the Senate amended the rules to require only a simple majority to end debate on a Supreme Court nomination, and it then voted to end debate on Gorsuch by a 55–45 vote. The votes on ending debate were overwhelmingly along party lines; the vote on amending the rules was entirely along party lines.

Overall, nominees' success in winning confirmation is best described as moderately good. Through 2019, by one count, twenty-nine nominations to the Supreme Court have not been confirmed—through an adverse vote, Senate inaction, or withdrawal of the nomination in the face of opposition.[31] These twenty-nine cases constitute nearly one-fifth of the nominations that have been submitted to the Senate. That rate of failure is far higher than the rate for nominations to the president's cabinet.

The overall success rate obscures wide variation over time. Twenty-two nominations failed in the nineteenth century, 30 percent of all nominations in that century. These failures had several different sources, including some presidents' political weakness, conflicts within the president's party, senators' disagreements with nominees' policy positions, and questions about nominees' qualifications.

In contrast, nominees did very well during the first two-thirds of the twentieth century. Between 1900 and 1967, only one nominee failed to win confirmation, Herbert Hoover's nominee John Parker in 1930. Only a few others faced a serious prospect of defeat. Some other nominees drew more than ten negative votes, but the most common outcome was confirmation without even a recorded vote.

The period from 1968 to 1994 can be regarded as a transitional era. During that period, four nominees were defeated: Abe Fortas, nominated by Lyndon Johnson for elevation to chief justice in 1968; two nominees of Richard Nixon, Clement Haynsworth in 1969 and G. Harrold Carswell in 1970 (both for the same vacancy); and Ronald Reagan nominee Robert Bork in 1987. Some others faced significant opposition, and one—Clarence Thomas, nominated by George H. W. Bush in 1991—won confirmation by only a four-vote margin.

In contrast, most nominees during that period were confirmed with little difficulty, and five received unanimous approval from the Senate. In that period, as in the one that preceded it, senators usually voted to confirm even those nominees whose ideological positions seemed quite distant from their own positions.[32] Still, even the nominees who faced little Senate opposition generally received closer scrutiny than those who were chosen earlier in the twentieth century. As Table 2-2 shows, as late as the period from 1954 to 1965, most nominees were confirmed without even a recorded vote. In contrast, no nominee after 1965 received that very favorable response from the Senate.

Table 2-2   Senate Votes on Supreme Court Nominations since 1953

Nominee	Year	Vote
Earl Warren	1954	NRV
John Harlan	1955	71–11
William Brennan	1956	NRV
Charles Whittaker	1957	NRV
Potter Stewart	1959	70–17
Byron White	1962	NRV
Arthur Goldberg	1962	NRV
Abe Fortas	1965	NRV
Thurgood Marshall	1967	69–11
Abe Fortas[a]	1968	No vote
Homer Thornberry	(1968)	No vote
Warren Burger	1969	74–3
Clement Haynsworth	1969	45–55
G. Harrold Carswell	1970	45–51

(Continued)

Table 2-2 (Continued)

Nominee	Year	Vote
Harry Blackmun	1970	94–0
Lewis Powell	1971	89–1
William Rehnquist	1971	68–26
John Paul Stevens	1975	98–0
Sandra Day O'Connor	1981	99–0
William Rehnquist[b]	1986	65–33
Antonin Scalia	1986	98–0
Robert Bork	1987	42–58
Douglas Ginsburg	(1987)	No vote
Anthony Kennedy	1988	97–0
David Souter	1990	90–9
Clarence Thomas	1991	52–48
Ruth Bader Ginsburg	1993	96–3
Stephen Breyer	1994	87–9
John Roberts	2005	78–22
Harriet Miers	(2005)	No vote
Samuel Alito	2006	58–42
Sonia Sotomayor	2009	68–31
Elena Kagan	2010	63–37
Merrick Garland	(2016)	No vote
Neil Gorsuch	2017	54–45
Brett Kavanaugh	2018	50–48

Source: David G. Savage, *Guide to the U.S. Supreme Court*, 5th ed. (Washington, D.C.: CQ Press, 2010), 1253–1254; table updated by the author.

Note: NRV = no recorded vote.

a. Elevation to chief justice; nomination withdrawn after the Senate vote of 45–43 failed to end a filibuster against the nomination (two-thirds majority was required).

b. Elevation to chief justice.

There were no vacancies on the Court between 1994 and 2005. The nomination of John Roberts in 2005 marked the beginning of the current era. From Roberts through Brett Kavanaugh in 2018, there were eight nominations, including the withdrawn nomination of Harriet Miers later in 2005. Of the other seven, only Merrick Garland in 2016 failed to win confirmation. But the others received substantial numbers of negative votes, and none received majority support from senators in the party that did not hold the presidency. This opposition, along with unanimous or near-unanimous support for nominees from senators in the president's party, marks a new era of unusually sharp partisan conflict over confirmation.

Although the earlier eras should be kept in mind, I will focus on the two most recent eras. What did those eras look like, and what brought them about?

The Transitional Era

In the 1950s and the 1960s, under Chief Justice Earl Warren, the Supreme Court made several major decisions expanding constitutional protections of civil liberties. There was considerable opposition to the Court's general direction and to some specific decisions, especially those in criminal justice. Some members of Congress denounced the Court, and the Court became an issue in the presidential elections of 1964 and 1968. But the Warren Court also had its defenders, people who strongly approved of the Court's work.

The Court's higher profile and the debate over its policies set the stage for increased conflict over confirmations of presidential nominees. The growth in activity by interest groups that cared about the Court's policies intensified this conflict. As a result, it became common for nominees to draw serious opposition. Nominees certainly received more intense scrutiny in the Senate: the median time between submission of a nomination to a Senate and its final action was seventy-one days during this transitional period, compared with fifteen days between 1937 and 1965.[33]

The votes in Table 2-2 highlight the wide variation in senators' responses to different nominations during the transitional era. The sources of those differences are suggested by two pairs of adjacent nominees.

The first pair was Antonin Scalia and Robert Bork, nominated by Republican president Reagan in 1986 and 1987. Scalia and Bork had both been well-regarded legal scholars, and both were clearly conservative. But Scalia was confirmed unanimously, while Bork was defeated. Bork had the disadvantage of a large body of writing that included highly conservative and unpopular views on some legal issues, but more important were the differences in the situations that the two nominees faced.

One key difference was that the Senate had a Republican majority in 1986 but a Democratic majority the next year. Presidents have done far better in winning confirmation for their nominees when their party holds a Senate majority. Another was that Scalia replaced another strong conservative but Bork would have replaced a moderate conservative on a Court that was closely divided between liberals and conservatives.

Finally, in 1986, liberal senators and interest groups focused their efforts on defeating William Rehnquist's nomination for chief justice and largely ignored

Scalia. In 1987, in contrast, liberal interest groups mounted a major campaign against Bork. This was a crucial step, because such a campaign could overcome the assumption that the nominee would be confirmed. The charge of extremism from interest groups and some Democratic senators was strengthened by some of Bork's statements at his confirmation hearing, and the Reagan administration was not as effective as it could have been in defending Bork. Ultimately, all but two of the Senate's Democrats voted against Bork, and they were joined by six Republicans. As a result, he lost by a 42–58 margin.

The second pair was David Souter and Clarence Thomas, chosen by Republican president George H. W. Bush in 1990 and 1991. They were nominated in similar situations: there were Democratic majorities in the Senate, and each nominee would replace a highly liberal justice. But Souter won confirmation with only nine negative votes, while forty-eight senators voted against Thomas and his confirmation was achieved with some difficulty.

One source of the difference was that Thomas's past policy positions indicated he was a strong conservative, while Souter's more limited record suggested he was more moderate. The other source was a perception that Souter was well qualified for the Supreme Court, while Thomas's qualifications might be questioned. Both nominees received some opposition from liberal interest groups, but the opposition to Thomas was broader and more intense. Partly as a result, most Democratic senators lined up against Thomas. Opposition became even more intense after an allegation of sexual harassment was made against Thomas, and a second set of committee hearings was convened to investigate the allegation. Ultimately Thomas received just enough support from Senate Democrats to win confirmation.

Robert Bork was one of the four nominees who failed to win confirmation during this transitional period. The other three defeats came near the beginning of the period. The first was Abe Fortas, a sitting justice whom President Johnson nominated to be chief justice in 1968. The Senate had a Democratic majority. But many of the Democrats were conservative, and the strong liberalism of the Warren Court and of Fortas himself aroused conservative opposition. Further, the nomination came in the last year of Johnson's term, and historically, last-year nominees have been successful less than 60 percent of the time. For one thing, presidents tend to become politically weak by the end of their terms, especially a second term. Further, senators from the other party would like to reserve a vacancy in case their party wins the presidential election.[34] Indeed, in 1968 half the Republican senators signed a statement saying that they would vote against confirming any Johnson nominee in his last year.[35]

Opponents of Fortas questioned his ethical fitness on two grounds: his continued consultation with President Johnson about policy matters while serving on the Court and an arrangement by which he gave nine lectures at American University in Washington, D.C., for a fee of $15,000 that was contributed by businesses. After the nomination went to the full Senate, it ran into a filibuster. A vote to end debate fell fourteen votes short of the two-thirds majority then required; the opposition came almost entirely from Republicans and southern Democrats. President Johnson then withdrew the nomination at Fortas's request.

In 1969, Fortas resigned from the Court. President Nixon selected Clement Haynsworth, chief judge of a federal court of appeals, to replace him. Haynsworth was opposed by labor groups and the National Association for the Advancement of Colored People (NAACP), both of which disliked his judicial record. Liberal senators, unhappy about that record themselves, sought revenge for Fortas's defeat as well. Haynsworth was also charged with unethical conduct: he had sat on two cases involving subsidiaries of companies in which he owned stock, and in another case he had bought the stock of a corporation in the interval between his court's vote in its favor and the announcement of that decision. These charges led to additional opposition from Senate moderates. Haynsworth ultimately was defeated by a 45–55 vote, with a large minority of Republicans voting against confirmation.

President Nixon then nominated another court of appeals judge, G. Harrold Carswell. After the fight over Haynsworth, most senators were inclined to support the next nominee. One senator predicted that any new Nixon nominee "will have no trouble getting confirmed unless he has committed murder—recently."[36] But Carswell drew opposition from civil rights groups for what they perceived as his hostility to their interests, and their cause gained strength from a series of revelations about the nominee that suggested active opposition to racial equality. Carswell was also charged with a lack of judicial competence. After escorting Carswell to talk with senators, one of Nixon's staffers reported to the president that "they think Carswell's a boob, a dummy. And what counter is there to that? He is."[37] The nomination was defeated by a 45–51 vote, with a lineup similar to the vote on Haynsworth.

The four defeats during the transitional period, different though they were, have some things in common. In each instance, many senators were inclined to oppose the nominee on ideological grounds. All but Fortas faced a Senate controlled by the opposite party, and Fortas was confronted by a conservative Senate majority. And each nominee was weakened by a "smoking gun" that provided a basis for opposition: the ethical questions about Fortas and Haynsworth, the allegations of racism and incompetence against Carswell, and the charge that Bork was outside the mainstream in his views on judicial issues. The combination of these problems led to enough negative votes to prevent confirmation in each instance.

The Current Era

President Bill Clinton's nominations of Ruth Bader Ginsburg in 1993 and Stephen Breyer in 1994 were the last ones made in the transitional era. Several conditions favored easy confirmations for Ginsburg and Breyer: the Senate had a Democratic majority, the nominees were well-regarded judges, and neither was expected to change the Court's ideological balance very much. As a result, efforts to mount opposition to these nominees had little success. Ginsburg was confirmed with three negative votes, Breyer with nine.

When George W. Bush nominated John Roberts as chief justice in 2005, the same conditions seemed equally favorable. The Senate had a moderately large Republican majority, Roberts had been an impressive advocate in the Supreme

Court as a lawyer before his service as a judge, and he made a favorable impression in his confirmation hearing. He was perceived as distinctly conservative, but so was the chief justice he would succeed, William Rehnquist. Yet half the Democratic senators voted against confirmation—not enough to threaten his confirmation, but a noteworthy number.

What had changed? The best single answer is that the growing polarization in politics was having a powerful effect on the confirmation process. Liberal Republicans and conservative Democrats had largely disappeared from the Senate, moderates had become more scarce, and hostility between the parties had increased. Senators were also feeling stronger pressure from interest groups associated with their party, groups that wanted them to support their own party's nominees and to oppose nominees from the other party. Also important was the continuing close balance between conservatives and liberals on the Court, combined with a perception that this balance had considerable effect on decisions that were important to the two parties.

When Harriet Miers withdrew a few weeks after Bush nominated her to succeed Sandra Day O'Connor later in 2005, that withdrawal reflected another aspect of polarization: the demand from groups associated with the Republican Party for a nominee whose strong conservatism was unquestionable. Bush's subsequent nomination of Samuel Alito for the same seat pleased those groups, but for the same

▶ **Photo 2-2** Harriet Miers with President George W. Bush, who nominated her for the Supreme Court in 2005. Miers' withdrawal under pressure from Republican conservatives underlined the importance of Supreme Court appointments to ideological groups that are associated with the two parties.

reason it aroused considerable unhappiness among liberal Democrats. Alito seemed considerably more conservative than O'Connor, so his appointment might have a significant effect on the Court's ideological balance.

The campaign against Alito was successful in mobilizing Democratic senators. But Alito's opponents could find nothing negative about him that would turn Republican senators against the nominee. Because Alito did not have the support of sixty senators, Democratic opponents could have mounted a filibuster against him. But many Democratic senators saw a filibuster as inappropriate or at least bad political strategy. After a 75–25 vote to end debate, Alito won confirmation by a 58–42 margin. One Republican and all but four Democrats voted against him.

Sonia Sotomayor entered the confirmation process with the great advantage of a Democratic majority in the Senate and the additional advantage that her replacement of David Souter was unlikely to change the Court's overall ideological balance very much. Still, some Senate Republicans joined conservative interest groups in expressing strong opposition to Sotomayor. She had said in one talk, "I would hope that a wise Latina woman with the richness of her experiences would more often than not reach a better conclusion than a white male who hasn't lived that life."[38] Opponents argued that this passage and other statements and actions indicated a lack of impartiality on her part. They also charged that some of her positions in court of appeals decisions were unduly liberal and departed from good interpretations of the law.

None of these criticisms constituted the kind of smoking gun that might have attracted Democratic opposition to the nomination. Indeed, no Democratic senator voted against Sotomayor. But the great majority of Republicans—thirty-one of forty—cast negative votes. Although those Republicans cited specific concerns about Sotomayor, their votes were primarily a product of ideological considerations: conservative senators and interest groups that were important to those senators saw the nominee as unduly liberal.

Elena Kagan benefited from the same Democratic majority as Sotomayor. And like Sotomayor, she was not expected to alter the ideological balance of the Court substantially. Indeed, some liberals complained that she was probably less liberal than Republican appointee John Paul Stevens, the justice she would succeed.

Yet Kagan still faced widespread opposition from Senate Republicans and conservative interest groups. Opponents cited her lack of judicial experience and her limited experience as a practicing lawyer. Even in the absence of a prior judicial record, they found evidence of what they saw as strongly liberal views. Republicans were especially critical of her actions as dean at Harvard Law School that limited the access of military recruiters to law students because of the military's prohibition of service by openly gay and lesbian people. Ultimately, Kagan won confirmation with even less Republican support than Sotomayor, with thirty-six of forty-one Republicans (and a single Democrat) voting against her.

The defeat of Merrick Garland in 2016 underlined how conditions had changed. Because this was the last year of President Obama's term, he could have expected that any nominee he chose would face close scrutiny from the Republican majority in the Senate. This was especially true because an Obama appointee to succeed Antonin Scalia was likely to create the first liberal majority on the Court since the early 1970s. The Republican Senate leadership acted preemptively, announcing shortly after Scalia's death in February 2016 that no Obama nominee would be considered by the Senate. Obama chose Garland in an effort to win support among Republicans: Garland was well respected and relatively moderate, and his age (sixty-three) made it likely that his tenure would be shorter than that of the average justice. But all the Republican senators held firm. Some were willing to meet with Garland, but no hearings were held and no vote ever taken. Any prospect of confirmation ended when Hillary Clinton was defeated in the presidential election.

Neil Gorsuch was on one of Donald Trump's lists of prospective nominees in 2016. Like nearly everyone else on the lists, he was a sitting judge with a strong conservative record. His selection by a Republican president and his conservatism virtually guaranteed that nearly all Senate Republicans would vote to confirm him. That conservatism and bitterness over the treatment of Merrick Garland guaranteed that nearly all Democrats would vote no. Opponents of Gorsuch, facing a small Republican Senate majority, could not provide a persuasive reason for the few moderate Republicans to vote against confirmation. Ultimately, all the Senate's Republicans (except one who was absent for health reasons) voted for Gorsuch, and three Democrats joined them; the vote was 54–45.

In some respects, the situation facing Brett Kavanaugh was similar to that for Gorsuch: a small Republican majority and a focus on a few senators who might be persuaded to diverge from their party colleagues. But the battle was more intense because of the perception that Kavanaugh would move the Court to the right and because some Democrats viewed him as a Republican partisan. The regular committee hearing on the nomination was punctuated by Democrats' complaints that documents related to Kavanaugh's work in the George W. Bush administration had not been released and their charges that Kavanaugh had not been fully truthful about that work. But there were no signs of Republican defections.

As Kavanaugh worked toward confirmation, a charge that he had committed sexual assault while he was in high school emerged. The Judiciary Committee held a second hearing on the charge, and the Federal Bureau of Investigation (FBI) carried out a limited investigation of that charge and a second one from Kavanaugh's college years. Ultimately, the charges had little effect on senators' positions: Kavanaugh was confirmed by a two-vote margin, with a favorable vote from one Democratic senator. One Republican was prepared to vote against him but abstained as a courtesy to a pro-confirmation Republican who could not be present for the vote.

Thus, the confirmation process has changed a good deal in the current era. This change is reflected in Justice Ginsburg's statement in 2011 that her work with the American Civil Liberties Union (ACLU) "would probably disqualify me" in the current era and Chief Justice Roberts's judgment in 2014 that neither Ginsburg nor Antonin Scalia "would have a chance" of confirmation today.[39] By the same token, at least half of the successful nominees between 2005 and 2018—those whose appointments were unlikely to change the Court's ideological balance very much—probably would have received only a few negative votes, if any, had they been nominated in the transitional era.

Political polarization has made senators' party affiliations the primary determinants of their votes.[40] In contrast with the votes on Abe Fortas, Clement Haynsworth, and G. Harrold Carswell in the transitional era, senators in the current era nearly always vote to confirm nominees from their own party even when confirmation is strongly contested. Across the five nominees from Samuel Alito to Brett Kavanaugh that the Senate considered, there were only two negative votes from members of the president's party, less than 1 percent of all their votes. In contrast, 89 percent of the votes from the other party were against confirmation. (Independents are counted as members of the party that they caucused with.) In both parties, activists help to rein in senators with the explicit or implicit threat that they will be opposed in primary elections if they stray from the party's position.[41]

As a result, party control of the Senate has become even more important than it was in past eras. None of the six successful nominees in the current era were in serious danger of defeat, because the president's party had a Senate majority in each instance. Even in the current era, Ginsburg and Scalia probably would have been confirmed so long as their party had a Senate majority. By the same token, Republican control of the Senate in 2016 allowed Merrick Garland to be denied consideration. Indeed, it is possible—as some Republican senators advocated—that if Hillary Clinton had been elected president in 2016, any nomination she made would have been blocked as long as Republicans maintained a Senate majority.

The history of Senate confirmation strongly suggests that the current era will end at some point. But for now, with sharp political polarization and bitter contention over ideological control of the Supreme Court, nominees will face a response from senators that falls overwhelmingly along partisan lines.

WHO IS SELECTED

The attributes of the people who become Supreme Court justices reflect the criteria that presidents use to select nominees. In turn, those attributes shape the collective choices that the Court makes. They also affect perceptions of the Court. Justice Kagan, for instance, has said that diversity in the justices' backgrounds "allows people to identify" with the Court.[42] Thus, it is important to know what kinds of people reach the Court, and why.

Career Paths

One way to understand these questions is by tracing the paths that people take to get to the Court. These paths have changed over time. To highlight that change, in this section I examine the set of thirty-nine justices who have been appointed since 1937, when Franklin Roosevelt made his first appointment. Recent justices are of particular interest, and Box 2-1 summarizes the careers of the justices who sat on the Court in 2019–2020.[43]

BOX 2-1

Careers of the Supreme Court Justices, 2019–2020

▶ **Photo 2-3**

John G. Roberts Jr. (born 1955)

Law degree, Harvard University, 1979

Law clerk, U.S. Court of Appeals, 1979–1980

Law clerk, Supreme Court, 1980–1981

U.S. Justice Department, 1981–1982

Office of White House Counsel, 1982–1986

U.S. Office of the Solicitor General, 1989–1993

Private law practice, 1986–1989, 1993–2003

Judge, U.S. Court of Appeals, 2003–2005

Appointed chief justice, 2005

▶ **Photo 2-4**

Clarence Thomas (born 1948)

Law degree, Yale University, 1974

Missouri attorney general's office, 1974–1977

Attorney for Monsanto Company, 1977–1979

Legislative assistant to a U.S. senator, 1979–1981

Assistant U.S. secretary of education, 1981–1982

Chair, U.S. Equal Employment Opportunity Commission, 1982–1990

Judge, U.S. Court of Appeals, 1990–1991

Appointed to Supreme Court, 1991

▶ **Photo 2-5**

Ruth Bader Ginsburg (born 1933)

Law degree, Columbia University, 1959

Law clerk, federal district court, 1959–1961

Law school research position, 1961–1963

Law school teaching, 1963–1980

Judge, U.S. Court of Appeals, 1980–1993

Appointed to Supreme Court, 1993

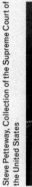

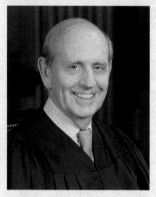

▶ **Photo 2-6**

Stephen G. Breyer (born 1938)

Law degree, Harvard University, 1964

Law clerk, Supreme Court, 1964–1965

U.S. Justice Department, 1965–1967

Law school teaching, 1967–1980

Staff, U.S. Senate Judiciary Committee, 1974–1975, 1979–1980

Judge, U.S. Court of Appeals, 1980–1994

Appointed to Supreme Court, 1994

▶ **Photo 2-7**

Samuel A. Alito Jr. (born 1950)

Law degree, Yale University, 1975

Law clerk, U.S. Court of Appeals, 1976–1977

Assistant U.S. attorney, 1977–1981

U.S. Office of the Solicitor General, 1981–1985

U.S. Justice Department, 1985–1987

U.S. attorney, 1987–1990

Judge, U.S. Court of Appeals, 1990–2006

Appointed to Supreme Court, 2006

(Continued)

(Continued)

▶ **Photo 2-8**

Sonia Sotomayor (born 1954)

Law degree, Yale University, 1979

Assistant district attorney, 1979–1984

Private law practice, 1984–1992

Judge, U.S. District Court, 1992–1998

Judge, U.S. Court of Appeals, 1998–2009

Appointed to Supreme Court, 2009

▶ **Photo 2-9**

Elena Kagan (born 1960)

Law degree, Harvard University, 1986

Law clerk, U.S. Court of Appeals, 1986–1987

Law clerk, Supreme Court, 1987–1988

Private law practice, 1989–1991

Law school teaching, 1991–1995

Positions in executive branch, 1995–1999

Law school teaching and administration, 1999–2009

U.S. Solicitor General, 2009–2010

Appointed to Supreme Court, 2010

▶ **Photo 2-10**

Neil Gorsuch (born 1967)

Law degree, Harvard University, 1991

Law clerk, U.S. Court of Appeals, 1991–1992

Law clerk, Supreme Court, 1993–1994

Private law practice, 1995–2005

U.S. Justice Department, 2005–2006

Judge, U.S. Court of Appeals, 2006–2017

Appointed to Supreme Court, 2017

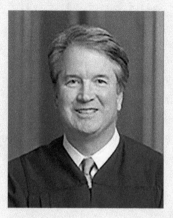

Brett Kavanaugh (born 1965)

Law degree, Yale University, 1990

Law clerk, U.S. Court of Appeals, 1990–1992

U.S. Office of the Solicitor General, 1992–1993

Law clerk, Supreme Court, 1993–1994

Associate independent counsel, investigation of President Clinton, 1994–1997, 1998

Private law practice, 1997–1998, 1999–2001

▶ **Photo 2-11**

Office of White House Counsel, 2001–2003

Assistant to the president, 2003–2006

Judge, U.S. Court of Appeals, 2006–2018

Appointed to Supreme Court, 2018

Source: Biographical Directory of Federal Judges, Federal Judicial Center, https://www.fjc.gov/history/judges. All photos: Steve Petteway, Collection of the Supreme Court of the United States.

Note: With the exception of Justice Breyer's Senate staff service, only the primary position held by a future justice during each career stage is listed.

The Legal Profession

The Constitution specifies no requirements for Supreme Court justices, so they need not be attorneys. In practice, however, this restriction has been absolute. Nearly everyone involved in the selection process assumes that only a person with legal training can serve effectively on the Court. If a president nominated a non-lawyer to the Court, this assumption—and the large number of lawyers in the Senate—almost surely would prevent confirmation.

Thus, a license to practice law constitutes the first and least flexible requirement for recruitment to the Court. Most justices who served during the first century of the Court's history took what was then the standard route, apprenticing under a practicing attorney. In several instances, the practicing attorney was a leading lawyer. James Byrnes (chosen in 1941) was the last justice to study law through apprenticeship. All the people appointed since then—like nearly all other lawyers in this period—had graduated from law school.

A high proportion of justices were educated at prestigious law schools. This has been especially true in the current era. From Sandra Day O'Connor in 1981 through Brett Kavanaugh in 2018, all thirteen appointees to the Court went to the law schools at Harvard, Yale, or Stanford. (Ruth Bader Ginsburg received her law degree from Columbia after spending her first two years at Harvard.) It may be that as scrutiny of nominees has increased, presidents have thought it desirable to choose people whose attendance at leading law schools suggests a high level of qualifications.

High Positions

If legal education is a necessary first step in the paths to the Court, almost equally important as a last step is attaining a high position in government or the legal profession. Obscure private practitioners or state trial judges might be superbly qualified for the Court, but their qualifications would still be questioned. A high position also makes a person more visible to the president and to the officials who identify potential nominees.

At the time they were selected, the justices appointed since 1937 held positions of four types. They were judges, executive branch officials, elected officials, or well-respected leaders in the legal profession.

Twenty-one of the justices appointed in this period were appellate judges at the time of selection. Nineteen sat on the federal courts of appeals, the other two on state courts. Seven of the nineteen federal judges came from the District of Columbia circuit, which is especially visible to the president and other federal officials.

Eleven justices served in the federal executive branch at the time of their appointment, eight of them in the Justice Department. The other three justices were chair of the Securities and Exchange Commission (William Douglas), secretary of the Treasury (Fred Vinson), and secretary of labor (Arthur Goldberg).

Of the other seven justices appointed since 1937, four held high elective office. Three were senators (Hugo Black, James Byrnes, and Harold Burton), and the fourth was the governor of California (Earl Warren). The other three held positions outside government. Each had attained extraordinary success and respect—as a legal scholar (Felix Frankfurter), a Washington lawyer (Abe Fortas), and a leader of the legal profession (Lewis Powell). Frankfurter and Fortas had also been informal presidential advisors.

The Steps Between

The people who have become Supreme Court justices took several routes from their legal education to the high positions that made them credible candidates for the Court. Frankfurter, Fortas, and Powell illustrate one simple route: entry into legal practice or academia, followed by a gradual rise to high standing in the legal profession. Some justices took a similar route through public office. Earl Warren held a series of appointive and elective offices, culminating in his California governorship. Clarence Thomas, Samuel Alito, and Brett Kavanaugh each served in several non-elected government positions and then as a judge on a federal court of appeals.

Since 1975, the most common route to the Court has been through private practice or law teaching, often combined with some time in government, before appointment to a federal court of appeals. Antonin Scalia, Ruth Bader Ginsburg, and Stephen Breyer were law professors. Anthony Kennedy and John Roberts were in private practice. Before becoming judges, all five had held government positions or participated informally in the governmental process. Neil Gorsuch was in private practice until he took a Justice Department position; a year later, he received a court of appeals appointment. Sonia Sotomayor left private practice to become a federal district judge and was later elevated to a court of appeals.

Justice O'Connor took a unique path to the Court. She spent time in private practice and government legal positions, with some career interruptions for family responsibilities, before becoming an Arizona state senator and majority leader of the state senate. O'Connor left the legislature for a trial judgeship. Her promotion to the state court of appeals through a gubernatorial appointment put her in a position to be considered for the Supreme Court.

Changes in Paths

Even within the period since 1937, there has been a striking change in justices' pre-Court careers. Put simply, those careers have come to involve less politics and more law. This change did not happen abruptly, but it is illustrated by a comparison of the justices who were appointed between 1937 and 1968 and the justices chosen since then. That comparison is shown in Table 2-3.

In their career backgrounds, the twenty-one justices appointed to the Court between 1937 and 1968 were fairly typical of those selected in earlier periods. About half had judicial experience, nearly as many had held elective office, and more than a quarter had headed a federal administrative agency.

Table 2-3 Selected Career Experiences of Justices Appointed since 1937 (in percentages)

| Years appointed | Experience during career | | |
	Elective office	Head of federal agency	Judgeship
1937–1968	38	29	48
1969–2019	6	6	83
	Position at appointment		
1937–1968	19	29	29
1969–2019	0	0	83

Source: *Biographical Directory of Federal Judges,* Federal Judicial Center, https://www.fjc.gov/history/judges.

Note: Federal agencies include cabinet departments and independent agencies. Heads of offices within departments (e.g., the Office of the Solicitor General in the Justice Department) are not counted.

The eighteen justices who arrived at the Court during the period from 1969 through 2019 were different. All but three came directly from lower courts. Only Sandra Day O'Connor had ever held elective office, only Clarence Thomas had headed a federal agency, and several had spent little or no time in government before winning judgeships. For the justices chosen in this era, the median proportion of their careers spent in what might be called the legal system—private practice, law school teaching, and the courts—was 85 percent. For the justices appointed between 1937 and 1968, the median had been 67 percent.[44] The high proportion for the period since 1969 is all the more striking because the Roberts Court's justices collectively had spent less time in private practice than did the justices of any prior era: it is teaching and the courts that account for the prominence of the legal system in the backgrounds of recent justices.[45]

These changes in justices' career paths seem to have two sources. The first is that long experience in the legal system and service as a judge are increasingly viewed as indications that a nominee is well qualified to serve on the Supreme Court. Indeed, Harriet Miers in 2005 and Elena Kagan in 2010 were criticized for the absence of judicial experience.

Second, and especially important, a substantial judicial record helps presidents and their advisors to predict the positions that prospective nominees might take as justices. In an era in which most presidents care a great deal about the Court's direction, any help in making these predictions is valued. Service on a federal court of appeals is especially helpful in prediction because the courts of appeals are the most similar to the Supreme Court in the kinds of issues they address.

The changes in paths to the Court may affect the justices' perspectives and their thinking about legal issues. For instance, some people have argued that the limited experience of recent justices in politics has made it more difficult for them to understand cases relating to politics. In 2016 the Court unanimously interpreted a federal bribery statute in a way that made it more difficult to secure convictions of public officials. One commentator—a former lobbyist who had been convicted and imprisoned for offenses related to political corruption—argued that the justices had misperceived the realities of politics "because none of them have been in the political process."[46]

Other Attributes of the Justices

Career experience is only one important characteristic of the people who become justices. Other attributes can be understood partly in terms of the career paths that take people to the Court.

Age

Since 1937, most Supreme Court justices have been in their fifties at the time of their appointments and the rest in their forties or early sixties. William Douglas was the youngest appointee, at age forty; at the other end of the spectrum, Lewis Powell was sixty-four.

The ages of Court appointees reflect a balance between two considerations. On the one hand, lawyers need time to develop the record of achievement that makes them credible candidates for the Court. On the other hand, presidents would like their appointees to serve for many years in order to achieve the maximum impact on the Court. Thus, a candidate such as Clarence Thomas, forty-three when George H. W. Bush appointed him, can be especially attractive. Relative youth was an important criterion in the selection processes that resulted in President Trump's nominations of Neil Gorsuch (forty-nine when nominated), Brett Kavanaugh (fifty-three), and Amy Coney Barrett (forty-eight).

Class, Race, and Sex

The Supreme Court's membership has diverged from the general population in regard to social class: most justices grew up in families that were relatively well off during their childhoods. One study found that about one-third of the justices were from high-income families and one-quarter from upper middle-income families. Less than one-quarter were from lower middle-income or low-income families. But the justices selected from the 1930s on have been less of a high-status group than their predecessors, with a far smaller proportion coming from wealthy families and about half from families at or below the middle-income category.[47]

The historic predominance of higher-status backgrounds can be explained by the career paths that most justices take. First, a justice must obtain a legal education. To do so is easiest for people from high-income families because of the cost of law school and the college education that precedes it. Early in the Court's history, when most justices had apprenticed with an attorney, people from advantaged families had the best opportunity to apprentice with leading lawyers. Similarly, those who can afford to attend elite law schools have the easiest time obtaining Supreme Court clerkships and positions in successful law firms. The increased availability of college and legal education to people of limited means helps to explain the changes in justices' collective economic backgrounds since the 1930s.

Until 1967, all the justices were white men. This pattern is not difficult to understand. Because of various restrictions, women and members of racial minority groups long had enormous difficulty pursuing a legal education. As a result, few members of these groups passed the first criterion for selection. In addition, discrimination limited their ability to advance in the legal profession and in politics. As a result, very few individuals who were not white men could achieve the high positions that people generally must obtain to be considered for nomination to the Court.

Since 1967, four women (Sandra Day O'Connor, Ruth Bader Ginsburg, Sonia Sotomayor, and Elena Kagan), two African Americans (Thurgood Marshall and Clarence Thomas), and a Hispanic American (Sotomayor) have won appointments to the Court. These appointments reflect changes in society that made it less difficult for people other than white men to achieve high positions. They also reflect the growing willingness of presidents to consider women and members of racial minority groups as prospective nominees.

As the Court has moved away from the long-standing monopoly of white men on the Court, and as fewer justices have come from high-income families, how have these changes affected its policies? People who do not share the traditional attributes of justices might bring new perspectives to the Court, and these perspectives might influence the thinking of their colleagues. For instance, both Ruth Bader Ginsburg and Sandra Day O'Connor expressed their view that the presence of female justices affects the Court's collective judgments in some cases.[48]

On the other hand, justices with similar backgrounds or life experiences may develop very different points of view. As Justice Sotomayor said, "You would think that Clarence Thomas and I would be more similar, wouldn't you, if you looked just at our background and upbringing."[49] And justices' social class origins might affect their views less than does the high professional status that they all achieved by the time they joined the Court. This may help to explain why the justices with relatively humble backgrounds have included conservatives such as Thomas and Warren Burger as well as liberals such as Sotomayor and Earl Warren.

In terms of race and sex, the current Court is the most diverse in history. It is also fairly diverse in terms of economic backgrounds. Still, the Court is homogeneous in the sense that from the time of their college education, all the justices became part of an elite group. All nine of the 2019–2020 justices graduated from private undergraduate schools, including seven who went to Ivy League schools. And all nine justices went to law school at Harvard or Yale. Some commentators have expressed concern about what they see as the insularity of a Court that comes from such a narrow range of schools. As Justice Kagan said, referring to Ruth Bader Ginsburg's law school transfer, "Know what our diversity is? Justice Ginsburg spent a year at Columbia."[50]

Partisan Political Activity

Even though today's justices spent the bulk of their pre-Court careers in the legal system, most shared with their predecessors some involvement in partisan politics. Seven of the 2019–2020 justices served in presidential administrations. Clarence Thomas worked with John Danforth when Danforth was the Missouri attorney general and a U.S. senator. Stephen Breyer interrupted his service as a law professor twice to work with Democrats on the Senate Judiciary Committee. Prior to his five years of service in the George W. Bush administration, Brett Kavanaugh was on the staff of independent counsel Kenneth Starr for the investigation of Bill Clinton that led to his impeachment.

This pattern reflects the criteria for selecting justices. Even when nominations to the Court are not used as political rewards, presidents look more favorably on people who have contributed to their party's success. Partisan activity also brings people to the attention of presidents, their staff members, and others who influence nomination decisions. Perhaps most important, it helps in winning the high government positions that make people credible candidates for the Court.

The Role of Chance

No one becomes a Supreme Court justice through an inevitable process. Rather, advancement from membership in the bar to a seat on the Court results from luck as much as anything else. This luck comes in two stages: achieving the high positions in government or law that make individuals possible candidates for the Court and then getting serious consideration for the Court and actually winning an appointment.

In that second stage, a potential justice gains enormously by belonging to a particular political party at the appropriate time. Every appointment to the Court between 1969 and 1992 was made by a Republican president. As a result, a whole generation of potential justices who were liberal Democrats had essentially no chance to win appointments. Further, someone whose friend or associate achieves a powerful position becomes a far stronger candidate for a seat on the Court. Elena Kagan accomplished a great deal, culminating in her appointment as dean at the Harvard Law School. But if she had not known Barack Obama, there is little chance that she would have become solicitor general and then won a Supreme Court appointment.

More broadly, everyone appointed to the Court has benefited from a favorable series of circumstances that build on each other. This does not mean that the effects of presidential appointments to the Court are random. Presidents and their aides increasingly make systematic efforts to identify the nominees who serve their goals best. But it does mean that specific individuals achieve membership on the Court through good fortune. As Kagan said, "It's a lot of chance that the nine of us are there rather than nine other people."[51]

LEAVING THE COURT

Opportunities to appoint new justices enable presidents to shape the Court's membership and influence the policies it makes. In the Supreme Court's first century, those opportunities sometimes arose from legislation that increased the Court's size to allow new appointments. Some prominent Democrats have talked about that possibility as a means to counterbalance President Trump's appointments, but the enactment of such legislation seems unlikely. Today, new members come to the Court only when a sitting justice departs.

Justices leave the Court involuntarily if they die or if they are removed through impeachment proceedings. In contrast with the nineteenth century, few justices in the past several decades have stayed on the Court until death. William Rehnquist, Antonin Scalia, and Ruth Bader Ginsberg are the only justices to die in office since Robert Jackson in 1954. And no justice has ever left the Court through impeachment proceedings. Thus, justices' Court tenure usually ends through their own decisions, though external pressures sometimes play a role in those decisions.

As Table 2-4 shows, over the last several decades, justices have left the Court for a variety of reasons. One reason that has become quite uncommon is the attraction of another position. In past eras, some justices did resign to seek or take another office. For instance, Charles Evans Hughes resigned to become the Republican nominee

Table 2-4   Reasons for Leaving the Court since 1965

Year	Justice	Age	Primary reasons for leaving	Length of time from leaving until death
1965	Goldberg	56	Appointment as ambassador to the United Nations	24 years
1967	Clark	67	Son's appointment as attorney general	10 years
1969	Fortas	58	Pressures based on possible ethical violations	13 years
1969[a]	Warren	78[b]	Age	5 years
1971	Black	85	Age and ill health	1 month
1971	Harlan	72	Age and ill health	3 months
1975	Douglas	77	Age and ill health	4 years
1981	Stewart	66	Age	4 years
1986	Burger	78	Uncertain: age, demands of service on a federal commission may have been factors	9 years
1987	Powell	79	Age and health concerns	11 years
1990	Brennan	84	Age and ill health	7 years
1991	Marshall	83[b]	Age and ill health	2 years
1993	White	76[b]	Desire to allow another person to serve, possibly age	9 years
1994	Blackmun	85	Age	5 years
2005	Rehnquist	80	Death	Same time
2006[a]	O'Connor	75	Spouse's ill health	NA
2009	Souter	69	Desire to return to New Hampshire	NA
2010	Stevens	90[b]	Age	9 years
2016	Scalia	79	Death	Same time
2018	Kennedy	82[b]	Desire to spend time with family, possibly age and health	NA
2020	Ginsburg	87	Death	Same time

Sources: Biographical sources, newspaper stories.

Note: NA = not applicable.

a. Warren originally announced the intent to leave the Court in 1968, O'Connor in 2005.

b. When they announced their intent to leave the Court, Warren was seventy-seven, Marshall eighty-two, White seventy-five, Stevens eighty-nine, and Kennedy eighty-one.

for president in 1916. (He lost the general election; fourteen years later he rejoined the Court as chief justice.) But the only justice to leave the Court for another position since 1942 was Arthur Goldberg, who resigned in 1965 to become U.S. ambassador to the United Nations. Goldberg did so with great reluctance, bowing to intense pressure from a president (Lyndon Johnson) who wanted to create a vacancy on the Court that he could fill. In contrast, Byron White rejected the idea of becoming FBI director when the Reagan administration sounded him out about it.

With the possibility of other positions largely irrelevant, justices face the choice between continued Court service and retirement. Financial considerations once played an important part in those choices: several justices stayed on the Court, sometimes with serious infirmities, to keep receiving their salaries. Congress established a judicial pension in 1869, and it is now quite generous. Justices who have served as federal judges for at least ten years and who are at least sixty-five years old can retire and continue to receive the salary they received at the time of retirement if their age and years of service add up to eighty or more. Justices can also receive any salary increases granted to sitting justices if they are disabled or if they perform a certain amount of service for the federal courts, generally equal to one-quarter of full-time work.

Thereby freed from financial concerns, older justices weigh the satisfactions of remaining on the Court against the prospective enjoyments of retirement and against concern about their capacity to handle their work. In the current era, the satisfactions of continued Court service seem to be quite substantial: since 1970 all the justices except Potter Stewart and David Souter have stayed on the Court past the age of seventy, and nine have served in their eighties. Even with the promise of generous pensions, some justices have remained on the Court after their health weakened considerably. During his last term on the Court in 1974 and 1975, William O. Douglas's mental condition had deteriorated so much that his colleagues issued no decisions in cases in which his vote would have been decisive.[52] William Rehnquist continued his service as chief justice in 2005 even when he was unable to participate fully in the Court's work because of cancer; he died later that year. Antonin Scalia had serious medical problems before his death in 2016, but it does not appear that those problems had much effect on his work as a justice.

Most justices do leave the Court when their infirmities become clear. Sandra Day O'Connor asked a former law clerk to monitor her work and let her know if she was no longer doing her job effectively.[53] John Paul Stevens asked his colleague David Souter to serve the same function for him. In early 2010, after Souter had retired, Stevens was troubled when he found himself stumbling over words for the first time while presenting his opinion in a case. That experience moved him toward retirement, which he announced three months later.[54]

Souter and Sandra Day O'Connor retired in the absence of health problems—Souter because of his preference for living in New Hampshire and O'Connor because of her need to care for her ailing husband. O'Connor's retirement came under unusual circumstances. With Chief Justice Rehnquist's own health deteriorating in 2004 and 2005, O'Connor talked with him about the timing of their retirements in light of their shared view that they should not create two Court vacancies in the same year. When Rehnquist made it clear that he would not retire in 2005, O'Connor concluded that she should retire herself rather than wait two years to retire in case Rehnquist left the Court in 2006. As it turned out, Rehnquist died in 2005 after O'Connor announced her retirement. The health of O'Connor's husband then declined so much that she could no longer care for him, which meant that she would have had no reason to leave the Court. O'Connor's seat was filled with the more conservative Samuel Alito, so her deference to Rehnquist made considerable difference for the Court. According to one account, O'Connor later wondered whether Rehnquist had maneuvered to get her to retire.[55]

Justices are well aware that the Court's future direction depends in part on which president gets to appoint their successor. The half dozen justices who retired most recently did so at a time when the president was ideologically compatible with them, and this pattern is not entirely accidental. For instance, a friend of David Souter's reported that Souter told him in 2008, "If Obama wins, I'll be the first one to retire."[56] Souter did announce his retirement three months after Obama took office. But health problems and other circumstances sometimes prevent justices from timing their retirements in this way.[57]

Just as some presidents have tried to create vacancies on the Court by inducing justices to take other positions, some have sought to secure the retirements of older justices. John Kennedy reportedly persuaded Felix Frankfurter to retire after ill health had decreased his effectiveness, but some other justices resisted similar efforts by Richard Nixon and Jimmy Carter.

When Donald Trump became president in 2017, three justices were at least seventy-eight years old. Democrats Stephen Breyer (seventy-eight at the time) and Ruth Bader Ginsburg (eighty-three) were quite unlikely to retire under a Republican president so long as they were in good health. Ginsburg had faced calls from liberals to retire while Barack Obama was president, but she chose to stay on the Court. With Trump in office, she continued to insist that she would not retire despite several serious health problems that she had overcome. She noted in 2019 that when she contracted cancer in 2009, a Republican senator "announced with great glee that I was going to be dead within six months. That senator . . . is now himself dead."[58] She remained on the Court until her death in 2020.

Anthony Kennedy, eighty years old when President Trump took office, was a fairly conservative Republican. During the 2016 campaign, lawyers working with Trump consulted Kennedy when they were creating a list of potential Court nominees, and Kennedy suggested several of his former law clerks. President Trump filled the Scalia seat with Neil Gorsuch, who had clerked for Kennedy in the Supreme Court. Trump later nominated three other former Kennedy clerks to federal courts of appeals. Trump spoke warmly of Kennedy. After Trump gave his first speech to Congress, he talked with Kennedy and praised his son Justin, who was acquainted with Donald Trump Jr. The administration got what it wanted when Kennedy announced his retirement in June 2018, though it is uncertain how much its efforts affected Kennedy's decision. In any event, it is very likely that he wanted to have a Republican president choose his successor.

▶ **Photo 2-12** Justice Anthony Kennedy at the 2018 ceremony in which his successor Brett Kavanaugh was sworn in. Like most other justices in the current era, Kennedy retired from the Court when a president who shared his ideological leaning was in office.

Under the Constitution, justices can be removed through impeachment proceedings for "treason, bribery, or other high crimes and misdemeanors."[59] President Thomas Jefferson actually sought to gain control of the largely Federalist (and anti-Jefferson) judiciary through the use of impeachment, and Congress did impeach and convict a federal district judge in 1803. Justice Samuel Chase made himself vulnerable to impeachment by participating in President John Adams's campaign for reelection in 1800 and by making some injudicious and partisan remarks to a Maryland grand jury in 1803. Chase was impeached, but the Senate acquitted him in 1805. His acquittal effectively ended Jefferson's plans to seek the impeachment of other justices.

No justice has been impeached since then, but the possible impeachment of two justices was the subject of serious discussion. Several efforts were made to remove William Douglas, most seriously in 1969 and 1970. The reasons stated publicly by advocates of impeachment were Douglas's financial connections with a foundation and his outside writings.[60] A special House committee failed to approve a resolution to impeach Douglas, and the resolution died in 1970.

Had Abe Fortas not resigned from the Court in 1969, he actually might have been removed by Congress.[61] Fortas had been criticized for his financial dealings at the time of his unsuccessful nomination to be chief justice in 1968. A year later, it was disclosed that he had a lifetime contract as a consultant to a foundation and had received money from the foundation at a time when the person who directed it was being prosecuted by the federal government. Under considerable pressure, Fortas resigned. The resignation came too quickly to determine whether an impeachment effort would have been successful. But almost certainly, it would have been serious.

The campaigns against Douglas and Fortas came primarily from the Nixon administration, which sought to replace the two strong liberals with more conservative justices. John Dean, a lawyer on Nixon's staff, later reported that Fortas's resignation led to "a small celebration in the attorney general's office," which "was capped with a call from the president, congratulating" Justice Department officials "on a job well done."[62] In contrast, according to Dean, the unsuccessful campaign against Douglas "created an intractable resolve by Douglas never to resign while Nixon was president."[63]

The Fortas episode seems unlikely to be repeated, in part because it reminded justices of the need to avoid questionable financial conduct. The occasional removal of federal judges through impeachment proceedings makes it clear that impeachment is a real option. But it is used only in cases with strong evidence of serious misdeeds, often involving allegations of corrupt behavior.

In practice, then, the timing of a justice's leaving the Court reflects primarily the justice's own inclinations, health, and longevity. Those who want to influence the Court's membership may have their say when a vacancy occurs, but they have little control over the creation of vacancies.

Justices who enjoy good health after their retirement often remain active, and that is true of the three most recent retirees. David Souter has served frequently in the federal court of appeals in Boston, near his New Hampshire home. In the decade after his 2009 retirement, he participated in about 400 decisions.[64] In the nine years between his 2010 retirement and his death, John Paul Stevens wrote three books and some lengthy book reviews, and he gave a number of speeches and interviews.

Before her health declined, Sandra Day O'Connor combined judicial and non-judicial activity. She participated in cases for eight years after her 2006 retirement, sitting with all eleven regional courts of appeals. She also spoke on behalf of causes such as replacement of state judicial elections with appointment systems. In 2009 she founded an organization that develops and distributes video games to teach students about the political system and to encourage political participation.[65] Her example—like those of Stevens and Souter—underlines the fact that many justices leave the Court while they still have the capacity to play active roles.

CONCLUSION

The recruitment of Supreme Court justices is a complex process. People do not rise to the Court in an orderly fashion. Rather, whether they become credible candidates for the Court and whether they actually win appointments depend on a wide range of circumstances. Indeed, something close to pure luck plays a powerful role in determining who becomes a justice.

The criteria that presidents use in choosing nominees and the balance of power between president and Senate have varied over the Court's history. The attributes of the people selected as justices have also varied. Justices today are relatively diverse in race, gender, and social class backgrounds, but they are also relatively narrow in their educational and career backgrounds.

In the current era of high political polarization, presidents choose nominees with close attention to their policy preferences, senators scrutinize nominees closely, and interest groups work hard to influence the selection of justices. That is not surprising. All these participants recognize the Court's power and prestige, and they also perceive a strong link between the Court's membership and its decisions.

The same considerations may help to explain the reluctance of most justices to leave the Court, even at an advanced age. In any event, that reluctance has meant that vacancies on the Court sometimes occur only after long intervals. But whatever the timing of vacancies may be, the importance of seats on the Court has made the selection of justices a subject of intense interest in the political world and the country as a whole.

NOTES

1. Henry J. Abraham, *Justices, Presidents, and Senators: A History of U.S. Supreme Court Appointments from Washington to Bush II*, 5th ed. (Lanham, Md.: Rowman & Littlefield, 2008), 146.
2. "Judging Brett Kavanaugh and the Supreme Court with John Yoo," *Uncommon Knowledge with Peter Robinson*, Hoover Institution, September 5, 2018, quoted in Ruth Marcus, *Supreme Ambition: Brett Kavanaugh and the Conservative Takeover* (New York: Simon & Schuster, 2019), 152.
3. Mollie Hemingway and Carrie Severino, *Justice on Trial: The Kavanaugh Confirmation and the Future of the Supreme Court* (Washington, D.C.: Regnery, 2019), 14–16. The quotations are from p. 16.
4. Jeffrey Budziak, "Blind Justice or Blind Ambition? The Influence of Promotion on Decision Making in the U.S. Courts of Appeals," *Justice System Journal* 34 (2013): 295–320; Ryan C. Black and Ryan J. Owens, "Courting the President: How Circuit Court Judges Alter Their Behavior for Promotion to the Supreme Court," *American Journal of Political Science* 60 (January 2016): 30–43.
5. These cases include *Jackson Women's Health Organization v. Dobbs* (5th Cir. 2019), *Kanter v. Barr* (7th Cir. 2019), *Trump v. Mazars USA, LLP* (D.C. Cir. 2019), and *United States v. Brown* (11th Cir. 2020). The term "auditioning" is discussed in Marcus, *Supreme Ambition*, 152.
6. Carl Hulse, *Confirmation Bias: Inside Washington's War Over the Supreme Court, from Scalia's Death to Judge Kavanaugh* (New York: HarperCollins, 2019), 168–169; Marcus, *Supreme Ambition*, 65–66.
7. Hulse, *Confirmation Bias*, 170–171.
8. See Paul M. Collins Jr. and Lori Ringhand, *Supreme Court Confirmation Hearings and Constitutional Change* (New York: Cambridge University Press, 2013).
9. Adam Liptak, "A Simple Script: Saying Nothing, Over and Over," *New York Times*, September 9, 2018, 1.
10. Kevin Liptak, "How Kavanaugh Maneuvered to Win His Confirmation Fight," *CNN*, October 8, 2018.
11. Ian Millhiser, "Trump Says He Will Delegate Judicial Selection to the Conservative Federalist Society," *ThinkProgress*, June 15, 2016.

12. Joan Biskupic, *Sandra Day O'Connor* (New York: HarperCollins, 2005), 72–73. Burger's role in the Nixon nominations is discussed in John W. Dean, *The Rehnquist Choice* (New York: Free Press, 2001), 19, 52, 179–185.

13. Hemingway and Severino, *Justice on Trial*, 52; Christopher Cadelago, Nancy Cook, and Andrew Restuccia, "How a Private Meeting with Kennedy Helped Trump Get to 'Yes' on Kavanaugh," *Politico*, July 9, 2018.

14. This discussion is based in part on John Anthony Maltese, *The Selling of Supreme Court Nominees* (Baltimore, Md.: Johns Hopkins University Press, 1995); and Gregory A. Caldeira and John R. Wright, "Lobbying for Justice: The Rise of Organized Conflict in the Politics of Federal Judgeships," in *Contemplating Courts*, ed. Lee Epstein (Washington, D.C.: CQ Press, 1995), 44–71.

15. Judicial Crisis Network, "Judicial Crisis Network Launches $10 Million Campaign to Preserve Justice Scalia's Legacy, Support President-Elect Trump Nominee," January 9, 2017, https://judicialnetwork.com/jcn-press-release/judicial-crisis-network-launches-10-million-campaign-preserve-justice-scalias-legacy-support-president-elect-trump-nominee/; Bill Allison and Greg Sullivan, "Kavanaugh Ads Flood the Airwaves," *Bloomberg News*, October 3, 2018.

16. Richard Davis, *Supreme Democracy: The End of Elitism in Supreme Court Nominations* (New York: Oxford University Press, 2017), 16.

17. The discussion of nomination decisions that follows draws much from Christine L. Nemacheck, *Strategic Selection: Presidential Nomination of Supreme Court Justices from Herbert Hoover through George W. Bush* (Charlottesville: University of Virginia Press, 2007); and David Alistair Yalof, *Pursuit of Justices: Presidential Politics and the Selection of Supreme Court Justices* (Chicago: University of Chicago Press, 1999).

18. Brian Lamb, Susan Swain, and Mark Farkas, eds., *The Supreme Court: A C-Span Book Featuring the Justices in Their Own Words* (New York: Public Affairs, 2010), 160.

19. Nemacheck, *Strategic Selection*, chap. 3; Sheldon Goldman, Elliot Slotnick, and Sara Schiavoni, "Obama's Judiciary at Midterm: The Confirmation Drama Continues," *Judicature* 94 (May–June 2011): 277.

20. Hulse, *Confirmation Bias*, 2–3.

21. Hulse, *Confirmation Bias*, 163.

22. The nomination process for Gorsuch is described in Adam Liptak, "Gorsuch Clinched Spot After a Lengthy Process," *New York Times*, February 7, 2017, A15; Hulse, *Confirmation Bias*, 160–163; and Hemingway and Severino, *Justice on Trial*, 58–62.

23. The nomination process for Kavanaugh is discussed in Mark Landler and Maggie Haberman, "Former Bush Aide Is Trump Pick for Court," *New York Times*, July 10, 2018, A1; Ashley Parker and Robert Costa, "President Wavered Late on Nominee Decision," *Washington Post*, July 11, 2018, A1; Hemingway and Severino, *Justice on Trial*, 20–24; and Marcus, *Supreme Ambition*, 67–92.

24. Richard A. Posner, "The Supreme Court After the Nuclear Option," *Slate*, April 8, 2017.

25. Robert Barnes, "Clinton Papers Illuminate the Selection Process," *Washington Post*, June 9, 2014, A13.

26. Matt Grossmann and David A. Hopkins, *Asymmetric Politics: Ideological Republicans and Group Interest Democrats* (New York: Oxford University Press, 2016), 72.

27. "Justice Anthony Kennedy: Surely Reagan's Biggest Disappointment," *Human Events*, May 31–June 7, 1996, 3.

28. Robert Scigliano, *The Supreme Court and the Presidency* (New York: Free Press, 1971), 95.

29. William O. Douglas, *The Court Years 1939–1975: The Autobiography of William O. Douglas* (New York: Random House, 1980), 247; John Paul Stevens, *Five Chiefs: A Supreme Court Memoir* (New York: Little, Brown, 2011), 60–61.

30. John Fritze, "President Trump on Supreme Court Nominee Brett Kavanaugh: 'I Don't Even Know Him,'" *USA Today*, October 2, 2018.

31. These figures on nominations and confirmations and figures presented later in the chapter are based on Denis Steven Rutkus and Maureen Bearden, *Supreme Court Nominations, 1789 to the Present: Actions by the Senate, the Judiciary Committee, and the President*, Congressional Research Service, Report RL33225 (2012); and Henry B. Hogue, *Supreme Court Nominations Not Confirmed, 1789–August 2010*, Congressional Research Service, Report RL31171 (2010), updated with the Gorsuch and Kavanaugh nominations and confirmations. In several instances, it is uncertain whether a nomination should be counted as failing to win confirmation, so the figure of twenty-nine failures should be regarded as approximate.

32. Charles M. Cameron and Jonathan P. Kastellec, "Are Supreme Court Nominations a Move-the-Median Game?" *American Political Science Review* 110 (November 2016): 778–797.

33. These figures are based on data in Rutkus and Bearden, *Supreme Court Nominations*, 33–39.

34. In computing this success rate, all nominations made in the fourth calendar year of a president's term or early in the fifth year before the term ended were counted as last-year nominations.

35. Laura Kalman, *The Long Reach of the Sixties: LBJ, Nixon, and the Making of the Contemporary Supreme Court* (New York: Oxford University Press, 2017), 141.

36. "Here Comes the Judge," *Newsweek*, February 2, 1970, 19.

37. Richard Reeves, *President Nixon: Alone in the White House* (New York: Simon & Schuster, 2001), 161.

38. Sonia Sotomayor, "A Latina Judge's Voice," *Berkeley La Raza Law Journal* 13 (Spring 2002): 92.

39. Jamie Stengle, "Ruth Bader Ginsburg Speaks at SMU," *Deseret News* (Salt Lake City), August 29, 2011; Brent Martin, "Chief Justice Roberts: Scalia, Ginsburg Wouldn't Be Confirmed Today," *Nebraska Radio Network*, September 19, 2014.

40. See Scott Basinger and Maxwell Mak, "The Changing Politics of Supreme Court Confirmations," *American Politics Research* 40 (July 2012): 737–763.

41. Davis, *Supreme Democracy*, 177.

42. Ed Enoch, "U.S. Supreme Court Justice Elena Kagan Speaks About Diversity," *Tuscaloosa News*, October 4, 2013.

43. This discussion of justices' backgrounds is based in part on John R. Schmidhauser, *Judges and Justices: The Federal Appellate Judiciary* (Boston, Mass.: Little, Brown, 1979), 41–100.

44. These proportions are based on biographies in the *Biographical Directory of Federal Judges*, compiled by the Federal Judicial Center, https://www.fjc.gov/history/judges.

45. Benjamin A. Barton, "An Empirical Study of Supreme Court Justice Pre-Appointment Experience," *Florida Law Review* 64 (September 2012): 1148–1151.

46. Carl Hulse, "Is the Supreme Court Naïve About Corruption? Ask Jack Abramoff," *New York Times*, July 6, 2016, A15. The decision was *McDonnell v. United States* (2016).

47. Lee Epstein, Jeffrey A. Segal, Harold J. Spaeth, and Thomas G. Walker, *The Supreme Court Compendium*, 6th ed. (Washington, D.C.: CQ Press, 2015), Table 4-2.

48. Bradley Blackburn, "Justices Ruth Bader Ginsburg and Sandra Day O'Connor on Life and the Supreme Court," *ABC News*, October 26, 2010.

49. Adam Liptak, "Two Justices Ponder a Cookie-Cutter Court," *New York Times*, September 6, 2016, A13.

50. Bruce Vielmetti, "Visiting MU, Justice Kagan Tells of Hunting with Scalia," *Milwaukee Journal Sentinel*, April 3, 2012. See Patrick J. Glen, "Harvard and Yale Ascendant: The Legal Education of the Justices from Holmes to Kagan," *UCLA Law Review Discourse* 58 (2010): 129–154.

51. Colleen Walsh, "Associate Justice Elena Kagan Provides Peek into Supreme Court's Everyday Workings," *Harvard Gazette*, September 4, 2014, http://news.harvard.edu/gazette/story/2014/09/court-sense.

52. John Paul Stevens, *The Making of a Justice: Reflections on My First 94 Years* (New York: Little, Brown, 2019), 141.

53. Evan Thomas, *First: Sandra Day O'Connor* (New York: Random House, 2019), 257.

54. Stevens, *Making of a Justice*, 499, 503.

55. Thomas, *First*, 371–380. See Mary Harris and Dahlia Lithwick, "Why Ruth Bader Ginsburg Didn't Retire During Obama's Presidency," *Slate*, January 18, 2019.

56. Robert Barnes, "Souter Reportedly Planning to Retire from High Court," *Washington Post*, May 1, 2009, A1.

57. Christine Kexel Chabot, "Do Justices Time Their Retirements Politically? An Empirical Analysis of the Timing and Outcomes of Supreme Court Retirements in the Modern Era," *Utah Law Review* 2019 (2019): 527–580.

58. Nina Totenberg, "Justice Ginsburg: 'I Am Very Much Alive,'" *Morning Edition*, National Public Radio, July 24, 2019, https://www.npr.org/templates/transcript/transcript.php?storyId=744633713.

59. U.S. Constitution, art. 2, § 4.

60. John Ehrlichman, *Witness to Power: The Nixon Years* (New York: Simon & Schuster, 1982), 122.

61. Laura Kalman, *Abe Fortas: A Biography* (New Haven, Conn.: Yale University Press, 1990), 359–376; Bruce Allen Murphy, *Fortas: The Rise and Ruin of a Supreme Court Justice* (New York: Morrow, 1988).

62. Dean, *Rehnquist Choice*, 11.

63. Dean, *Rehnquist Choice*, 26.

64. Information on participation in cases by Justices Souter and O'Connor was drawn from the LexisNexis archive of court of appeals decisions.

65. Natasha Singer, "Trailblazing Justice Now Has Games on Docket," *New York Times*, March 28, 2016, B1.

CHAPTER THREE

THE CASES

In the term that ended in July 2020, the Supreme Court issued fifty-four decisions in cases that it had accepted for full consideration on the merits—that is, to address the legal issues in those cases. The cases that the Court put on its agenda and then decided were a very small proportion of all the court cases and potential cases that could have led to decisions by the Court. This chapter examines the process of agenda setting that produces those rare events. In the first stage of that process, people make a series of decisions that bring their cases to the Supreme Court. In the second stage, the Court selects from those cases the few—currently about 1 in 100—that it will fully consider and decide. Except for a few special sets of cases, when the Court agrees to hear a case it does so formally by granting a writ of certiorari to call the case up from a lower court.

Several sets of people and institutions help set the Court's agenda. In the first stage, litigants file cases and bring them through the legal system to the Court. Most of these litigants are represented by lawyers in at least part of this process, and some receive direct or indirect help from interest groups.

The Court itself plays no direct part at this stage. But people's expectations about how the Court might respond to their case affect their decision whether to bring it to the Court. After Justice Antonin Scalia died in 2016, the leaders of the New York State Rifle and Pistol Association decided not to take their challenge of a state gun law to the Court because it had become highly unlikely that the group could win a majority in the Court. "It's just the wrong time," the Association president said.[1] But in 2018, after Neil Gorsuch's appointment to succeed Scalia and Brett Kavanaugh's nomination to succeed Anthony Kennedy, it appeared that the Court would be more receptive to arguments against gun regulations. The Association then brought a challenge of a New York City gun law to the Court.[2]

Justices sometimes try to shape litigants' thinking about the desirability of bringing certain kinds of cases, typically by using opinions to encourage certain kinds of cases. For instance, Justice Kavanaugh's opinion in *Paul v. United States* (2019) indicated that he would welcome a case in which the Court could consider narrowing the ability of Congress to delegate authority to administrative agencies. That signal was especially powerful because the other four conservative justices had expressed similar views in an earlier decision in which Kavanaugh did not participate.[3]

In the second stage of the process, in which the Court chooses cases to hear, the justices are the sole decision makers. And because they receive so many petitions for certiorari, they have a wide range of legal and policy issues from which to choose. But their choices may be influenced by the litigants, lawyers, and interest groups that participate in cases. For their part, the other branches of the federal government structure both stages by setting the Court's jurisdiction and writing other statutes and rules that affect cases, and the executive branch participates directly in many cases.

The two sections of this chapter examine the two stages of agenda setting in the Court. In the first section, I examine how and why cases are brought to the Court. In the second, I discuss how and why the justices choose certain cases to decide on the merits. In the last part of that section, I consider why the Court now hears a relatively small number of cases each year.

REACHING THE COURT: LITIGANTS, ATTORNEYS, AND INTEREST GROUPS

Litigants, their attorneys, and interest groups are all important to the Supreme Court. The federal government is the most frequent and most distinctive participant in Supreme Court cases. I will discuss all these sets of participants, giving particular attention to their roles in bringing cases to the Court.

Litigants

Every case that comes to the Supreme Court has at least one formal party, or litigant, on each side. For a case to reach the Court, one or more of the parties must initiate the litigation and move it upward through the court system.

Litigants in the Court are diverse. Among the petitioners who ask the Court to hear cases, the great majority are individuals. Most of these individuals are criminal defendants or prisoners; the others occupy a variety of roles. Among respondents—the litigants who are on the other side from petitioners—the largest category consists of governments and government agencies at all levels. Individuals are also respondents in many cases. Businesses frequently appear as petitioners or respondents. Other kinds of organizations, such as nonprofit groups and labor unions, are parties in some Court cases.

Table 3-1 shows the attributes of the competing litigants in the cases that the Court decided after oral argument in the 2019 term. The table underlines the prominence of governments (including government officials) and businesses (mostly corporations) in the Court's cases alongside individuals. The most common pairing of parties, appearing in more than one-third of the cases, was an individual versus government.

Table 3-1   Percentages of Cases with Oral Argument Involving Various Sets of Competing Litigants, 2019 Term

Competing litigants	Percentage
Criminal defendant or prisoner vs. government	19
Other individual vs. government or government employee (majority were immigration related)	17
Business vs. government or government employee	19
Business vs. business	11
Business vs. individual (majority were employment related)	10
Interest group vs. government	10
Government vs. government	5
Other	10

Note: Business category includes individuals operating businesses. Consolidated cases are counted once unless they include cases that fall in different categories in the table.

One key question about litigants is why they become involved in court cases and carry those cases to the Supreme Court. We can think of litigants' motives as falling into two categories: advancing a direct personal or organizational interest, and seeking to shape political outcomes or public policy. Cases in which the first motive is dominant can be called ordinary litigation, while those in which the second motive is dominant can be called political litigation.

I use the term *ordinary litigation* because the overwhelming majority of court cases are motivated by the direct interests of the parties. Indeed, the great majority of cases brought to the Supreme Court are essentially ordinary litigation. Many are criminal cases in which a convicted defendant wants to get out of prison or to stay out. Other cases involve efforts by individuals to obtain monetary benefits from government agencies or monetary damages from private entities. Some cases come from businesses that have a significant economic stake in a dispute with other businesses or with a government body.

Ordinary litigation is typified by a case that arose from Puerto Rico's 2017 declaration of bankruptcy. As one attorney for an investment firm was arguing the constitutional question in the case, Justice Samuel Alito pressed him to identify the firm's financial stake in the outcome. The attorney noted that over $100 billion in debt was at stake in the case. Alito interjected, "Right, and your client wants more of it."[4] In *Monasky v. Taglieri* (2020), the issue involving interpretation of an international treaty arose in a child custody battle between two parents. The father who brought the case to court and the mother who successfully petitioned the Supreme Court to hear the case were not motivated by the legal issue in the case. Rather, these estranged parents each wanted to have custody of their child in their own country.[5]

In political litigation, the most common goal is gaining a judicial decision that favors the litigant's policy goals. Litigants with that purpose usually care more about shaping the law than about simply winning the case. That attribute is underlined by *New York State Rifle & Pistol Association v. City of New York* (2020), the case in which the Association and three individuals challenged a restriction on the transporting of guns that the city had adopted. After the Supreme Court accepted the case, the city eliminated that restriction and New York state acted to reinforce that change in the law. But the Association and other gun rights groups were not satisfied, because they sought a ruling by the Court that established broad limits on gun regulations. For that reason the Association disputed the city's assertion that the case had become moot. As one commentator put it, the challengers of the law "aren't taking victory for an answer."[6] In contrast, when one litigant whose petition for certiorari had attracted support from a broad coalition of interest groups was offered more money to drop his petition than he had been awarded by a trial court, he took the offer. From his perspective, his case was ordinary litigation.[7]

Although political litigation is the exception to the rule in cases brought to the Supreme Court, it is more common in the Court than in lower courts. Ordinary litigation usually ends at an early stage because the parties find it advantageous to settle their dispute or even to accept defeat rather than to fight on. In contrast, political litigants often want to get a case to the highest court, where a victory may establish a national policy they favor. In addition, political litigation sometimes attracts the support of interest groups that help to shoulder the costs and other burdens of carrying a case through the judicial system. Those costs are substantial; one litigant who won a favorable Supreme Court decision in 2019 reported that the case had cost him and his supporters more than $1.5 million.[8] Political litigation is especially common among the cases that the Court agrees to hear because political cases are more likely than ordinary litigation to contain broad legal issues that interest the justices.

Rules of legal standing require that a litigant have a direct stake in a case. So even when lawyers or interest groups orchestrate a case on the basis of their policy goals, they must bring the case in the name of one or more people or organizations that would be affected by the outcome. As a result, what looks like political litigation from the perspective of lawyers and interest groups might have a large element of ordinary litigation from the point of view of the litigants they support or recruit.

Some cases cannot easily be labeled as ordinary or political litigation, because the litigants have mixed motives. In cases brought by government agencies, ordinary and political elements may be difficult to separate. For instance, prosecutors file criminal cases to advance the specific mission of their agencies, but that mission is linked to the broader policy goal of attacking crime.

Individuals can have mixed motives as well. Sometimes they initiate a case to win something specific but become increasingly interested in the broader impact of their case. Simon Tam challenged the federal government's denial of a trademark that he sought for his rock band's name under a statutory provision that prohibited trademarks for "matter which may disparage . . . persons, living or dead, institutions, beliefs, or national symbols."[9] Tam became increasingly interested in the broad implications of his case as it was transformed from a dispute over interpretation of the statutory provision to a dispute over whether the provision violated the First Amendment—an issue that Tam's attorney initially raised "as an afterthought" but that ultimately won him a unanimous victory in the Court.[10]

Some litigants help to publicize their causes before and after the Supreme Court's decision. Others are drawn involuntarily into the public arena. People who challenge school practices that have strong community support on issues such as racial segregation and religious observances are often subject to negative reactions that can include "insults, hate mail, intimidating telephone calls, and even death threats."[11] In contrast, most litigants stay in the background, largely unnoticed, even as their cases shape legal policy on major issues.

Litigants also differ in the extent to which they participate in decisions about the handling of their case. Organizations sometimes play active roles in those decisions. That is not often true of individuals, who are more likely to leave decision making to their attorneys. As one reporter put it, the people in whose name a case was brought "often play bit roles in battles waged by legal advocacy groups pursuing policy changes."[12] In contrast, the lead petitioner in a 2019 case about class action settlements, an attorney associated with an interest group, presented oral argument on his own behalf before the Court.[13]

When lawyers take cases in order to advance policies they care about, they might not fully serve their clients' interests. Indeed, this seems to occur in some cases that get to the Court. But it appears that even policy-oriented lawyers usually give a high priority to those interests.

Attorneys

Of all the appearances that lawyers made in the Supreme Court's oral arguments during the 2019 term, about half were made by members of private law firms and about one-third by attorneys in the U.S. Department of Justice. The remainder were by employees of state and local governments, law professors, and employees of private interest groups.

Nearly all the lawyers in the Justice Department who presented oral argument were from the Office of the Solicitor General, which is the primary representative of the federal government in the Supreme Court. These lawyers regularly write briefs and present oral arguments in the Court, so they quickly become experienced and expert.

In the mid-twentieth century, the lawyers in the solicitor general's office and those who represented a few federal agencies that took their own cases to the Court stood out in this respect. Even though the cases that the Supreme Court accepts for oral argument usually have high stakes for the litigants and often for the country as a whole, the lawyers who represented litigants other than the federal government typically had little or no prior experience in the Court. There were only a few exceptions, most notably lawyers for interest groups such as the NAACP Legal Defense Fund that had a good many cases in the Court.

Since the 1980s, that situation has changed a good deal. As a group, lawyers in the solicitor general's office continue to stand out for the numbers of cases they handle in the Court. Those who remain in the office for most of their careers can amass very large numbers of oral arguments: Lawrence Wallace argued 157 cases during his thirty-five years in the office, and two other lawyers in the office (one who retired in 2019 and the other still active) have argued more than 100 cases. But increasingly, parties other than the federal government are also represented by experienced Supreme Court litigators.

Most of these experienced litigators are in private law firms that have Supreme Court litigation as one of their major areas of practice. They represent a range of litigants in the Court, but their primary clients are businesses that can pay their high fees—for one leading Supreme Court practitioner, more than $1,700 an hour.[14] The law firms with successful Supreme Court practices have become increasingly prominent in the Court: in the Court's 2019 term, lawyers from nine law firms presented one-third of all the oral arguments for litigants other than the federal government and nearly half of the arguments by attorneys in private practice. Many of the lawyers in these firms who handle cases in the Court had prior experience in the solicitor general's office, as law clerks in the Court, or both.

Table 3-2 shows how the experience of lawyers in the Court has grown since the mid-1990s, when specialization in Supreme Court advocacy was just beginning to develop. Again leaving aside the lawyers who represent the federal government, the proportion of oral arguments in the Court that were presented by lawyers who argued at least one other case over a five-year period jumped from one-quarter in the 1994 term to three-fifths in the 2019 term. Only two arguments in the 1994 term were presented by lawyers with more than five arguments over a five-year period—both by future chief justice John Roberts, who had made the preponderance of his prior arguments when he was in the solicitor general's office. In contrast, more than one-quarter of the arguments in the 2019 term came from lawyers with that level of experience. The growth in specialization is symbolized by the fact that Paul Clement has now argued more than 100 cases in the Court, about half of them since he left the solicitor general's office for private practice in 2008.

But the figures in Table 3-2 also indicate that advocates who appear before the Court only on rare occasions—often a single time over their careers—have hardly disappeared. These lawyers are even more common at the stage of petitioning the Court for hearings. One example is Matthew Weisberg, who practices in a small Pennsylvania law firm. After losing a debt collection case in the lower federal courts, he submitted his first petition for certiorari in 2018 on behalf of his consumer client. His petition was successful, perhaps aided by his recognition of the justices' preference for brevity: the petition was eight pages long, far shorter than average.[15]

Table 3-2 Numbers of Oral Arguments over a Five-Term Period by Lawyers Arguing Cases in the 1994 and 2019 Terms (lawyers for federal government excluded)

Number of arguments	1994 (percentage)	2019 (percentage)
1	74.7	40.2
2	16.0	19.6
3–5	8.0	10.3
6–10	0.0	19.6
11–15	0.0	2.8
16–25	1.3	7.5

Note: For lawyers who argued cases in the 1994 term, the five-term period is 1990–1994; for lawyers who argued cases in 2019, the period is 2015–2019. Lawyers who argued multiple cases in 1994 or 2019 are counted each time they argued a case. Thus, the 7.5 percent in the lower-right cell of the table means that, leaving aside arguments by lawyers for the federal government, 7.5 percent of the oral arguments in the 2019 term were made by lawyers who had 16–25 arguments in the 2015–2019 terms.

Some lawyers with no experience in the Court go on to present oral argument in their cases after their petitions are accepted, though most (including Weisberg) do not. These lawyers receive numerous inquiries from lawyers with Supreme Court practices who want to present the argument. Those inquiries are one reflection of the increasingly intense competition among Supreme Court "regulars" for the limited number of argument slots each term. For the same reason, when the Court accepts multiple cases and consolidates them for argument, the lawyers involved in the various cases on the same side usually vie with each other to participate in the argument.

Inevitably, lawyers vary in their effectiveness as advocates in the Court. On the whole, those who participate frequently in Court cases have a higher level of skills. Some of the justices have spoken of this difference. Justices Elena Kagan and Sonia Sotomayor have said that it is unfortunate when criminal defense lawyers argue before the Court rather than enlisting an experienced Supreme Court advocate. Sotomayor said that "I think it's malpractice for any lawyer who thinks this is my one shot before the Supreme Court and I have to take it."[16]

As these judgments suggest, justices have welcomed the growing role of experienced Supreme Court lawyers. As Kagan put it, these lawyers "really know the court" and "what it is we like."[17] Justice Clarence Thomas said that it made sense for litigants to hire the best lawyers to represent them in the Court. "If there is a .400 hitter, you will go with someone who will increase your odds."[18]

Lawyers who practice regularly before the Court become familiar to the justices, and some interact with them outside the Court. Two justices knew Theodore Olson, one leading Supreme Court advocate, well enough to attend his 2006 wedding. He was also a regular guest at the New Year's Eve dinners that Justice Ginsburg hosted.[19] Even in the formal setting of oral argument, this familiarity sometimes becomes evident in the interactions between justices and lawyers.

In the legal system as a whole, there is a positive correlation between the wealth of an individual or institution and the quality of the legal services available to that party. To a degree, this is true of the Supreme Court. The experienced Supreme Court advocates in private practice are most readily available to large corporations and other prosperous organizations that can afford their substantial fees. Further, because their firms regularly represent business firms, many of these lawyers will not represent consumers or employees in conflicts with businesses.[20] And one study verified that criminal defendants are more likely to have inexperienced Supreme Court advocates than other litigants, including the prosecution in criminal cases.[21]

But several mechanisms improve the position of people with limited resources. Because Supreme Court cases are both scarce and attractive to lawyers, Supreme Court specialists sometimes offer their services at no cost to litigants whose cases have been accepted by the Court. (The Court itself appoints an attorney to represent any indigent litigant whose case it accepts if that litigant does not have a lawyer from another source.) Further, more than a dozen law schools have established clinics to work on Supreme Court cases for no charge. These clinics assist litigants in many of the cases that the Court hears, sometimes in cooperation with law firms that have Supreme Court specialists, and faculty members associated with the clinics often present oral argument. Because of these mechanisms, one commentator argued that "there is plenty of good lawyering to go around."[22] Still, as a group, those litigants who can afford to hire the most experienced advocates have an advantage over those who cannot.

Many litigants—most of them prison inmates—have no attorneys when they file petitions for certiorari. Most people who cannot hire lawyers to write their petitions are at a considerable disadvantage. But in its 2019 term the Court heard two cases in which prison inmates successfully petitioned for certiorari without a lawyer's assistance.[23] Some prisoners use the assistance of "jailhouse lawyers," fellow inmates who have developed some expertise in the law. Calvin Johnson, a Louisiana inmate who was paid 20 cents an hour to assist other prisoners with their legal cases, became so knowledgeable that lawyers sought his advice. Freed in 2011, he helped to develop the challenge to nonunanimous jury verdicts in criminal cases that achieved a favorable ruling by the Court in 2020.[24]

Although people can petition for certiorari in their own cases without lawyers, arguing cases that the Court has accepted is another matter. The last non-lawyer who presented oral argument in his own case in the Court did so in 1978 (he won in a unanimous decision), and after that, the Court regularly prohibited specific litigants from following his example when they sought to do so.[25] In 2013, the Court adopted a blanket rule limiting oral argument to lawyers.

Occasionally the Court appoints a lawyer to argue for a position in a case that neither of the parties has taken.[26] This occurs most often when the lawyers for both sides agree that a lower-court decision should be overturned and the justices want to hear the arguments in favor of affirmance. In *Seila Law LLC v. Consumer Financial Protection Bureau* (2020), a federal court of appeals ruled that the statutory provision limiting the president's power to remove the director of the Bureau did not violate the constitutional separation of powers. Reflecting the view of the Trump administration, the solicitor general agreed with the petitioner's challenge to the court of appeals decision. After accepting the case, the Court appointed Paul Clement to argue that the statutory provision did not violate the Constitution.

Attorneys are eligible to participate in cases if they join the Supreme Court bar, for which the most important requirement is that they have been admitted to practice in a state for at least the past three years. But lawyers who cannot meet this requirement usually are allowed to argue cases they have brought to the Court.

Most lawyers join the Supreme Court bar primarily for the prestige. A few thousand join each year, and the great majority will never participate in a Supreme Court case. The Court is vigilant about disbarring lawyers who have been suspended or disbarred from the practice of law in their state. In 2017, the cases in which the Court suspended lawyers in the expectation that they would be disbarred included two instances of mistaken identity. In the second instance, the unlucky lawyer had once worked at the Court for several years. Informed of its mistakes, the Court quickly rescinded its actions.[27]

Interest Groups

Leaders of political interest groups must decide how to allocate their group's time, effort, and money in order to advance their policy goals. Groups vary considerably in how much attention they give to the Supreme Court. One key consideration is the relevance of courts in general and the Supreme Court in particular to a group's goals. Groups that advocate broad protections of civil liberties typically devote a good deal of work to litigation, because constitutional provisions that protect liberties provide a basis for lawsuits challenging government actions.

Another consideration for groups is the Court's likely receptiveness to a group's arguments. During the 1960s, when the Court was highly liberal, groups that favored liberal policies played the most active roles in the Court. As the Court has become more conservative over the past half century, it has also become more attractive to groups that advocate conservative policies. Conservative groups increasingly play a proactive role, seeking change in the Court's legal policies, while liberal groups sometimes try to keep issues out of the Court when the prospects for victory are not good.

Interest groups have another reason to participate in Supreme Court litigation. Group leaders want to maintain and enhance the strength of their organizations, and they may use their involvement with the Court as a means to attract members or financial contributions. That is especially true in an era in which the Court is the subject of great interest among people who care about politics and public policy.

The Array of Groups in the Court

Interest group activity aimed at the Supreme Court has increased dramatically in the past half century. One reason for this growth is that the number of active interest groups and the level of their activity have increased considerably. Another is a growing recognition of the importance of Supreme Court decisions to the goals of interest groups. Finally, the apparent success of some groups in shaping the Court's policies has encouraged other groups to seek similar success.

Hundreds of interest groups now participate in Supreme Court cases in some way. Among them are nearly all the groups that are most active in Congress and the executive branch. Box 3-1 provides a sampling of this participation by listing some of the groups that submitted amicus curiae briefs to the Court in the 2019 term. (Amicus briefs are submitted by individuals and organizations that are not parties to cases.)

BOX 3-1

A Sampling of Groups Submitting Amicus Curiae Briefs to the Supreme Court in the 2019 Term

---

Economic Groups: Business and Occupational

> Chamber of Commerce of the United States
>
> Service Employees International Union
>
> Intellectual Property Owners Association
>
> Mortgage Bankers Association
>
> National Association of Home Builders of the United States
>
> American Medical Association

Noneconomic Interests

> NAACP Legal Defense and Educational Fund, Inc.
>
> United States Conference of Catholic Bishops
>
> National PTA
>
> Fond du Lac Band of Lake Superior Chippewa

Ideological and Issue Groups

> National Women's Law Center
>
> ACLU Foundation of Louisiana

Pacific Legal Foundation

Criminal Justice Legal Foundation

Citizens United

Governments and Government Officials

State of Illinois

National School Boards Association

National League of Cities

Members of Congress

Former National Security Officials

As Box 3-1 shows, the groups that participate in Supreme Court cases can be placed in four broad categories. The first is economic: individual businesses, trade associations, professional groups, labor unions, and farm groups. Much of the Court's work affects the interests of economic groups, on issues that range from employment discrimination to regulation of product safety. The business community is especially well represented in the Court. Individual businesses frequently are parties to cases, and businesses and business groups regularly submit amicus briefs.

The most prominent economic group in the Supreme Court is the U.S. Chamber Litigation Center, the litigation arm of the U.S. Chamber of Commerce.[28] The Center frequently brings lawsuits in the name of the Chamber of Commerce, and occasionally these lawsuits reach the Supreme Court. The Center is very active as an amicus, submitting briefs in about one-quarter of the cases in which the Court heard oral arguments in its 2019 term; in calendar year 2019 the Center submitted eighteen briefs at the certiorari stage. The Center also holds moot courts to prepare lawyers who represent business interests for their arguments in the Court.

In the second category are groups that represent segments of the population defined by something other than economics. Most of these groups are based on personal attributes such as race, gender, age, and sexual orientation. The prototype for these groups is the NAACP Legal Defense and Educational Fund (often called the NAACP Legal Defense Fund, or simply LDF). LDF has engaged in substantial activity in several areas, including voting rights, school desegregation, criminal justice, and employment. Its successes in the Supreme Court encouraged the creation of organizations that were concerned with discrimination on grounds other than race.

The groups in the third category represent broad ideological positions or more specific issue positions rather than the interests of a specific segment of society. Here, the prototype is the American Civil Liberties Union (ACLU).[29] Established in 1920 to protect civil liberties, the ACLU involves itself in nearly every area of

> ▶ **Photo 3-1** Sherrilyn Ifill, president of the NAACP Legal Defense & Education Fund. Pictured behind her is Thurgood Marshall, first head of the Fund (and later a justice). This organization has played an active role in litigating issues involving civil rights over several decades.

civil liberties law. The ACLU has created special projects to undertake concerted litigation campaigns in specific areas of concern such as women's rights, capital punishment, and national security. Among the other groups that work to achieve liberal policy goals are the Constitutional Accountability Center, which litigates on a wide range of issues, and the Planned Parenthood Federation of America, for which abortion is a major concern.

Some conservative litigating groups have broad agendas. The Institute for Justice litigates against government regulation of economic activity and government action to take private property, and it involves itself in other issues as well. It sponsored the successful lawsuit to apply the Eighth Amendment's prohibition of excessive fines to the states through the Fourteenth Amendment in *Timbs v. Indiana* (2019) and the successful challenge to prohibitions of government financial aid to students in religious schools in *Espinoza v. Montana Department of Revenue* (2020). Similarly, the Center for Individual Rights participates in a wide range of cases.

Other groups have a more specific focus. Alliance Defending Freedom, a conservative group concerned with religious issues, has won a series of Supreme Court cases that it sponsored in recent years on issues such as the right of a baker to refuse to make cakes for same-sex marriages and a local sign regulation that affected notices of church services.[30] Edward Blum, a conservative activist, heads two organizations that oppose affirmative action programs, one of which (Project on Fair Representation) also sponsors cases dealing with election law.

The final category consists of governments and groups of government officials. Governments regularly appear as interest groups in the Court. The federal government is a special case, discussed later in this section. State and local governments often come to the Court as litigants. They regularly file amicus briefs as well—frequently with many states acting together on behalf of a shared point of view. The Court sometimes grants states' requests to participate as amici in oral argument.[31]

Forms of Group Activity

As the discussion so far suggests, interest groups attempt to influence the Court in multiple ways. First, they can try to exert influence from outside the litigation process. Some groups lobby the Court indirectly through marches and demonstrations. On a different level, groups try to get information that favors their positions to the Court through vehicles such as newspaper op-eds and blog posts. What two legal scholars have labeled "virtual briefing" through these vehicles has become increasingly common, and justices and their law clerks sometimes pay attention to this source of information.[32]

Occasionally, groups seek to bolster their positions on legal issues by sponsoring empirical research. The National Rifle Association (NRA) supported research by scholars to help build the case that the Second Amendment guarantees gun rights for individuals. This research made its way into briefs in the case that the Court heard on this issue and provided one basis for its 2008 ruling in favor of the NRA's position.[33]

Legal scholars and other lawyers who are associated with groups or sympathetic to their goals also develop arguments that can be used to support their positions in court. In the current era the network of lawyers who are active in the Federalist Society and other conservative groups has identified and refined legal arguments for conservative positions on an array of issues. Those arguments have won support from conservative justices on issues such as the extent of congressional power to regulate interstate commerce, a question that arose in the first legal challenge to President Obama's health care plan.[34]

Second, as discussed earlier, groups can enter cases by submitting amicus briefs on the question of whether a case should be accepted or, in accepted cases, directly on the merits. With the consent of the parties to a case or of the Court, any person or organization may submit an amicus brief to supplement the arguments of the parties. (Governments do not need to obtain consent.) Most of the time, the parties agree to the submission of amicus briefs on both sides. When the Court's consent is needed, it seldom is denied—five times between 2004 and early 2018.[35]

Interest groups ordinarily refrain from submitting amicus briefs opposing certiorari, because such briefs might have the undesired effect of indicating that a case raises an important issue. Amicus briefs favoring certiorari appear in only a small minority of cases, but that proportion has grown considerably in the past few decades. Some cases attract several briefs. In a 2019 case arising from a challenge to a religious monument on public land, sixteen briefs supported the petition for certiorari.[36]

Far more common are amicus briefs after the Court accepts cases for decisions on the merits. The great majority of these briefs are submitted by interest groups, and the proliferation of amicus briefs is an indication of the growth in interest group activity in the Court. In cases in which the Court heard oral arguments in the 1956–1965 terms, it received an average of 0.63 briefs per case.[37] In contrast, in most recent terms the Court has received an average of more than ten briefs per case.[38] In the 2019 term, the average was seventeen. In that term, amicus briefs were submitted in all but three of the cases in which the Court heard oral argument, 71 percent of the cases had at least five briefs, and 61 percent had at least ten briefs.[39] In cases that affect the interests of a broad range of interest groups, the

Court sometimes receives massive numbers of briefs—136 in the challenges to the Affordable Care Act ("Obamacare") that the Court addressed in 2012, 147 in the 2015 challenge to state prohibitions of same-sex marriage.[40] And because groups or individuals regularly join in submitting a brief, the number of participants is much larger than the number of briefs.

Amicus briefs are popular for several reasons. First, although the costs of preparing them are substantial, they are considerably cheaper than funding the litigant on one side of a case. Second, writing and submitting an amicus brief is straightforward, so that any group with the needed financial resources can do so. Finally, there is a widespread perception that amicus briefs sometimes influence the Court's decisions.

Although interest groups can act on their own in submitting amicus briefs, it has become increasingly common for the lawyers who represent parties in Supreme Court cases to coordinate amici on their side of the case.[41] What Allison Orr Larsen and Neal Devins call "the amicus machine" can be expensive to operate: one side in a 2013 case reported spending more than half a million dollars in what was later described as "soliciting and coordinating amici support."[42]

Direct participation in litigation is the third form of interest group activity in the Court. If a group has legal standing, it can initiate a case in its own name. In the Court's 2019 term, the NAACP, the Hawaii Wildlife Fund, and the Sierra Club were among the litigants.

More often, a group sponsors a case on behalf of another party—sometimes a litigant that the group has recruited. A group sponsor provides legal services to the litigant, bears other costs, and directs the course of the case. Carrying a case all the way to the Supreme Court is expensive, and it can be difficult to accomplish. But it is also very rewarding when it is successful, so groups with the necessary resources and expertise often seek to achieve that end.

Some of these groups engage in long-term litigation campaigns by sponsoring a series of cases in an issue area. Under the leadership of Thurgood Marshall, the NAACP Legal Defense Fund successfully attacked racial segregation of public schools in a series of cases that culminated in *Brown v. Board of Education* (1954). As head of the ACLU Women's Rights Project, Ruth Bader Ginsburg adopted the same kind of long-term strategy for advancing legal equality that Marshall had developed.[43] Indeed, the LDF's approach has served as a model for interest groups with a wide range of policy goals. Encouraged by the presence of a sympathetic Supreme Court in the current era, some conservative groups have engaged in litigation campaigns on issues such as affirmative action in school admissions and labor union fees for government employees.

These kinds of litigation campaigns are usually accompanied by efforts to influence the general public and the other branches of government.[44] Support for a group's goals outside the judiciary might have an indirect effect on court decisions. More important, victories in the legislative and executive branches could produce the same policies that groups seek from the courts, and the other branches shape the long-term effects of court decisions.

Polarization and Interest Group Activity

Inevitably, the growth in political polarization has affected interest group activity in litigation. The hardening of ideological divisions has encouraged groups to challenge policies with which they disagree. Similarly, groups increasingly use litigation to secure an advantage for the political party they favor. And on most controversial issues, the lawyers and interest groups that support one side with amicus briefs are overwhelmingly conservative and Republican, the other side liberal and Democratic.[45]

These changes are reflected in the activities of attorneys general as legal representatives of their states.[46] Today, attorneys general frequently submit amicus briefs on issues that do not affect state governments directly but on which they have strong policy views. As a result, it has become common for two coalitions of states to take opposing positions in amicus briefs, dividing primarily or entirely on the basis of the party affiliations of attorneys general.[47] Such conflicts arise most often on controversial issues such as affirmative action, abortion, and gun policy, and on issues that affect the fortunes of the political parties. In *Bostock v. Clayton County* (2020), a case about whether federal law prohibited discrimination based on sexual orientation, the fourteen attorneys general on one side were all Republicans; the twenty-two on the other side (including the District of Columbia) were all Democrats.

Attorneys general increasingly use litigation to attack federal policies with which they disagree when the president is from the opposing party. Alongside the policy issues that are at stake, such litigation is sometimes aimed at weakening the political standing of the president and the president's party. The use of litigation by states and other interest groups as a means to challenge a broad range of policies that were sponsored or adopted by a president accelerated during the Obama administration. That development was underlined by the long-term legal campaign against the Affordable Care Act, the federal health care law of 2010 that President Obama had sponsored.[48] Democratic attorneys general and liberal interest groups have taken similar actions against the Trump administration on issues such as immigration. The challenges to the administration's plan to terminate the Deferred Action for Childhood Arrivals (DACA) program were brought by twenty states alongside local governments and private interest groups.

The Significance of Interest Groups

Interest groups can influence both whether the Supreme Court grants certiorari to hear a case and the Court's rulings in the cases it does accept. Influence at those two stages is discussed later in this chapter and in Chapter 4. Here, I consider groups' effect on whether cases get to the Court in the first place. In this respect, cases may be placed in three categories.

The largest category contains the cases that come to the Court without any participation by interest groups. The issues in most of these cases are too narrow to interest any group. They reach the Court because the parties and attorneys have strong incentives to seek a Supreme Court hearing and sufficient resources to finance the litigation. It is not surprising that criminal defendants bring so many cases to the Court. Defendants who face lengthy prison terms have the needed incentive, and indigent defendants need not pay lawyers' fees or other expenses to get a case to the Court.

The second category consists of cases that would have reached the Court without any interest group involvement but in which groups are involved in some way. An interest group may assist one of the parties by providing attorneys' services or financing, or it may submit an amicus brief supporting a petition for hearing.

The third category includes cases that would not reach the Court without group sponsorship. There are many important legal questions in civil liberties that no individual litigant would take to the Supreme Court without help. For example, most of the individuals whose cases the ACLU takes could not have gone to court in the first place without the group's assistance.

Because group sponsorship of cases in the Court is relatively rare, only a small proportion of cases brought to the Court fall into this third category. But groups are most likely to provide full or partial sponsorship for cases that have a good chance to be heard by the Court and to produce major legal rulings. Indeed, much of the Court's support for legal protections for civil liberties over the past century was made possible by interest group action.[49]

The Federal Government

Of all the litigants in the Supreme Court, the federal government appears most frequently. Table 3-3 shows that the solicitor general's office as representative of the government participated in nearly 80 percent of the Court's decisions in cases with oral argument in the 2018 and 2019 terms, either as a party or as an amicus.

Table 3-3   Participation of Solicitor General's Office in Cases Decided after Oral Argument, 2018 and 2019 Terms (in percentages)

| | Did the solicitor general's office participate? | | |
| | Yes | | |
Role of office	As party	As amicus	No
Submitted brief on merits and participated in oral argument	34.1	44.5	21.4
Submitted brief at certiorari stage	34.1	13.5	52.4

Note: In cases that came to the Court as appeals, the stage at which the Court decided whether to hear oral argument is treated as the certiorari stage.

In almost half of the cases decided on the merits, the office also submitted a brief at the certiorari stage. The federal government's frequent participation helps to make it the most important interest group in the Court.

In turn, the group of about two dozen lawyers in the solicitor general's office has more impact on the Court than any other set of attorneys. Lawyers in the office represent the federal government in the Supreme Court. They decide whether to petition for certiorari in cases that the federal government has lost in lower courts. They also do the bulk of the government's legal work in Supreme Court cases, including briefs and oral arguments. Only a few federal agencies can act on their own in the Court rather than working through the solicitor general's office.

As head of the office, the solicitor general is a significant policy maker. Presidents and their aides seek to appoint someone with strong legal credentials. In the current era, ideological credentials are quite important as well. Noel Francisco, who served from 2017 to 2020, met both those criteria well. After their service, solicitors general often go into private practice and continue to argue cases before the Court. Since the office was created in 1870, six solicitors general later served on the Court. The most recent is Elena Kagan, appointed to the Court by President Obama in 2010 after one year as his solicitor general.

The solicitor general's office occupies a complicated position. On the one hand, it represents the president and the executive branch, functioning as their law firm. In this role, the office helps to carry out the president's policies. But the office also has a unique relationship with the Supreme Court, one in which it serves as an advisor as well as an advocate. The office's unique relationship with the Court rests on the fact that it represents a unique litigant. For one thing, the executive branch and the Supreme Court are both part of the federal government. And because the executive branch is involved in so many potential and actual Supreme Court cases, the solicitor general has the opportunity to build a mutually advantageous relationship with the Court.

One way the solicitor general uses this opportunity is by exercising self-restraint in requesting that the Court hear cases. The federal government petitioned for certiorari in forty-two cases in 2018 and 2019, a small fraction of all the cases it had lost in the courts of appeals.[50] In contrast, the government's opponents file many hundreds of petitions for certiorari each term. When she was serving as solicitor general, Elena Kagan said that she regularly turned down requests by other federal officials to bring cases to the Court. "Because I say the Court won't take it, our credibility is on the line, the Court will wonder why on earth we're filing this cert. petition."[51]

The solicitor general's office also seeks to maintain credibility by taking a more neutral stance than other litigants. Occasionally, the office even "confesses error," recommending that the Court overturn a victory for the federal government in the lower courts. Lawyers in the office also try to maintain a high level of accuracy in briefs and oral argument so that the justices will rely on their statements, although there have been at least a few instances of significant inaccuracies.[52]

Traditionally, the office has taken other steps to maintain its standing with the Court. One is to adhere to the position that a prior administration has taken in a case even though the new administration has a different point of view. Another is to defend federal laws against constitutional challenges, whether or not the president agrees with those laws.

For their part, the justices have given the solicitor general's office a unique status, one that is reflected in some of its practices. The Court frequently "invites" (in reality, orders) the solicitor general to file amicus briefs at the certiorari stage because the justices are interested in the government's view about whether the Court should hear a case. (In the absence of those invitations, the government seldom supports petitions for certiorari with amicus briefs.) If one of these cases is accepted, the solicitor general's office almost always submits a brief at the merits stage and participates in oral argument. The office often asks permission to present oral arguments in other cases, and the Court seldom denies that permission. Other governments and interest groups as amici are far less successful when they ask the Court for argument time.[53] These practices help explain the high proportions of cases in which the solicitor general participates.

The office's special relationship with the Court leads to a degree of independence from the president and the attorney general, who understand the value of maintaining that relationship. But the office operates in a climate created by the president and the attorney general. These superiors occasionally intervene in the office's handling of specific cases, typically cases that involve major policy issues. After a debate within his administration that went on for several months, President Trump in 2020 decided that the solicitor general's office would argue in a pending case for full invalidation of the Affordable Care Act.[54]

The office also interacts with administrative agencies that have an interest in particular cases. Ordinarily, the office is free to make the decision its lawyers favor, even if other agencies disagree. The 2020 case on the question of whether the federal law that prohibits sex discrimination in employment applies to transgender status arose from a lawsuit filed by the Equal Employment Opportunity Commission (EEOC) against an employer. But when the case reached the Supreme Court, the solicitor general's office took the employer's side, apparently over objections from the EEOC but in line with the Justice Department's policy.[55] Sometimes the conflict is wider. In a 2019 case involving disability benefits for Vietnam War veterans, two cabinet departments took opposing positions and members of Congress lobbied the office on whether to petition for certiorari. After requesting extra time from the Court to make its decision, the office ultimately decided not to petition.[56]

The impact of a presidential administration on the solicitor general's choices varies with the situation.[57] Because of the government's interests, there are certain positions that the office would take regardless of who the president is. For instance, when the office acts as an amicus in a state criminal case, it almost always supports the prosecution because the federal government also prosecutes criminal cases. In many other cases, the solicitor general chooses a position without regard to the liberalism or conservatism of the administration. But there are some cases, such as those involving contentious civil liberties issues, in which the ideological coloration of the administration affects the solicitor general's position. Thus, the government's amicus briefs support state restrictions on abortion during Republican administrations and oppose those restrictions during Democratic administrations. One study has found that in the aggregate, the positions of the office in amicus briefs are considerably more liberal under Democratic presidents than under Republicans.[58]

There have always been exceptions to the practices that the solicitor general's office uses to maintain its standing with the Court. For instance, the office sometimes changes its position on an issue after a new president comes into office, and it sometimes declines to defend a federal law with which the administration disagrees.

In an era of political polarization, these exceptions have become more common. The Trump administration reversed the position that the Obama administration had taken in four major cases that the Court heard in the 2017 term. Both the Obama and Trump administrations refused to defend important federal laws in the Court, instead arguing that they were unconstitutional.[59] In preliminary stages of cases, the Trump administration has stood out for the frequency with which it requests that the Court issue stays of lower-court decisions to keep them from going into effect or that the Court grant certiorari to hear cases before courts of appeals had reached decisions.[60] It does not appear that the solicitor general's relatively assertive stance during the Trump administration has damaged its relationship with the Court. At least in large part, this is because most of the government's positions have accorded with the views of a majority of justices.

DECIDING WHAT TO HEAR: THE COURT'S ROLE

The Supreme Court reaches judgments about petitions for certiorari throughout the nine months that it sits during each term. In June of 2020 it considered and rejected petitions on several significant issues. One was a First Amendment challenge to state requirements that lawyers belong and pay dues to state bar associations. Another challenged the federal law under which President Trump had imposed tariffs on $6.6 billion worth of imported steel. A third was the federal government's challenge to California's "sanctuary state" law that limited the state's cooperation with federal immigration officials. And a fourth contested the procedure that the federal government planned to use when it resumed executions after seventeen years.[61]

In that month the Court also turned down ten petitions challenging gun regulations and nine petitions asking it to reconsider the doctrine of "qualified immunity," under which public officials could not be sued for violations of constitutional rights if the courts had not already established that the specific type of action they took was unconstitutional.[62] Both sets of petitions arose out of litigation campaigns. One was the effort by gun rights advocates to get the Court to overturn regulations that arguably violated the Second Amendment right to individual gun ownership that the Court had established in 2008. The other involved an unusual coalition of conservative and liberal groups arguing against qualified immunity on the ground that it unduly protected public officials from legal responsibility for violations of rights.

In a statistical sense, the Court's actions in those cases were hardly noteworthy. In its 2018 term, typical of recent years, the Court considered more than 6,000 petitions for hearings. The Court granted certiorari and full consideration in only eighty-six of those cases.[63] Of the thousands of other petitions, the overwhelming majority were simply denied, allowing the lower-court decision to become final. Many of these cases had high stakes for the people who petitioned the Court, and some raised important legal and policy issues. Nonetheless, the Court chose not to hear them. In doing so, the Court exercised its power to determine what questions it will and will not consider.

Options

In screening petitions for hearings, the Court makes choices that are more complicated than simply accepting and rejecting individual cases. To begin with, cases are not always considered in isolation from one another. The justices regularly accept cases to clarify or expand on earlier decisions in the same policy area. They often accept multiple cases that raise the same issue. They may reject a case because they are looking for a more suitable case on the same issue.

When the Court does accept a case, it does not necessarily adopt the legal questions that were presented in the petition for hearing. The Court made some modification to the set of questions raised by the petition in about one-quarter of the cases that it heard in the 2019 term. Most often, it accepts only one of the questions in the petition. But sometimes it reformulates a question in the petition or adds a new question. In one 2020 case, the Court asked the parties to address a question that added a new dimension to the case two weeks before oral argument. In another, the Court asked the parties to address a new question in supplemental briefs *after* oral argument.[64] Occasionally the Court decides a case on the basis of an issue that the parties did not have a chance to argue, and such an action may provoke a dissent from justices who see it as inappropriate. In *Lozman v. City of Riviera Beach* (2018), Justice Thomas said that the Court had not decided the question for which it granted certiorari but instead decided a different question that the litigants had had no chance to address. "No one," he said, "briefed, argued, or even hinted at the rule that the Court announces today."[65]

In accepting a case, the Court also determines what kind of consideration the case will receive. It may give the case full consideration, which means that the Court receives a new set of briefs on the merits from the parties and holds oral argument, then issues a decision on the merits with a full opinion explaining the decision. Alternatively, it may give the case summary consideration. This usually means that the case is decided without new briefs or oral argument.

In most summary decisions, typically several dozen each term, the Supreme Court issues a one-sentence GVR order—that is, Granting certiorari, Vacating the lower-court decision, and Remanding the case to that court for reconsideration.

The great majority of GVR orders are issued because some event after the lower-court decision—usually a recent Supreme Court decision—is relevant to the case. Typically, even justices who dissented from the Court's recent decision accept a GVR order. But in recent years some justices have objected to GVRs that they see as inappropriate. In 2019, for instance, the Court followed the solicitor general's recommendation that a case be sent back to a court of appeals for reconsideration. Four justices dissented, arguing in an opinion by Chief Justice Roberts that the remand was pointless.[66]

In a much smaller number of summary decisions, the Court actually reaches a decision on the merits and issues an opinion of several paragraphs or even several pages. This opinion typically is labeled per curiam, meaning "by the Court," rather than being signed by a justice. But it has the same legal force as a signed opinion. These summary decisions typically are used when most of the justices think that the lower court's decision was seriously in error and requires correction.[67]

Finally, the Court sometimes issues summary decisions with very brief opinions in the appeals from three-judge federal district courts that it is required to decide—meeting in a minimal way its obligation to reach a decision on the merits. *Republican Party of Louisiana v. Federal Election Commission* (2017) involved a First Amendment challenge to a federal statutory provision that limited spending by state and local party organizations in connection with presidential and congressional elections. A three-judge court upheld the provision. The challengers of the law then appealed to the Supreme Court, which issued a four-word opinion: "The judgment is affirmed."

Even after accepting a case, the Court occasionally avoids a decision by issuing what is called a DIG, for "dismissed as improvidently granted." The great majority of DIGs occur when the parties' briefs on the merits or the oral arguments suggest to the justices that the case is inappropriate for a decision. But the Court occasionally DIGs a case in order to avoid a decision with no majority opinion. And in a few cases, the Court has used a DIG because they think a litigant engaged in a "bait-and-switch" in which they petition for certiorari on the basis of one issue but then emphasize a different issue in their brief on the merits.[68] (In a 2019 case, Justice Alito's dissent argued that the Court *should* have DIGged the case because of a bait-and-switch, but "instead, the majority rewards counsel's trick."[69]) Like GVRs, DIGs sometimes draw heated dissents from justices who think they are inappropriate in a particular case.

Screening Procedures

The Court screens petitions for hearings through multiple steps, which are made more complex by two distinctions. The first distinction is between the certiorari cases, over which the Court's jurisdiction is discretionary, and the cases labeled appeals, which the Court is required to decide. Few appeals reach the Court. As *Republican Party v. Federal Election Commission* illustrates, the Court has the option of deciding an appeal without holding oral argument or issuing a full opinion. The second distinction, between paid cases and paupers' cases, requires more extensive discussion.

Paid Cases and Paupers' Cases

In recent years, only about one-fifth of the requests for hearings that arrive at the Supreme Court have been paid cases, for which the petitioner pays the Court's filing fee of $300. The remaining cases are brought *in forma pauperis* by people who are indigent, people for whom the fee is waived and requirements for the format of litigants' written materials are relaxed. The great majority of the paupers' petitions (also called "unpaid") are brought by federal and state prisoners. A person responding to a petition can also be given pauper status.

Criminal defendants who have had counsel provided to them in the lower courts because of their low incomes are automatically entitled to bring paupers' cases in the Supreme Court. Other litigants must submit an affidavit supporting their motion for leave to file as paupers. The Court has never developed precise rules for when a litigant can claim pauper status. However, it denies many litigants the right to proceed as paupers in particular cases on the grounds that they are not

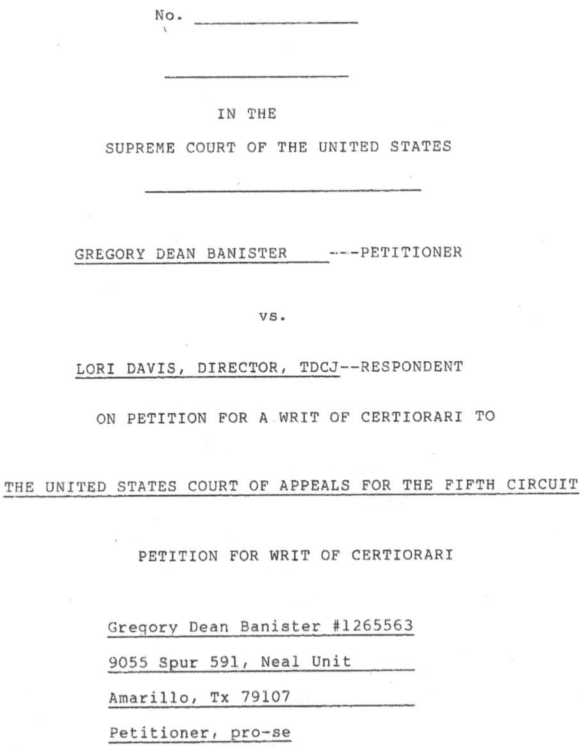

```
No. _____
    \
    _____

         IN THE
SUPREME COURT OF THE UNITED STATES
    _____


GREGORY DEAN BANISTER    ----PETITIONER

            vs.

LORI DAVIS, DIRECTOR, TDCJ--RESPONDENT

  ON PETITION FOR A WRIT OF CERTIORARI TO

THE UNITED STATES COURT OF APPEALS FOR THE FIFTH CIRCUIT


     PETITION FOR WRIT OF CERTIORARI


   Gregory Dean Banister #1265563

   9055 Spur 591, Neal Unit

   Amarillo, Tx 79107

   Petitioner, pro-se
```

▶ **Photo 3-2** The cover page of Gregory Banister's petition for certiorari, submitted to the Court from a Texas prison in 2018. "Paupers' petitions" for certiorari are accepted by the Court at a very low rate, but Banister won a full hearing from the Court—and then a decision in his favor in 2020.

truly indigent or that their petitions are frivolous or malicious. The Court also issues a general denial of pauper status in noncriminal cases to some litigants who have filed large numbers of paupers' petitions.

A very small percentage of the paupers' petitions for certiorari are granted. The low acceptance rate reflects the lack of inherent merit in many of these cases and the fact that many litigants have to draft petitions without a lawyer's assistance. It may also be that the justices and law clerks look less closely at paupers' petitions than at the paid petitions. There is some evidence that, all else being equal, the Court is less likely to accept a pauper's petition than a paid petition.[70] Because there are so many paupers' petitions, even the small proportion that are accepted add up to a significant number of cases, an average of eight per term in the 2015–2019 terms. The great majority of these accepted paupers' cases are criminal, and they constitute a substantial part of the Court's work on issues of criminal procedure.

Prescreening: The Discuss List

Under its rule of four, the Court grants a writ of certiorari and hears a case on the merits if at least four justices vote at conference to grant the writ. But petitions for hearings are considered at conference only if they are put on the Court's discuss list. The chief justice creates the initial discuss list, but other justices can and do add cases to it. Cases left off the discuss list are denied hearings automatically. Retired Justice Anthony Kennedy reported in 2018 that the Court puts about 500 cases on the discuss list each year, less than one in ten of the cases brought to it.[71]

The discuss list procedure serves to limit the Court's workload. But this procedure also reflects a belief that most petitions do not require collective consideration because they are such poor candidates for acceptance. It is easy to reject petitions that raise only very narrow issues or make weak legal claims.

Action in Conference

In conference, the chief justice or the justice who added a case to the discuss list opens consideration of the case. In order of seniority, from senior to junior, the justices then speak and usually announce their votes. If the discussion does not make the justices' positions clear, a formal vote is taken, also in order of seniority. Despite the prescreening of cases, a large majority of the petitions considered in conference are denied.

Most cases receive only brief discussion in conference. Some cases get more consideration, which sometimes extends beyond the initial discussion. In conference, any justice can ask that a case be "distributed" once again for a later conference. This step might be taken to obtain additional information in the case. A justice also might ask for another distribution in order to circulate an opinion dissenting from the Court's tentative denial of a hearing and thereby try to win the necessary four votes to grant certiorari. Some cases are considered at more than half a dozen conferences, and occasionally several months elapse between the justices' first consideration of a case and their ultimate decision to grant or deny certiorari. In recent years, the great majority of cases that the Court agrees to hear have been considered at multiple conferences. It may be that justices are now giving a second look to cases they are inclined to accept in order to make sure that these cases are appropriate for decisions by the Court.[72]

When it accepts a case, the Court also decides whether to allow oral argument or to decide the case summarily on the basis of the written materials. Four votes are required for oral argument. For summary decisions, including GVRs, the grant of certiorari and the disposition of the case are typically announced at the same time.

The Court does not issue opinions to explain its acceptance or rejection of cases. Nor are individual votes announced. But justices occasionally record their dissents from denials of petitions for hearings, sometimes accompanied by dissenting opinions. There were thirty-nine cases with such dissents in the 2019 term, twenty-two of them dissents by Justices Sotomayor and Justice Ginsburg on a recurring issue in criminal law. Altogether, the two justices dissented from denials of certiorari in more than forty cases involving that issue between 2018 and 2020 before announcing that they were giving up their effort.[73]

Sometimes justices write opinions in which they voted against granting certiorari, as they did in ten cases in the 2019 term. Some of these opinions encourage litigants to bring new cases related to the issues in the present one. In one 2019 case, Justice Thomas wrote a lengthy opinion concurring in the denial of certiorari in order to argue that the Court should reconsider both its landmark 1964 ruling that gives public officials an additional requirement to meet in suits they bring for libel and the later decisions that extended the requirement to public figures.[74]

The Clerks' Role

One of the primary jobs of the Court's law clerks is to scrutinize requests for hearings. As of 2020, all of the justices except Samuel Alito and Neil Gorsuch are part of the "cert. (for certiorari) pool." Petitions and other materials on each case are divided among the clerks for the justices in the pool. The clerk who has responsibility for a case writes a memorandum, one that typically includes a summary of the case and a recommendation that the petition be granted or denied. On the whole, clerks who write pool memos are cautious about recommending that the Court hear a case. One reason is that they know such recommendations will be scrutinized more closely than recommendations to deny certiorari. And it would be embarrassing for a clerk to suggest that the Court take a case and have the Court follow that suggestion, only to have the case disposed of with a DIG later because the clerk had missed an important fact about the case.

Because there are so many petitions, and because pool memos are the most extensive source of information about them, that information surely has some impact on the justices' judgments about petitions. But the extent of that impact is uncertain.[75] Two factors limit the impact of the pool on certiorari decisions. First, the great majority of petitions would elicit a denial from any justice or clerk. Justice Stephen Breyer said in 2010 that of the approximately 150 petitions that the Court received each week, "there are only about 10 or 12 that are even possible, that anyone would think of considering for granting."[76] Second, the justices, with help from their own clerks—who have a justice's views in mind—undertake some independent review of cases. This independent review is reflected in the fact that in a substantial proportion of the cases that the Court decides to hear, the pool memo had not recommended that the Court accept the case.[77] In other words, to some degree justices correct for the pool clerks' caution.

Criteria for Decision

In deciding whether to accept or deny petitions, the justices look for cases whose attributes make them desirable to hear. The Court's Rule 10 lists some of those attributes, which are based on the Court's role in enhancing the certainty and consistency of the law. Rule 10 indicates that the Court is more interested in hearing cases if they contain important issues of federal law that the Court has not yet decided, if there is conflict between lower courts on an important legal question or between a lower court's decision and the Supreme Court's prior decisions, or if a federal court of appeals has drastically departed "from the accepted and usual course of judicial proceedings" or allowed a lower court to do so.

The Court's pattern of screening decisions and evidence from other sources indicate the significance of several types of considerations, both those described in Rule 10 and those that it does not mention. These considerations can differ in their weight from justice to justice.[78]

Technical Criteria

The Court will reject a petition for hearing if it fails to meet certain technical requirements. Some of these requirements are specific to the Court. For example, paid petitions must comply with the Court's Rule 33, which establishes requirements on matters such as the size of print and margins used, type of paper, format and color of the cover, and maximum length.

The Court also imposes the same kinds of technical requirements that other courts apply. One specific requirement is that petitions for hearing be filed within ninety days after judgment is entered in the lower court, unless the Court has extended the time in advance. The Court consistently refuses to allow the filing of petitions that are brought after the deadline.

More fundamental are the requirements of jurisdiction and standing. The Court cannot accept a case for hearing that clearly falls outside its jurisdiction.

For example, the Court could not hear a state case in which the petitioner had raised no issues of federal law in the state courts.

The rule of standing holds that a court may not hear a case unless the party bringing the case is properly before it. The most important element of standing is the requirement that a party in a case have a real and direct legal stake in its outcome. This requirement precludes hypothetical cases, cases brought on behalf of another person, "friendly suits" between parties that are not really adversaries, and cases that have become moot (in effect, hypothetical) because the parties can no longer be affected by the outcome.

Because of the mootness rule, the Court generally must dismiss a case if the parties have reached a settlement or if the only party on one side has died. Other circumstances can take a case out of the Court's hands. *Mathena v. Malvo* (2020) concerned the scope of a 2012 Court decision that prohibited sentencing rules requiring life sentences with no possibility of parole for certain crimes committed by juveniles. After the Court heard oral argument, Virginia enacted a statute that made parole possible for Malvo. The two sides asked the Court to dismiss the case, and it did so. Twelve days later the Court accepted another case raising the same issue, and that action underlined how often the justices can find cases on issues that they want to address.[79]

Conflict between Courts

In 2019, the Court granted certiorari in a case involving the application of federal maritime law to language in a contract between a ship owner and a company that chartered the ship. One commentator said that the certiorari grant "will settle once and for all the question of what is the dullest case the Supreme Court has ever taken."[80] Even allowing for exaggeration, the case was not very exciting. Nor would the Court's decision have broad impact on legal policy. Why, then, did the Court decide to hear the case? Three federal courts of appeals had interpreted the contract language that was at issue in this case, and one of those courts disagreed with the other two about its meaning. At least four justices thought that the conflict should be resolved.

This case illustrates the reality that Rule 10 suggests: conflict among lower courts is a major criterion for acceptance of cases. Indeed, the existence of a clear legal conflict, typically between federal courts of appeals, increases enormously the chances that a case will be accepted.[81] When the Court's opinion indicates why the case had been accepted, by far the most common reason it cites is the existence of a conflict between lower courts.

The significance of conflict is underlined by justices' willingness to hear some kinds of cases in which they have only limited interest. Conflict between courts of appeals is the primary reason why the Court accepts cases involving the federal tax laws. Similarly, as one commentator noted, the Roberts Court "agrees to hear securities cases because there is a circuit split, not because it is anxious to impose its mark on the field of securities law."[82]

▸ **Photo 3-3** The Athos I in the Delaware River after a collision with an abandoned anchor caused a large spill of oil from the ship. The justices' willingness to address a seemingly narrow dispute over liability for the oil spill illustrates their interest in resolving conflicts in legal interpretation between lower courts.

This does not mean that the Court accepts every case involving conflict between courts. Indeed, one study found that the Court ultimately resolves only one-third of the conflicts that arise between courts of appeals.[83] Rule 10 emphasizes the importance of the issue on which a conflict has arisen as a criterion for the Court, and this criterion undoubtedly affects the justices' choices of which conflict cases to hear. Yet the Court occasionally accepts a case to resolve a conflict that does not seem highly significant, such as the maritime contract dispute in 2019.

Importance of the Issues

Of all the cases in which litigants petition for a writ of certiorari, the great majority involve narrow issues. Frequently, the "questions presented" at the beginning of the petition ask only whether the case was wrongly decided. Those cases are easy to turn away because the justices seldom see any point in allocating part of the limited space on their agenda to cases in which a decision would have little effect beyond the immediate parties. Rather, the best way for the Court to maximize its impact is to decide the cases that raise the most important legal and policy questions.

Importance is a more subjective matter than conflict between courts, so different justices may assess the importance of a case quite differently. In general, justices look for cases in which a decision would have a broad effect on courts, government, or society as a whole. In some of the cases that meet this criterion, the issues are dramatic. In others, the issues are dry and technical but nonetheless important. The number of amicus briefs supporting petitions for certiorari is correlated with the likelihood that the Court will accept a case, either because those briefs alert the justices to the importance of a case or because briefs are simply more likely to be submitted in important cases.[84]

Just as the Court rejects some cases that involve conflicts between lower courts, it also rejects some cases that raise important issues—such as the ones described at the beginning of this section. One reason for such denials is the same reason why the Court does not resolve all conflicts between lower courts: the number of cases with significant issues is considerably larger than the number the Court is able and willing to hear. Justices sometimes have more specific reasons to vote against hearing such cases. To take two examples, they may agree with the lower-court decision or want to delay before tackling a difficult issue.

Policy Preferences

Rule 10 does not mention justices' personal conceptions of good policy as a criterion for accepting or rejecting cases, but those conceptions have considerable effect on the Court's choices. Because the Court's agenda helps determine its role as a policy maker, members of the Court inevitably use the agenda-setting process to advance their own policy goals.

Justices can act on their policy goals primarily in two ways. First, they may vote to hear a case because they disagree with the lower-court decision in the case: tentatively concluding that the lower court established an undesirable policy, they want to correct it. Second, they may act strategically by voting to hear a case when they think the Court would reach a decision they favor on policy grounds if it decided the case on the merits and voting against certiorari when they think the Court would produce what they consider to be bad policy. For either approach, the limits on the number of cases that the Court hears require justices to be selective. For instance, if they strongly disagree with a lower-court decision but think that the case has only narrow policy implications, they are likely to pass it by. (In some cases of this type, the Court issues a summary decision reversing the lower-court decision without getting additional briefs or holding oral argument.)

The justices' use of the first approach is made clear by the Court's decisions on the merits. The Court overturns the lower court altogether or in part in more than two-thirds of its decisions. The comparable rate for the federal courts of appeals, which lack the Court's power to screen the cases brought to it, is under 10 percent.[85] One reason for the Court's high reversal rate is that it accepts so many cases in order to resolve conflicts between lower courts: in that set of cases, there is something like a 50–50 chance that the Court will overturn the decision it reviews.

Even so, the reversal rate could not be nearly as high as it is if the justices were not inclined to hear cases when they have doubts about the validity of the lower court's decision. And the Court seems to accept some cases simply because four or more justices concluded that the lower court got the law wrong and did a serious injustice with its decision. One commentator referred to these cases as the Court's "outrage docket."[86]

Of course, there is considerable room for disagreement in these tentative judgments, and that disagreement often falls along ideological lines. Indeed, judges on the federal courts of appeals sometimes use a dissenting opinion to signal ideological allies on the Court that they should consider hearing the case. In the current era, because of the Court's conservative majority, all or nearly all these cues come from conservative judges.

The justices sometimes use the second, strategic approach as well. When the Court denied certiorari in a 2020 case, Justice Alito wrote an opinion saying that the court of appeals had made a bad decision but the Court was right not to take the case because Justice Kavanaugh had recused. Alito may have concluded that Kavanaugh's vote would be needed for a majority favoring Alito's position on the issue in the case.[87]

Strategic considerations might help to explain the course of the Court's agenda on firearms and abortion. After the Court ruled that the Second Amendment protected individual gun ownership in 2008 and extended this right to the state level in 2010, it turned away a large number of challenges to regulations of firearms in the years that followed. By one count in 2017, the Court had denied petitions for certiorari in more than seventy gun regulation cases since 2008.[88] It has continued to avoid hearing cases involving gun regulations, except for the case brought by the New York State Rifle and Pistol Association that it set aside as moot in 2020. Although some conservative justices dissented from denials of certiorari in gun cases over the years, both liberals and other conservatives may have shied away from these cases because they were unsure of what the Court would rule in them.

Similarly, after the Court established a new standard for constitutional challenges to laws that restrict abortion in 1992, states enacted a variety of restrictive laws that were challenged in court. But between 1993 and 2020 the Court reached full decisions on whether these restrictions were constitutional in only four cases, two involving prohibitions of one method of performing abortions and the other two involving requirements for the operation of abortion clinics.[89] As with gun cases, justices on both sides of the abortion issue may have feared that the Court would rule in the wrong direction from their perspective if they heard challenges to regulation of abortion.

It is uncertain how often the justices act strategically in their certiorari votes. Almost surely, justices concentrate their strategic calculations on the relatively small proportion of petitions that are good candidates for acceptance on other grounds. And they are probably more inclined to take the Court's prospective decisions into account when they are part of the Court's ideological minority, because members of the minority have the most reason to worry about what the Court might decide.

These two ways of acting on policy goals are likely to have the greatest impact when they reinforce each other. If a case is a good candidate for acceptance on other grounds, justices who disagree with a lower-court decision and who think that the Court would agree with them on the merits have strong incentives to vote for certiorari.

Problematic Cases and Issues

Sometimes the Court collectively chooses not to hear a case in order to avoid a problem. Justices might vote against hearing a case because they want to await more decisions on the issue in the lower courts, decisions that may refine the issue or give the justices a better chance to assess it. And sometimes they see a case as a "bad vehicle" for resolution of an issue because of its factual circumstances or the presence of other issues that complicate the case.

Another possible concern is that resolving a particular issue might embroil the Court in controversy. Perhaps the classic example is the Court's unwillingness to hear any case involving a challenge to the legality of U.S. participation in the Vietnam War. Some petitions for hearing in those cases received positive votes from individual justices, but never enough to accept a case. In 2014 the Court turned away three cases on the question of whether state prohibitions of same-sex marriage were unconstitutional despite the clear importance of that issue, and at least some justices may have hoped that the Court could avoid involvement in the contention over that issue. The Court accepted a new set of cases a few months later, after the ruling in those cases created a conflict of decisions between federal courts of appeals and thus left the justices with little choice but to resolve the conflict.[90]

Still, what stands out is the justices' willingness to address issues that have the potential to create controversy. One striking example is *Bush v. Gore* (2000), a case in which the Court's decision resolved the outcome of the presidential election that year. In 2013 retired justice Sandra Day O'Connor expressed her concern about the effect of the case on the Court's reputation. "Maybe," she mused, "the court should have said, 'We're not going to take it, goodbye.'"[91]

Indeed, in a period in which justices worry about perceptions that the Court is a partisan body, they are still willing to accept cases that might feed those perceptions. In the 2018 term, the Court heard cases about partisan gerrymandering and the Trump administration's effort to add a question about citizenship to the 2020 Census, both of which evoked disagreement among people along partisan lines.[92] In the 2019 term, the Court heard cases about the administration's immigration policies and subpoenas of the president's financial records.[93] Whether out of duty or for other reasons, the justices collectively have been willing to accept the possibility of widespread criticism by taking such cases.

Identities of the Participants

Every petition for certiorari involves at least two competing parties. In most paid cases and many paupers' cases, the petitioner is represented by a lawyer. And in some cases, the petitioner is supported by one or more interest groups in amicus briefs. The identities of those participants might have an impact on the Court's decisions whether to grant certiorari.

One participant, the federal government, stands out for its success in winning hearings from the Court. Of the petitions for certiorari that the government submitted in the years 2018 and 2019, the Court accepted about two-thirds.[94] That success rate is enormously high in comparison with the low overall rate of success for petitioners.

Undoubtedly, one source of this level of success is the special relationship that the solicitor general's office has developed with the Court through its frequent participation in litigation and the steps it takes to maximize its credibility. This credibility is strengthened by the solicitor general's selectivity in filing petitions, which gives greater weight to the petitions it does file and which may lead to gratitude from justices because it limits their workload. Selectivity improves the office's success rate in another way as well: its lawyers can choose the cases that are most likely to be accepted, and almost any litigant who could be so selective would enjoy a relatively high winning percentage at the certiorari stage.

Another advantage of the solicitor general is the expertise that attorneys in the office develop through their frequent participation in Supreme Court cases. As a result, the federal government can do more than most other litigants to make cases attractive to the justices. Still another possibility is that the justices defer to the executive branch as a fellow branch of government.

Although no other set of lawyers can match the solicitor general's success, the lawyers in private practice who frequently appear in the Court and other lawyers in firms with Supreme Court specializations also do well. One study found that a set of "elite" lawyers did far better than other lawyers in getting petitions from businesses accepted by the Court, and they did enormously better in getting petitions from individuals accepted.[95]

This level of success may be somewhat misleading, because there is probably a tendency for elite lawyers to take cases that are relatively strong. But the skills of the best advocates undoubtedly make considerable difference at the certiorari stage. At that stage, justices and clerks have to deal with large numbers of petitions for certiorari, and the briefs on the two sides are their primary source of information. As a result, the ability of lawyers to make persuasive cases for hearing a case makes a difference.

The reputations of lawyers also have an impact. Justice Kennedy said that "we look at the names of counsel for lawyers we trust."[96] Moreover, the involvement of prominent Supreme Court advocates in a case, representing one of the parties or an amicus, may signal law clerks and justices that the petition merits serious consideration.[97] Indeed, it is common for those lawyers to "ghostwrite," leaving their names off of briefs that oppose petitions for certiorari. This is because justices and clerks might read their involvement as an indication that a case deserves consideration by the Court. Carter Phillips, one of the leading Supreme Court advocates, said in 2017 that "I have been ghostwriting opposition briefs for more than 30 years."[98]

Amicus briefs on behalf of petitioners improve the chances that a petition will be accepted, because they indicate that a case has significance that extends beyond the parties. And specific interest groups may have special credibility with some justices because they regularly submit high-quality briefs or because the justices respect the groups themselves.[99]

Ultimately, of course, the justices have the final say. In *City of Boise v. Martin* (2019), the lawyer whose name appeared first on the petition for certiorari was one of the leading advocates in the Court. The petition was supported by twenty amicus briefs, perhaps a record at the certiorari stage. The amici included seven states, an array of other governmental groups, and several business groups. The Court denied certiorari.[100]

Summary

When Supreme Court justices vote on petitions for hearings, they act on a complex set of considerations. All justices take these considerations into account, but justices with different goals and perspectives respond differently to petitions. Some give a higher priority to resolving lower-court conflicts than others. Justices assess the importance of cases in various ways. And they act on quite different sets of policy preferences.

It follows that the Court's selection of cases to decide fully, like everything else it does, is affected by its membership. The great majority of petitions would not be accepted no matter who is on the Court. But the composition of the cases the Court actually accepts reflects the identities of the justices who sit on the Court at the time.

Setting the Size of the Agenda

Over the Supreme Court's history, there has been considerable fluctuation in the number of full decisions on the merits that the Court hands down. As Figure 3-1 shows, that has been true of the past half century. There was a substantial increase in the number of decisions in the early 1970s and an even steeper decline in the early 1990s, from 139 decisions in the 1989 term to 79 decisions in the 1995 term. Since then, the number has fluctuated but has moved to a slightly lower level, and the Court is now hearing about half the number of cases each term that it did in the terms between 1971 and 1986. As Justice Thomas put it in 2016, "We're not exactly killing it."[101]

That is a noteworthy change. Of course, cases that the Court hears are not equal in their significance. Even so, it is striking that the Court is addressing far fewer legal issues today than it did forty years ago. This decline is even more striking because the number of cases that litigants brought to the Court doubled between the 1970s and the first decade of the twenty-first century. Indeed, the number of petitions for hearings increased by about one-third at the same time as the precipitous drop in the number of decisions in 1989–1995. Why have those trends run in opposite directions?

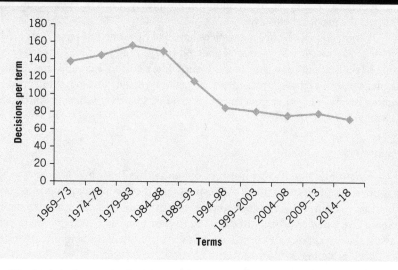

Figure 3-1 Numbers of Decisions with Full Opinions per Term, Averaged over Five-Term Periods, 1969–2018 Terms

Source: "The Statistics," *Harvard Law Review*, November issues ("Opinions of Court").

An answer to that question requires some historical perspective. The number of cases brought to the Court went up dramatically over several decades in a trend that culminated in the 1960s. That growth seemed to have several sources. Outside the Court, these sources included an apparent increase in "rights consciousness," which led people to bring more legal claims; the increased availability of lawyers and the development of interest groups that assisted litigants in carrying cases through the courts; and increased activity by the federal government, which produced new laws and legal questions. The Court itself contributed to the growth in its caseload. Most important, its positive responses to claims that government actions violated civil liberties encouraged people who felt that their rights had been violated to bring cases to the Court.

After a period of relative stability in the number of cases brought to the Court, a new period of rapid growth began in the late 1980s, peaking in the first decade of this century before the numbers fell back. This second period of growth was quite different from the earlier one. As Figure 3-2 shows, it was limited to paupers' petitions. The number of paid petitions per term was fairly stable in the 1980s and 1990s, and after that it fell by more than 20 percent before stabilizing at 1,500 to 1,600 cases per term. (There was a one-term jump to 1,718 paid petitions in 2017 that was reversed in 2018.) In contrast, the number of paupers' petitions, which hovered around 2,000 per term from the late 1960s to the mid-1980s, grew to a high of about 7,100 in the 2006 term before undergoing its own 20 percent decline.

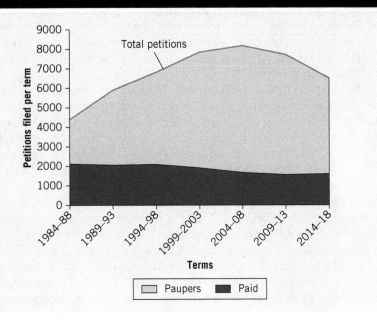

Figure 3-2 Paid and Paupers' Cases Filed in the Supreme Court per Term, by Five-Year Averages, 1984–2018 Terms

Total petitions

Petitions filed per term

Terms

Paupers   Paid

Sources: Gerhard Casper and Richard A. Posner, *The Workload of the Supreme Court* (Chicago: American Bar Foundation, 1976), 34; "Statistical Recap of Supreme Court's Workload during Last Three Terms," *United States Law Week*, various years; "Statistics" in the Supreme Court's *Journal*, various years.

The great majority of paupers' petitions come from prisoners, and the number of adults in prison nearly quintupled between 1980 and 2005.[102] This trend accounts for most if not all of the increase in paupers' cases. The substantial fall in the numbers of paupers' petitions since their peak in 2006 parallels a decline in criminal and habeas corpus cases in the federal courts of appeals, so it likely reflects broader changes in the criminal justice system.

The pattern of growth in the Court's caseload over the last two decades helps to explain why the Court is not hearing more cases than it did in the mid-1980s. Paupers' petitions are always accepted at relatively low rates, and a Court that has become less sympathetic to claims by prisoners undoubtedly finds fewer of those petitions worthy. But there was little decline in the number of paid petitions until long after the steep drop in the number of cases that the Court accepted. Why did that drop occur, and why has the smaller agenda persisted?

Commentators and the justices themselves have offered several answers to that question.[103] Some possible explanations lie outside the Court. In 1988, Congress greatly reduced the types of cases that are classified as appeals (rather than petitions for certiorari), which the Court is required to decide. As a result, the number of appeals in which the Court reaches full decisions has dropped from an average of twenty-eight per term in the decade before that change to about two per term today (though the Court hears other cases that would have been classified as appeals prior to 1988). And two justices have pointed to attributes of the cases that come to the Court: less major legislation by Congress that requires interpretation by the Court (Justice Thomas), and fewer legal conflicts between federal courts of appeals (Justice Breyer).[104]

Yet these changes in inputs cannot fully explain the reduced number of decisions. Even taking into account the reduction in the number of appeals, it seems unlikely that there were 139 cases that merited consideration in the 1989 term and only 79 in 1995. Thus the justices' own choices almost surely came into play. We do know that change in the Court's membership had an impact: on the whole, the justices who joined the Court in the late 1980s and early 1990s were less inclined to vote for certiorari than the justices they succeeded.[105] And other justices may have shared a desire to hear fewer cases.

Once the bulk of the decline occurred in the 1990s, the justices became accustomed to a smaller number of decisions each term, a number that reduced their workloads and gave them more time for other pursuits. Justice Kagan told a congressional committee in 2019 that "I don't think anybody would want to go back to" the period when the Court was hearing around 140 cases a year. She also said that "I think we would all like to have some more" cases, perhaps around ninety per term rather than seventy, but the justices' application of their criteria for case acceptance to the petitions they get results in the lower number.[106] However, those criteria likely have changed over the years, perhaps in ways that the justices do not fully recognize.

In any event, the difficulty of gaining a hearing in the Supreme Court has increased considerably. In its 1985 term, the Court accepted for full consideration about one in twelve of the paid petitions for certiorari. In the 2018 term, that rate was one in twenty-three. For paupers' petitions the decline was precipitous, from an already low 1 in 108 in 1985 to a very low 1 in 562 in 2018. Given the worsening odds and the significant costs of filing paid petitions for those who use lawyers' services, it is not surprising that the number of paid petitions has declined since the late 1990s.

CONCLUSION

Like other courts, the Supreme Court can decide only the cases that come to it. For that reason, people and institutions outside the Court have great influence on the Court's agenda. Ultimately, however, the Court determines which cases it hears. From the wide variety of legal and policy questions brought to the Court, the justices can choose the few they will address fully. They can also choose which issues in a case they will decide. And the justices help determine which cases are brought to them by indicating with their opinions what kinds of legal claims they view favorably.

The Court is sometimes criticized for its choices of cases to hear and turn aside. In recent years, it has also been criticized for the small number of cases it accepts each term. Whatever the validity of these criticisms may be, the justices employ their agenda-setting powers rather well to serve their purposes. They accept and reject cases on the basis of individual and collective goals such as avoiding troublesome issues, resolving conflicts in the interpretation of federal law, and establishing legal rules that the justices favor. The justices' selection of cases for full decisions helps them shape the Court's role as a policy maker. They also use that process to limit their workloads.

After the Court selects the cases to hear, of course, it decides those cases. In the next chapter, I will examine the Court's decision-making process and the forces that shape its choices.

NOTES

1. Kenneth Lovett, "Lovett: Antonin Scalia's Death Halts Lawsuit to Fight Cuomo's Gun Control Law," *New York Daily News*, March 7, 2016.
2. *New York State Rifle & Pistol Association v. City of New York* (2020).
3. That decision was *Gundy v. United States* (2019). See Jonathan H. Adler, "Justice Kavanaugh on Delegation and Major Questions (Updated)," *The Volokh Conspiracy*, November 25, 2019.
4. Oral argument, *Financial Oversight and Management Board for Puerto Rico v. Aurelius Investment, LLC*, 18-1334, 60. See Jesse Barron, "Isle of Debt," *New York Times Magazine*, December 1, 2019, 43.
5. Sabrina Eaton, "U.S. Supreme Court to Hear International Child Custody Dispute from Cleveland Area," cleveland.com, December 10, 2019.
6. Matt Ford, "The Supreme Court's First Major Gun Case in a Decade," *The New Republic*, August 14, 2019.
7. Jay Schweikert and Clark Neily, "As Supreme Court Considers Several Qualified Immunity Cases, A New Ally Joins the Fight," *Cato at Liberty*, January 17, 2020. The case was *Allah v. Milling* (2018).
8. Robert Barnes, "An Alaskan Moose Hunter Beat the Odds at the Supreme Court. It Cost $1.5 Million," *Washington Post*, November 3, 2019. The case was *Sturgeon v. Frost* (2019).
9. This provision is 15 U. S. C. §1052(a).
10. Simon Tam, *Slanted: How an Asian American Troublemaker Took on the Supreme Court* (Nashville: Troublemaker Press, 2019). The quotation is from p. 191. The case was *Matal v. Tam* (2017).
11. Justin Driver, *The Schoolhouse Gate: Public Education, the Supreme Court, and the Battle for the American Mind* (New York: Pantheon Books, 2018), 15.
12. Greg Stohr, "That Feeling When You Win a Supreme Court Case . . . and Get Nothing," *Bloomberg Business*, December 3, 2015.

13. The case was *Frank v. Gaos* (2019).

14. Tony Mauro and Marcia Coyle, "What New Supreme Court Cases Reveal About Big Law Billing Rates," *Supreme Court Brief* (*National Law Journal*), September 6, 2019.

15. The case was *Rotkiske v. Klemm* (2019). Weisberg's participation is discussed in Tony Mauro and Marcia Coyle, "An 8-Page Petition Strikes Gold," *Supreme Court Brief* (*National Law Journal*), March 6, 2019.

16. Janet Roberts, Joan Biskupic, and John Shiffman, "Special Report: In Ever-Clubbier Bar, Eight Men Emerge as Supreme Court Confidants," *Reuters*, December 8, 2014.

17. Marcia Coyle, "Kagan Says Repeat Players at SCOTUS 'Know What It Is We Like,'" *National Law Journal*, September 13, 2017.

18. Tony Mauro, "Clarence Thomas Praises High Level of Supreme Court Advocacy," *National Law Journal*, June 3, 2019.

19. Roberts, Biskupic, and Shiffman, "Special Report: In Ever-Clubbier Bar."

20. Joan Biskupic, Janet Roberts, and John Shiffman, "Special Report: The Echo Chamber," *Reuters*, December 8, 2014.

21. Andrew Manuel Crespo, "Regaining Perspective: Constitutional Criminal Adjudication in the U.S. Supreme Court," *Minnesota Law Review* 100 (May 2016): 2001–2017.

22. Tom Goldstein, "The Supreme Court Bar as a Tool of Business," *SCOTUSblog*, January 6, 2015.

23. *Banister v. Davis* (2020); *Lomax v. Ortiz-Marquez* (2020).

24. Adam Liptak, "Jailhouse Lawyer Propels a Case to the Supreme Court," *New York Times*, August 6, 2019, A9. The case was *Ramos v. Louisiana* (2020).

25. Jessica Gresko, "Only Lawyers Now Can Argue before Supreme Court," Associated Press, July 1, 2013. The 1978 case was *Securities and Exchange Commission v. Sloan* (1978).

26. Katherine Shaw, "Friends of the Court: Evaluating the Supreme Court's Amicus Invitations," *Cornell Law Review* 101 (September 2016): 533–596.

27. Mark Sherman, "U.S. Supreme Court Suspends the Wrong Lawyer Again," Associated Press, November 28, 2017. The Court's orders correcting the errors were *In the Matter of Sullivan* (2017) and *In the Matter of James A. Robbins* (2017).

28. Information on activities of the U.S. Chamber Litigation Center is available at its website, https://www.chamberlitigation.com/.

29. See Samuel Walker, *In Defense of American Liberties: A History of the ACLU*, 2nd ed. (Carbondale: Southern Illinois University Press, 1999); Michael Chabon and Ayelet Waldman, eds., *Fight of the Century: Writers Reflect on 100 Years of Landmark ACLU Cases* (New York: Simon & Schuster, 2020).

30. These cases were *Masterpiece Cakeshop v. Colorado Civil Rights Commission* (2018) and *Reed v. Town of Gilbert* (2015).

31. Dan Schweitzer, "State Attorneys in the Supreme Court," *The Green Bag*, 2d series, 22 (Winter 2019): 143–159.

32. Jeffrey L. Fisher and Allison Orr Larsen, "Virtual Briefing at the Supreme Court," *Cornell Law Review* 105 (2019): 85–136.

33. David Cole, *Engines of Liberty: The Power of Citizen Activists to Make Constitutional Law* (New York: Basic Books, 2016), chap. 8. The case was *District of Columbia v. Heller* (2008).

34. *National Federation of Independent Business v. Sebelius* (2012). See Josh Blackman, *Unprecedented: The Constitutional Challenge to Obamacare* (New York: Public Affairs, 2013).

35. Eugene Volokh, "Should U.S. Supreme Court Litigants Decline Consent for Filing of Amicus Briefs?" *The Volokh Conspiracy*, April 28, 2018.

36. The case was *American Legion v. American Humanist Association* (2019).

37. Joseph D. Kearney and Thomas W. Merrill, "The Influence of Amicus Curiae Briefs on the Supreme Court," *University of Pennsylvania Law Review* 148 (January 2000): 754 n26.

38. Anthony J. Franze and R. Reeves Anderson, "A Calm but Impressive 2018–19 Term for 'Friends of the Court'," *Supreme Court Brief* (*National Law Journal*), November 25, 2019.

39. Consolidated cases were counted as a single case.

40. Franze and Anderson, "A Calm but Impressive 2018–19 Term." The cases were, respectively, *National Federation of Independent Business v. Sebelius* (2012) and *Obergefell v. Hodges* (2015).

41. The discussion in this paragraph is based on Allison Orr Larsen and Neal Devins, "The Amicus Machine," *Virginia Law Review* 102 (December 2016): 1901–1968.

42. Brief of Respondent, *Kirtsaeng v. John Wiley & Sons, Inc.*, 15-375 (2016), 10. The 2013 case had the same title.

43. Jeffrey Rosen, *Conversations with RBG: Ruth Bader Ginsburg on Life, Love, Liberty, and Law* (New York: Henry Holt, 2019), 23–24.

44. Cole, *Engines of Liberty*, 223–224.

45. Ann Southworth, "Elements of the Support Structure for Campaign Finance Litigation in the Roberts Court," *Law & Social Inquiry* 43 (Spring 2018): 319–359.

46. The discussion in this paragraph draws much from Paul Nolette, "State Litigation During the Obama Administration: Diverging Agendas in an Era of Polarized Politics," *Publius: The Journal of Federalism* 44 (July 2014): 451–474.

47. Lisa F. Grumet, "Hidden Nondefense: Partisanship in State Attorneys General Amicus Briefs and the Need for Transparency," *Fordham Law Review* 87 (April 2019): 1865–1867.

48. See Blackman, *Unprecedented*; and Josh Blackman, *Unraveled: Obamacare, Religious Liberty, and Executive Power* (New York: Cambridge University Press, 2016).

49. Charles R. Epp, *The Rights Revolution: Lawyers, Activists, and Supreme Courts in Comparative Perspective* (Chicago: University of Chicago Press, 1998), 44–70.

50. The government actually filed forty-seven petitions for certiorari, but some of the cases were linked to each other.

51. Adam Chandler, "The Solicitor General of the United States: Tenth Justice or Zealous Advocate?" *Yale Law Journal* 121 (December 2011): 733.

52. Regina Jefferies, "Tragedy of Errors: The Solicitor General, the Supreme Court, and the Truth," *Just Security* blog, May 23, 2018.

53. Darcy Covert and A. J. Wang, "The Supreme Court Takes a Small Step in the Direction of Judicial Independence," *Slate*, April 22, 2020; Adam Liptak, "Justices Greet Old 'Friend' at the Bar," *New York Times*, March 10, 2020, A19.

54. Devlin Barrett, "Trump Vows Complete End of Obamacare Law Despite Pandemic," *Washington Post*, May 6, 2020.

55. Marcia Coyle, "EEOC Doesn't Sign Trump DOJ's Supreme Court Brief Against Transgender Employees," *National Law Journal*, August 26, 2019. The case was *R.G. & G.R. Harris Funeral Homes v. Equal Employment Opportunity Commission* (2020), decided with *Bostock v. Clayton County* (2020).

56. Marcia Coyle, "Justice Department Will Not Challenge Benefits for Blue Water Navy Vets," *National Law Journal*, June 5, 2019. The lower-court decision was *Procopio v. Wilkie* (Fed. Cir. 2019).

57. Richard L. Pacelle Jr., "Amicus Curiae or Amicus Praesidentis? Reexamining the Role of the Solicitor General in Filing Amici," *Judicature* 89 (May–June 2006): 317–325.

58. Thomas G. Hansford, Sarah Depaoli, and Kayla S. Canelo, "Locating U.S. Solicitors General in the Supreme Court's Policy Space," *Presidential Studies Quarterly* 49 (December 2019): 860.

59. The laws were the Defense of Marriage Act (*United States v. Windsor*, 2013) and the Affordable Care Act (*California v. Texas*, pending).

60. Stephen J. Vladeck, "The Solicitor General and the Shadow Docket," *Harvard Law Review* 133 (December 2019): 123–163.

61. These cases were, in order, *Jarchow v. State Bar of Wisconsin* (2020), *American Institute for International Steel v. United States* (2020), *United States v. California* (2020), and *Bourgeois v. Barr* (2020).

62. The gun regulation cases are discussed in Amy Howe, "After Long Wait, Court Spurns Gun-Rights Challenges," *SCOTUSblog*, June 15, 2020.

63. These figures and other figures in this section on the Court's receipt and disposition of petitions are based on "Statistics" for each term in the Court's *Journal*, at http://www.supremecourt.gov/orders/journal.aspx.

64. The cases were *Trump v. Mazars, USA* (2020) and *Babb v. Wilkie* (2020).

65. *Lozman v. City of Riviera Beach*, 201 L. Ed. 2d 342, 354 (2018).

66. *Myers v. United States* (2019).

67. William Baude, "Foreword: The Supreme Court's Shadow Docket," *New York University Journal of Law and Liberty* 9 (2015): 19–46.

68. Kevin Russell, "Practice Pointer: Digging into DIGs," *SCOTUSblog*, April 25, 2019.

69. *Madison v. Alabama*, 203 L. Ed. 2d 103, 120 (2019).

70. Ryan C. Black and Christina L. Boyd, "U.S. Supreme Court Agenda Setting and the Role of Litigant Status," *Journal of Law, Economics, & Organization* 28 (June 2012): 286–312.

71. Marcia Coyle, "Anthony Kennedy Walks Through His Secret Retirement Plans," *National Law Journal*, November 28, 2018.

72. Michael Kimberly, John Elwood, and Ralph Mayrell, "The Statistics of Relists, OT 2016 Edition: Has the Relist Lost Its Mojo? Not Quite," *SCOTUSblog*, September 27, 2017.

73. *Patrick v. United States* (2020). See R. J. Vogt, "In Dissent: Why 2 Justices Keep Spotlighting Career Offenders," *Law 360*, February 2, 2020.

74. *McKee v. Cosby* (2019). The 1964 decision was *New York Times Co. v. Sullivan*.

75. Ryan C. Black and Christina L. Boyd, "The Role of Law Clerks in the U.S. Supreme Court's Agenda-Setting Process," *American Politics Research* 40 (January 2012): 147–173; Sara C. Benesh, David A. Armstrong, and Zachary C. Wallander, "Advisors to Elites: Untangling Their Effect," *Journal of Law & Courts* 8 (Spring 2020): 51–74.

76. Bryan A. Garner, "Justice Stephen G. Breyer," *Scribes Journal of Legal Writing* 13 (2010): 152.

77. Barbara Palmer, "The 'Bermuda Triangle?' The Cert Pool and Its Influence Over the Supreme Court's Agenda," *Constitutional Commentary* 18 (Spring 2001): 111; David R. Stras, "The Supreme Court's Gatekeepers: The Role of Law Clerks in the U.S. Supreme Court's Agenda-Setting Process," *Texas Law Review* 85 (March 2007): 976–980.

78. Gregory A. Caldeira and Daniel Lempert, "Justice-Level Heterogeneity in Certiorari Voting: U.S. Supreme Court October Terms 1939, 1968, and 1982," presented at the annual conference of the Western Political Science Association, May 2020.

79. Amy Howe, "Justices Grant Replacement for D.C. Sniper Case," *SCOTUSblog*, March 9, 2020. The case was *Jones v. Mississippi* (pending).

80. John Elwood, "Reschedule Watch Returns," *SCOTUSblog*, April 24, 2019. The case was *CITGO Asphalt Refining Co. v. Frescati Shipping Co.* (2020).

81. Ryan C. Black and Christina L. Boyd, "Selecting the Select Few: The Discuss List and the U.S. Supreme Court's Agenda-Setting Process," *Social Science Quarterly* 94 (March 2013): 1133.

82. A. C. Pritchard, "Securities Law in the Roberts Court: Agenda or Indifference?" In *Business and the Roberts Court*, ed. Jonathan H. Adler (New York: Oxford University Press, 2016), 141.

83. Deborah Beim and Kelly Rader, "Legal Uniformity in American Courts," *Journal of Empirical Legal Studies* 16 (September 2019): 448–478.

84. Jessica A. Schoenherr and Ryan C. Black, "Friends with Benefits: Case Significance, Amicus Curiae, and Agenda Setting on the U.S. Supreme Court," *International Review of Law and Economics* 58 (2019): 43–53.

85. The proportion for the Supreme Court is based on data in the "Statistics" postings at *SCOTUSblog*, http://www.scotusblog.com/statistics/. The proportion for the courts of appeals is based on data in the Administrative Office of the United States Courts, *Judicial Business of the United States Courts: Annual Report of the Director*, http://www.uscourts.gov/statistics-reports/analysis-reports/judicial-business-united-states-courts.

86. Pamela S. Karlen, "This Term, the Justices Chose Cases that 'Sear the Conscience,'" *Slate*, June 21, 2017.

87. *Archdiocese of Washington v. Washington Metropolitan Area Transit Authority* (2020).

88. Cody Jacobs, "Do the Justices Look More Favorably on Gun Regulation than Many Fear?" *SCOTUS Now*, IIT Chicago–Kent School of Law, December 5, 2017, http://blogs.kentlaw.iit.edu/iscotus/justices-look-favorably-gun-regulation-many-fear/.

89. The decisions were *Stenberg v. Carhart* (2000), *Gonzales v. Carhart* (2007), *Whole Women's Health v. Hellerstedt* (2016), and *June Medical Services v. Russo* (2020).

90. The Court's decision in those cases was *Obergefell v. Hodges* (2015).

91. Dahleen Glanton, "Retired Justice O'Connor: *Bush v. Gore* 'Stirred up the Public'," *Chicago Tribune*, April 26, 2013.

92. The cases were, respectively, *Rucho v. Common Cause* (2019) and *Department of Commerce v. New York* (2019).

93. The most important immigration case was *Department of Homeland Security v. Regents of the University of California* (2020). The financial records cases were *Trump v. Vance* (2020) and *Trump v. Mazars USA, LLC* (2020).

94. This figure counts consolidated cases only once and does not include GVRs (grant-vacate-remand). Some of these petitions were not counted because they were still pending at the certiorari stage at the end of the 2019 term.

95. Biskupic, Roberts, and Shiffman, "Special Report: The Echo Chamber."

96. "Notes on Justice Kennedy," *Southern California Appellate News*, February 4, 2010, http://www.socal-appellate.blogspot.com/2010/02/notes-on-justice-kennedy.html.

97. Kevin T. McGuire, *The Supreme Court Bar: Legal Elites in the Washington Community* (Charlottesville: University Press of Virginia, 1993), 175–180.

98. Tony Mauro, "Why Top Advocates Are Ghostwriting SCOTUS Briefs," *National Law Journal*, August 9, 2017.

99. Richard J. Lazarus, "Advocacy Matters: Transforming the Court by Transforming the Bar," in *Business and the Roberts Court*, ed. Adler, 82–83.

100. The case is discussed in Adam Liptak, "Supreme Court Won't Consider Revoked Law Banning Sleeping Outdoors," *New York Times*, December 17, 2019, A13.

101. Adam Liptak, "Reticent on the Bench, but Effusive About It," *New York Times*, November 1, 2016, A15.

102. *ProQuest Statistical Abstract of the United States 2019* (Lanham, Md.: Rowman and Littlefield, 2019), 241.

103. Ryan J. Owens and David A. Simon, "Explaining the Supreme Court's Shrinking Docket," *William & Mary Law Review* 53 (March 2012): 1219–1285; Kenneth W. Moffett, Forrest Maltzman, Karen Miranda, and Charles R. Shipan, "Strategic Behavior and Variation in the Supreme Court's Caseload Over Time," *Justice System Journal* 37 (2016): 20–38.

104. Liptak, "Reticent on the Bench, but Effusive About It"; Andrew Hamm, "Breyer on the Court's Shrinking Docket, Foreign Law, and More," *SCOTUSblog*, September 17, 2015.

105. David R. Stras, "The Supreme Court's Declining Plenary Docket: A Membership-Based Explanation," *Constitutional Commentary* 27 (Fall 2010): 151–161.

106. "Supreme Court Fiscal Year 2020 Budget," hearing before Subcommittee of House Appropriations Committee, March 7, 2019 (C-SPAN transcript), https://www.c-span .org/video/?458421-1/justices-alito-kagan-testify-supreme-courts-budget.

CHAPTER FOUR

DECISION MAKING

Once the Supreme Court determines which cases to hear, the justices get to the heart of their work: reaching decisions in those cases. This chapter examines how and why the Court makes its decisions.

COMPONENTS OF THE COURT'S DECISION

A Supreme Court decision on the merits, in which the Court decides the legal issues in a case, has two components: the immediate outcome for the parties to the case and a statement of general legal rules. In cases that the Court fully considers, it nearly always presents the two components in an opinion. In the great majority of cases, at least five justices subscribe to this opinion. As a result, it constitutes an authoritative statement by the Court.

Except in the few cases the Court hears under its original jurisdiction, the Court describes the outcome in relation to the lower-court decision it is reviewing. The Court can affirm the lower-court decision, leaving that court's treatment of the parties undisturbed. Alternatively, it can reverse or vacate the lower-court decision. According to the Court's Style Manual, "The Court should reverse if it deems the judgment below to be absolutely wrong, but vacate if the judgment is less than absolutely wrong."[1]

When the Court does disturb a lower-court decision, it occasionally makes a final judgment in the case. But far more often, it remands the case to the lower court, sending it back for reconsideration. The Court's opinion provides guidance on how the case should be reconsidered. For example, the opinion in a tax case may say that a court of appeals adopted the wrong interpretation of the federal tax laws and that this court should reexamine the case on the basis of a different interpretation.

In itself, the outcome of most cases has little impact beyond the parties themselves. Rather, what makes most decisions consequential is the statement in the Court's opinion of legal rules that apply to the nation as a whole. Any court must follow those rules in a case to which they apply, and the rules often apply to other public officials as well. As a result, a decision frequently affects thousands or millions of people who were not parties in the case.

The Court chooses which legal rules it establishes in a case, just as it chooses the outcome for the parties. In some cases, a ruling for one of the parties could be based on any of several rules or sets of rules. The rules chosen by the Court largely determine the long-term impact of its decision. If the Court overturns the death sentence for a particular defendant, it might base that decision on an unusual error in the defendant's trial, and the decision would affect few other defendants. Alternatively, the Court could declare that the death penalty is unconstitutional under all circumstances and thereby make a fundamental policy change.

THE DECISION-MAKING PROCESS

When the Court accepts a case for a decision on the merits, it initiates the decision-making process for that case. This process varies from case to case, but it typically involves several stages.

Presentation of Cases to the Court

The written briefs that the Court receives when it considers whether to hear a case usually give some attention to the merits of the case. Once a case has been accepted for oral argument and decision, attorneys for the parties submit new briefs that usually address only the merits. In the great majority of cases that reach this stage, amicus curiae briefs are submitted with their own arguments on the merits.

Most of the material in these briefs concerns legal issues. The parties muster evidence and logic to support their interpretations of relevant constitutional provisions and statutes. Briefs frequently offer arguments about policy as well, seeking to persuade the justices that support for their position constitutes not only good law but good public policy.

Material in the briefs is supplemented by attorneys' presentations in oral argument before the Court. In most cases, each side is provided a half hour for its argument. Attorneys for the parties sometimes share their time with the lawyer for an amicus—usually the federal government.

Justices today are considerably more active in oral arguments than they were in earlier eras, usually leaving lawyers with only short stretches of time to speak in between questions and comments from the bench.[2] Reflecting this change, the Court announced in 2019 that in the future justices "generally" would not interrupt lawyers who represent the parties in the first two minutes of their arguments. But in the Court's first sitting after this announcement, justices sometimes spoke up in the first two minutes.[3] Justices even interrupt each other from time to time, and male justices are especially likely to interrupt female colleagues.[4]

When the Court began to hear oral arguments by telephone during the coronavirus pandemic, this chaotic format was replaced by a more systematic structure. After a lawyer's opening statement, the justices asked questions in order of seniority, with Chief Justice John Roberts beginning the questioning, calling on his colleagues,

▶ **Photo 4-1** Justice Elena Kagan at the University of Minnesota in 2019. Kagan has suggested that the quality of briefs submitted to the Court by lawyers has greater impact than the quality of their oral arguments.

and sometimes cutting off a lawyer's response (or, less often, a justice's question) when it was time to move on to the next justice. One consequence of the new structure was that Justice Clarence Thomas, who had asked questions in only two cases since 2006, participated actively in the arguments. Thomas has indicated his disapproval of the course of the arguments in their usual form, and the absence of that chaos seemed to make the difference for him.[5] For whatever period this new structure continues, arguments will sound somewhat different from the pattern of the past few decades.

For the justices, oral argument serves three broad functions. First, it allows them to gather information about the strengths and weaknesses of the parties' positions and about other aspects of the case that interest them. In this way, it can help them reach their judgment about the case.

Second, and probably more important, the argument gives them an opportunity to shape their colleagues' perceptions of a case. Justice Anthony Kennedy reported that "we do not talk to each other about the cases before oral argument."[6] As a result, the argument provides justices with their only opportunity to persuade each other before the Court meets to reach its tentative decision at conference. As one commentator said, "The lawyer at the lectern is the medium through whom they send one another messages."[7] To a considerable degree, then, the justices act as advocates in oral argument.[8]

Because of this advocacy role, justices tend to ask more questions of the side they ultimately vote against, and their questions to that side tend to be more negative in content and tone.[9] One reporter referred to Justice Samuel Alito as "setting traps" for lawyers whose positions he opposed.[10] In contrast, when justices ask questions of the lawyer whose position they favor, the questions are often designed to shore up the lawyer's case. Thus, in the 2019 argument in which Justice Thomas made one of his then-rare interventions, his questions were designed to expose a weakness in a lawyer's case. Justice Sotomayor immediately followed with questions designed to repair any damage that Thomas had done to the lawyer's case.[11] Not surprisingly, when the Court issued its decision both justices voted in the direction that their questions indicated.

For at least some justices, oral argument serves a third function. As two scholars put it, "The Justices sometimes seem to regard oral argument not as a serious or important part of the decisional process, but as an opportunity to demonstrate their quickness or cleverness."[12] Justices frequently try to evoke laughter with their comments, often at the expense of attorneys.[13] The growing audience for oral arguments that has been facilitated by the availability of transcripts and audiotapes may encourage this behavior.

Understandably, oral arguments with their direct interactions between lawyers and justices receive far more attention than the written briefs from the parties. When the Court holds arguments in its courtroom, people line up very early—sometimes days early—for the small numbers of seats available to the general public, and it has become standard practice to pay people to wait in line on behalf of others who want to attend arguments.[14]

In an important sense, oral arguments do not merit this disproportionate attention. Justices get far more information from the briefs and other written case materials than they do from oral argument, so the potential for influence from these written materials almost surely is greater. As Justice Elena Kagan put it, "If you're going to have to choose between having a great brief and making a great oral argument, you should always choose to write the great brief."[15] And as one frequent litigator in the Court has said, the influence of lawyers' skills on the justices should not be exaggerated. "Supreme Court litigation is not a moot court competition. The Supreme Court rules for the better case, not the better lawyer."[16]

Even so, what justices hear during oral argument can have an impact on their thinking, and this impact is sometimes decisive. One study compared the tentative votes of two justices to affirm or reverse prior to the argument with their votes in conference a few days after the argument. The votes of Lewis Powell shifted 7 percent of the time and those of Harry Blackmun 10 percent of the time. Patterns in these shifts suggest that many of them resulted from the influence of the oral argument itself.[17] And as Justice Alito has pointed out, the argument may affect the justices' specific positions on the issues in a case even when their tentative votes for one side or the other are unchanged.[18]

Tentative Decisions

After oral argument, the Court discusses each case in one of its conferences later the same week. The chief justice begins the discussion of a case, which continues with the other justices from most senior to most junior. As the justices speak, they indicate their votes in the case and the reasons for their positions.

Once each justice has spoken, there is often little or no further discussion. This reflects the fact that, as Antonin Scalia put it, the discussion of a case in conference "is not really an exercise in persuading each other, it's an exercise in stating your views while the rest of us take notes."[19] Scalia would have preferred more extensive discussion of cases; he once noted that "I thrash out the cases with my law clerks much more than with my colleagues."[20] Even when the discussion is more extensive, it generally has little impact. Elena Kagan reported that "sometimes we go around the table and people are where they are and I know nothing is going to change and we just keep talking and we just keep annoying each other."[21]

After each two-week sitting, the writing of the Court's opinion in each case is assigned to a justice. If the chief justice voted with the majority, the chief assigns the opinion. In other cases, the most senior associate justice in the majority makes the assignment.

Reaching Final Decisions

The justice who was assigned the Court's opinion writes an initial draft, guided by the views that were expressed in conference. Ordinarily, the justice's clerks do most of the drafting. Once this opinion is completed and circulated, justices who were in the majority at conference sign on to it most of the time.[22] As a result, the opinion may get majority support with no difficulty. But justices often hold back rather than sign on, either because they have developed doubts about their original vote or because they disagree with language in the draft opinion. The language is important because justices are reluctant to join an opinion when they disagree with its reasoning. Members of the original minority also read the draft opinion for the Court, and they sometimes sign on to the opinion because their view of the case has changed.

Justices who do not immediately sign on often express fundamental disagreement with the opinion, so that no revision would satisfy them. Exaggerating somewhat, Clarence Thomas has described such responses: "Dear Clarence, I disagree with everything in your opinion except your name. Cheers."[23] But justices sometimes indicate that they would be willing to join an opinion if certain changes are made. Justices who had voted with the majority are especially likely to ask for changes. Their memos initiate a process of explicit or implicit negotiation in which the assigned justice tries to gain the support of as many colleagues as possible. At the least, the assigned justice wants to maintain the original majority for the outcome supported by the opinion and to win a majority for the language of the opinion so that it becomes the official statement of the Court. This negotiation process operates primarily through written memos, sent on paper rather than by e-mail. But justices occasionally interact directly, and law clerks may gather information from clerks for other justices to identify what revisions are needed to gain a colleague's support for an opinion.[24]

In the majority of cases, the justice who was assigned the Court's opinion competes with colleagues who write alternative opinions supporting the opposite outcome or arguing for the same outcome with a different rationale. Most of the time, assigned justices succeed in winning a majority for their opinions, though sometimes with substantial alterations to satisfy colleagues. Even after opinion writers secure majority support, they may continue to redraft their opinions to address other justices' arguments. Justice Ruth Bader Ginsburg reported that in one major decision, she wrote eighteen drafts of her majority opinion.[25]

More often than not, justices who were assigned the Court's opinion fail to win unanimous support for their opinion. As shown in Table 4-1, which summarizes attributes of the Court's decisions in the 2018 and 2019 terms, full unanimity for a single opinion was achieved only 27 percent of the time. (In another 9 percent of the cases, there was a unanimous vote on the outcome for the parties to the case.)

Table 4-1	Selected Characteristics of Supreme Court Decisions, 2018 and 2019 Terms
Characteristic	**Percentage**
Unanimous decision[a]	35.8
Support for Court's opinion	
Unanimous for whole opinion	26.7
Unanimous for part of opinion	4.2
Majority but not unanimous	60.0
Majority for only part of opinion	4.2
No majority for opinion	5.0
One or more concurring opinions[b]	43.3
Two or more concurring opinions	12.5
One or more dissenting opinions[c]	64.2
Two or more dissenting opinions	17.5

Note: The decisions included are those decided with opinions after oral argument.

a. "Decision" refers to the outcome for the parties. Partial dissents are not counted as votes for the decision.

b. Some concurring opinions are in full agreement with the Court's opinion.

c. Opinions labeled "concurring and dissenting" are treated as dissenting opinions.

Occasionally, no opinion gains the support of a majority. That occurred six times in the 2018 and 2019 terms, along with five decisions in which there was majority support for only part of an opinion. Without a majority opinion, there is no authoritative statement of the Court's position on the legal issues in the case. But the opinion on the winning side with the greatest support—the "plurality opinion"—may specify the points for which majority support exists.

On rare occasions, the justices find themselves unable to reach a final decision in a case before the term ends. They then schedule the case for a second set of oral arguments in the following term. The Court took this route in two landmark cases, *Brown v. Board of Education* (1954) and *Roe v. Wade* (1973). Occasionally, a case is reargued in order to break a 4–4 tie once a ninth justice is available to participate. In *Knick v. Township of Scott* (2019), the Court held the second argument in the same term, with new Justice Brett Kavanaugh casting the tie-breaking vote after that argument.

Concurring and Dissenting Opinions

Disagreement with the majority opinion that emerges from the decision process can take two forms. In the first form a justice dissents, disagreeing with the result reached by the Court as it affects the parties to a case. If a criminal conviction is reversed, for example, a justice who believes it should have been affirmed will dissent. In the second form a justice concurs with the Court's decision, agreeing with the result in the specific case but disagreeing with the rationale expressed in the Court's opinion.

Ordinarily, a justice who disagrees with the majority opinion writes or joins in a dissenting or concurring opinion. When the conference vote is not unanimous, the senior dissenting justice assigns the dissenting opinion. This opinion is written at the same time as the assigned opinion for the majority, and often one goal is to persuade enough colleagues to change their positions that a minority becomes a majority.

That goal is no longer relevant after the Court reaches its final decision, but a dissenting opinion can serve several other purposes. For one thing, dissenting opinions give justices the satisfaction of expressing unhappiness with the result in a case and justifying their disagreement. They sometimes have more concrete purposes as well. Through their arguments, dissenters may try to set the stage for a later Court to adopt their view. In the short term, a dissenting opinion may be intended to subvert the Court's decision by pointing out how lower courts can interpret it narrowly or by urging Congress to overturn the Court's reading of a statute.

When more than one justice dissents, the dissenters usually join in a single opinion—most likely the one originally assigned. But often there are multiple dissenting opinions, each expressing the particular view of the justice who wrote it but sometimes indicating agreement with another opinion.

A concurring opinion that disagrees with the majority opinion on the legal rationale for a decision is labeled a special concurrence. In some cases, the disagreement is limited. In some other cases, the majority and concurring opinions offer fundamentally different rationales for the outcome they favor. In *American Legion v. American Humanist Association* (2019), the Court ruled that a religious monument on public land in Maryland did not violate the establishment of religion clause of the First Amendment as it applied to the states through the Fourteenth Amendment. One concurring opinion, by Neil Gorsuch, concluded that the Court should not have decided that question because the challengers of the monument lacked legal standing to bring their case. Another concurring opinion, by Clarence Thomas, argued that the Court did not need to analyze the establishment clause question because that clause should not be incorporated into the Fourteenth Amendment.[26]

Another type of concurring opinion, a regular concurrence, is written by a justice who joins the majority opinion. Authors of regular concurrences agree with both the outcome for the litigants and the legal rules that the Court establishes. In light of this agreement, why would justices write separate opinions? Most often, regular concurring opinions offer their own interpretation of the majority opinion as a means to influence the responses of lower courts and other policy makers to the decision. In a 2020 concurrence, Justice Alito wrote that "I write to emphasize what we are not deciding."[27] Sometimes regular concurring opinions suggest how Congress might respond to the decision. When the Court ruled in 2019 that a provision of federal trademark law was unconstitutional, Alito said that "our decision does not prevent Congress from adopting a more carefully focused statute" and outlined what that statute might say.[28] And some concurring opinions offer suggestions about directions that the Court itself might take in the future.

Content and Style of Opinions

Majority opinions vary in form, but they usually begin with a description of the background of the case before it reached the Court. The opinion then turns to the legal issues, discussing the opposing views on those issues and describing the Court's conclusions about them. The opinion ends with a summary of the outcome for the parties.

Concurring and dissenting opinions do not need to be comprehensive, so they often focus on specific aspects of the case, and some are brief. There is also a difference in style, as Justice Alito has explained. "If you're writing a majority opinion, where you have to have at least four people agree with you, you're limited in what you can say. In my dissents I'm writing for myself, so they're more freewheeling." Alito noted that among the opinions he has written, all of his favorites were concurring and dissenting opinions.[29] Dissents sometimes include strong language criticizing the Court's decision. In a 2019 dissent, Justice Kagan said that "in throwing up its hands, the majority misses something under its nose: What it says can't be done *has* been done."[30] In another 2019 case, Chief Justice John Roberts said that the primary opinion for the Court's majority "devotes five pages to planting trees in hopes of obscuring the forest."[31]

Especially in concurring and dissenting opinions, justices seem to have moved toward a less formal style of writing. Responding to a passage in the majority opinion in one case, Stephen Breyer's dissent said, "Good reply. But no cigar."[32] This more colloquial style may reflect justices' awareness that their opinions are now readily available to a wide audience, including interested non-lawyers.

Both majority opinions and dissents are usually written as arguments for the conclusion they reach rather than presenting the considerations on both sides in an evenhanded way. They typically treat their conclusion as clearly correct, even if an opinion on the other side makes strong arguments for its own conclusion. As part of that style, opinions emphasize evidence about the law and other aspects of cases that are favorable to their conclusion. They draw that evidence primarily from the briefs and other materials in the case. But in the Internet era, justices' opinions frequently cite facts related to cases that justices and their law clerks have drawn from their own reading and research. Neither the factual information that justices take from briefs nor the information they gather independently is always well founded.[33]

The Decision Announcement and Later Events

The decision-making process for a case ends when all the opinions have been put in final form and all justices have determined which opinions they will join. The Supreme Court is unusual in that it announces its decisions in a Court session, though it dispensed with those sessions during the coronavirus pandemic. Typically, the justice who wrote the majority opinion reads a portion of the opinion. Occasionally—nine times over the 2017 and 2018 terms—the authors of dissenting opinions also read portions of their opinions. As Justice Ginsburg said in describing her own practice, justices do so when they think the Court's decision is "egregiously" wrong.[34] In announcing her dissent from the Court's decision in *Trump v. Hawaii* (2018), Justice Sonia Sotomayor concluded by saying that "history will not look kindly on the court's misguided decision today, nor should it."[35]

The length of time required for a case to go through all the stages from filing in the Court to the announcement of a decision varies a good deal. Of the cases that the Court decided in its 2018 term, the time from the petition for certiorari to oral argument varied from three months to twenty months, and the time from oral argument to decision varied from a little over a month to more than eight and a half months—nearly the full length of the Court's term.[36] The Court's decision often comes many years after the incident that triggered the case.

After the Court decides a case or declines to hear it, the losing party may petition for a rehearing. These petitions are rarely granted.

The language of the "slip opinions" that the Court issues when it hands down a decision is sometimes revised during the several years before an opinion is officially published in final form. Some revisions correct typographical errors, but others make more substantive changes.

INFLUENCES ON DECISIONS: INTRODUCTION

Of all the questions that might be asked about the Supreme Court, the one that has intrigued scholars and other observers the most is how the Court's decisions are best explained. Cases present the justices with choices: which litigant to support, what rules of law to establish. On what bases do they make their individual and collective choices?

This question is difficult to answer. Like policy makers elsewhere in government, Supreme Court justices act on multiple considerations, those considerations are intermixed, and their relative importance varies among justices and cases.[37] Further, the justices' choices can be explained at multiple levels. For instance, some recent research presents explanations based on the justices' personality traits.[38] In part because of these complexities, people who study the Court disagree a good deal about how best to explain the Court's decisions.

Those disagreements are primarily about two issues. The first is the goals that drive the justices' choices, either consciously or unconsciously. Some scholars think that when justices choose between alternatives in a case, their choice is based almost solely on their policy preferences, their judgments about how best to achieve what they see as desirable public policy. Other scholars think that policy considerations are important to the justices, but legal considerations are also important because justices want to interpret the law as accurately as possible.

The second issue is the extent to which justices are influenced by their colleagues and by people and institutions outside the Court. One point of view is that justices are essentially autonomous, making their choices without much influence from other justices or from the Court's political and social environment. This view is incorporated into a perspective called the attitudinal model, one in which justices simply adopt the alternatives that best fit their personal conceptions of good policy.[39]

In contrast, some observers think that the justices are subject to substantial influence from inside and outside the Court. Justices might be influenced by their colleagues or by people and institutions outside the Court for a variety of reasons. However, such influence is often thought to result from strategic considerations. When making choices in order to achieve their goals, strategic justices take into account the potential reactions of others to those choices rather than automatically adopting their own preferred position. From this perspective, a policy-oriented justice would compromise with colleagues on the wording of an opinion in order to move the Court as a whole to the best feasible collective decision from the justice's perspective. To take another example, a justice who thinks in strategic terms also takes into account the potential reactions of Congress to the Court's decisions, trying to avoid reaching decisions that legislators would act to override.

Possible variation among justices and cases merits some emphasis. For instance, justices' policy preferences may have greater impact on issues they care more about. Legal considerations may play a larger role when the law seems to lean heavily in favor of one side. And some justices may be more susceptible than others to influence from particular sets of people outside the Court. These and other kinds of variation should be taken into account in considering the factors that shape decision making on the Court.

The rest of this chapter considers these factors in relation to the two issues I have described. The next two sections relate to the first issue, examining the state of the law and justices' policy preferences as factors shaping the Court's decisions. The last two sections consider the second issue, examining justices' influence on each other and influence from the world outside the Court.

THE STATE OF THE LAW

Every case requires the Supreme Court to interpret the law, usually in the form of provisions of the Constitution or federal statutes. In this sense, a justice's job differs from that of a legislator: when justices make law with their decisions, they do so by interpreting existing law. For this reason, the existing state of the law is a good starting point for explanation of the Court's decisions.

Judges use primarily three broad sources of information as bases for interpretation of the law. The first is called the plain meaning of the language of legal provisions. The second is the intent of the lawmakers who wrote those provisions. The last is precedents, courts' prior interpretations of legal provisions. Examination of each of those sources provides a way to probe the role of legal considerations in the Court's decisions. After working through these sources, I will consider the role of those considerations more broadly.

Plain Meaning

Nearly everyone agrees that interpretation of a legal provision should begin with a search for the plain meaning of constitutional and statutory provisions— what the words and sets of words in those provisions mean. This is not always an easy task. The plain meaning of a legal provision is sometimes uncertain, and this is especially true in the cases that the Supreme Court hears. The provisions of the Constitution that the Court interprets most frequently are written in broad language whose meaning can be difficult to determine. This is true, for instance, of the Fourteenth Amendment provision that prohibits the states from depriving people "of life, liberty, or property, without due process of law." Understandably, the justices have had great difficulty in determining what "due process of law" requires.

Most federal statutes are written with greater specificity than the Constitution, but the statutory questions that the Court addresses typically involve matters on which Congress has not spoken with much clarity. In these cases, justices can do their best to ascertain the most reasonable interpretation of the words in a statute, but there may be considerable room for disagreement. Title VII of the Civil Rights Act of 1964 prohibits discrimination in employment practices "because of sex." Does discrimination on the basis of an employee's sexual orientation or transgender status constitute discrimination because of sex? When the Supreme Court faced that question in *Bostock v. Clayton County* (2020), the advocates on both sides made quite plausible arguments based on the language of Title VII.

In interpreting the law, justices might seek to ascertain the meaning of its language at the time it was written or what that language means to people today. The school of interpretation called originalism, strongly supported by justices such as Clarence Thomas and Neil Gorsuch, holds that only the original meaning counts.[40] Some other justices believe that the current meaning should be taken into account. But even justices who take the same position on this question may reach different conclusions. In *Bostock*, Justice Gorsuch's majority opinion employed originalism and found that discrimination based on sexual orientation or transgender status did violate the prohibition of sex discrimination in Title VII. The dissenting opinion by Samuel Alito also employed originalism and disagreed sharply with Gorsuch's analysis.

Even when a legal provision appears to have a clear meaning, the justices do not always adhere to it. That is especially true in constitutional law. Over time, the Court has adopted several interpretations of the Constitution that seem to depart from the language of its provisions. Although the language of the Fourteenth Amendment's due process clause requires only that government follow proper procedures in taking "life, liberty, or property," the Court interprets the clause to encompass rights that are substantive rather than procedural, such as freedom of expression and freedom of religion.[41] The Court interprets the same due process language in the Fifth Amendment as a protection against discrimination by the federal government.[42] And for more than a century, the Court has read the Eleventh Amendment's prohibition of lawsuits against states "by citizens of another state" to prohibit most lawsuits against a state by the state's own residents as well.[43]

Why have justices adopted and maintained these seemingly inaccurate interpretations? The primary reason is that doing so advances values that are important to them, values such as protecting freedom of speech. The general acceptance of what can be called constitutional fictions shows that no justice always adheres to the plain meaning of the law.

But the plain meaning of legal provisions still exerts an impact on the justices' conclusions. That is especially true in statutory interpretation, because of statutes' relative specificity. This may help to explain why the proportion of unanimous decisions in cases interpreting statutes is much higher than the proportion in constitutional cases: statutory language as applied to a case is more likely to lead all the justices to the same conclusion.

Intent of Framers or Legislators

When the plain meaning of a legal provision is unclear, justices can seek to ascertain the intentions of the lawmakers who wrote the provision. There is evidence about legislative intent in places such as congressional committee reports and the records of debates on the floor of the two houses, which constitute what is called the legislative history of a statute or a constitutional amendment. For provisions of the original Constitution, evidence is found in reports of deliberations at the Constitutional Convention of 1787 and other sources.

Sometimes the intent of Congress or the framers of the Constitution is clear. Frequently, however, it is not. The body that adopted a provision may not have spoken on an issue; the members of Congress who wrote the broad language of the Fourteenth Amendment could hardly indicate their intent about all the issues that have arisen under that amendment. Further, evidence about intent may be misleading and even contradictory, in part because of efforts to influence the courts by members of Congress and congressional staff who create the legislative history of statutes.

Justices disagree about the use of legislative intent in interpreting statutes. Textualists argue that judges should focus on the plain meaning of legal provisions and that they should ignore evidence of legislative intent. In contrast with textualists, some judges and commentators argue that it is both legitimate and desirable to take evidence of legislative intent into account.[44] One school of thought that takes this view is called purposivism, because it emphasizes the value of ascertaining the purposes that underlie provisions of law. Justice Breyer is the most visible supporter of purposivism on the current Court.

The continuing debate among justices over the use of legislative intent to guide interpretation of the law was reflected in the opinions in *Digital Realty Trust v. Somers* (2018). All the justices agreed on the Court's interpretation of a statutory provision that protected certain "whistleblowers" from retaliation by their employers. But Clarence Thomas wrote a concurring opinion that strongly disagreed with the majority opinion's use of legislative history as one basis for the decision. Thomas was joined by Samuel Alito and Neil Gorsuch. Sonia Sotomayor, joined by Breyer, wrote a concurring opinion in response, arguing for the relevance of legislative history to interpretation of statutes.

As the lineup of justices in *Digital Realty* suggests, disagreements between schools of legal interpretation tend to fall along ideological lines. Textualism and originalism, which Justice Antonin Scalia described as a "sort of subspecies of textualism,"[45] receive their strongest support from conservatives. Indeed, those two approaches have become powerful symbols for conservatives in the legal community, including some of the justices. During his first year on the Court, Justice Gorsuch spoke at the conservative Federalist Society and reported to an enthusiastic audience that "originalism has regained its place, and textualism has triumphed, and neither is going anywhere on my watch."[46]

Conservatives' identification with these two schools of interpretation stems largely from a belief that deviations from them have produced liberal judicial policies. Although some liberals on the Court and in the legal community argue against textualism and originalism, liberal justices also employ these approaches in support of their own conclusions. A classic example was *District of Columbia v. Heller* (2008), in which the Court held that the Second Amendment protects the right of individuals to possess firearms. Justice Scalia's majority opinion that focused on the original meaning of the Second Amendment was countered by Justice John Paul Stevens's dissent that interpreted the evidence on original meaning quite differently.

▶ **Photo 4-2** Justice Neil Gorsuch, speaking at the Federalist Society in 2017. In his speech, Gorsuch emphasized his strong support for originalism and textualism as approaches to legal interpretation.

Precedent

The Supreme Court's past decisions, its precedents, provide another guide to decision making. A basic doctrine of the law is stare decisis (let the decision stand). Under this doctrine, a court is bound to adhere to the rules of law established by courts that stand above it. No court stands above the Supreme Court, but stare decisis includes an expectation that courts will generally adhere to their own precedents.

Technically, a court is expected to follow not everything stated in a relevant precedent but only the rule of law that is necessary for decision in that case—what is called the holding. In the *Heller* decision, the Court's ruling that the Second Amendment protects the right of individuals to possess guns was the holding of the case. The Court's opinion also described some types of gun regulations that were "presumptively lawful." Because those regulations were not involved in this case, that part of the Court's opinion was "dictum," which has no legal force. Since dicta in the Court's opinion represent the majority view in the Court, however, they can have an impact on other policy makers. The dictum in *Heller* affected responses to the decision by lower courts and legislatures.

The practice of adhering to precedent would not eliminate ambiguity in legal interpretation even if the justices always followed that practice. Most cases before the Supreme Court concern issues that are at least marginally different from those decided in past cases, so precedents do not lead directly to a particular outcome.

Indeed, justices often "distinguish" a precedent, holding that it does not govern the current case.

The Court does abandon some of its precedents, although its opinions are not always clear about whether a precedent has been abandoned. The rate at which precedents are overruled has been much higher since the late 1930s than in the Court's earlier history; the 1937–2019 period constitutes 36 percent of the Court's history, but by one count 82 percent of the overrulings have come in that period. Figure 4-1, based on that source, also shows considerable variation within the post-1937 period.[47] There is a tendency for the rate to increase after the Court's ideological position shifts substantially, a tendency suggested by the large numbers of overrulings in the 1940s and 1960s. The decline since the 1970s may result in part from the absence of a strong ideological majority on either the conservative or liberal sides. But even in the decade from 2010 to 2019, when the Court rejected precedents in only a dozen cases, some of those overrulings were on issues of major importance such as regulation of campaign funding, same-sex marriage, and the drawing of legislative districts.[48]

The great majority of overrulings are in constitutional cases. The Court's special reluctance to overrule statutory precedents is based on a rationale that Justice Kagan described in a 2015 opinion for the Court: "Unlike in a constitutional case,

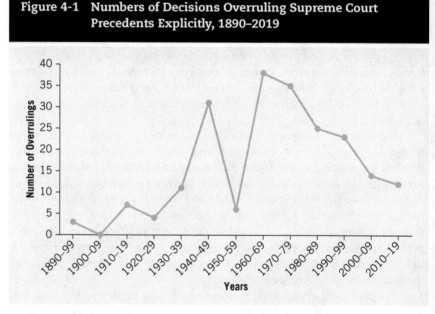

Figure 4-1   Numbers of Decisions Overruling Supreme Court Precedents Explicitly, 1890–2019

Source: Calculated from list in Congressional Research Service, *The Constitution of the United States of America: Analysis and Interpretation,* Table of Supreme Court Decisions Overruled by Subsequent Decisions, https://constitution.congress.gov/resources/decisions-overruled/.

critics of our ruling can take their objections across the street, and Congress can correct any mistake it sees."[49] The Court has used this rationale to adhere for a century to its position that professional baseball is exempt from the antitrust laws, even though the exemption has been increasingly regarded as an anomaly. However, the justices may also have been motivated by a concern about disturbing the status quo in baseball. (Congress did limit the exemption in one respect in 1998.)[50]

The number of times the Court overrules precedents is a small fraction of the times when it follows them. The same is true of individual justices. But most of the time when justices follow a precedent, its validity is not in question, or they simply agree with it. What do justices do when they confront a precedent with which they strongly disagree?

One way to identify such disagreement arises when a justice dissents from a legal rule at the time the Court first establishes it. Most of the time, justices continue to reject that precedent in later cases, engaging in what one legal scholar called "perpetual dissents."[51] Yet justices sometimes vote to uphold precedents that they originally opposed. More broadly, the Court as a whole adheres to a good many precedents that no longer accord with the views of most justices. Thus, few of the Warren Court's liberal precedents from the 1960s have been overruled by the more conservative Courts of the post-Warren era, although some of those precedents have been narrowed considerably by subsequent decisions.

On the current Court, Justice Thomas stands out for his belief that the Court gives too much weight to precedent. He wrote a long concurring opinion in a 2019 case to argue for that position, stating that "when faced with a demonstrably erroneous precedent, my rule is simple: We should not follow it."[52] Thomas frequently writes concurring and dissenting opinions that question the validity of existing precedents, and in recent years he has questioned major constitutional precedents on issues such as the exclusion of illegally obtained evidence from use in criminal trials, limits on libel suits by public officials and public figures, and the right to counsel for indigent defendants.[53]

With the establishment of a fairly solid conservative majority on the current Court, conservative justices have expressed greater willingness to question precedents while liberal justices decry that willingness. In a 2019 decision the Court overruled a precedent by a 5–4 vote along ideological lines, and Justice Breyer said in his dissenting opinion that "today's decision can only cause one to wonder which cases the Court will overrule next." A month later, when the Court overruled another precedent by the same vote, Justice Kagan wrote, "Well, that didn't take long. Now one may wonder yet again."[54]

The occasional overruling of precedents by the Court, the ideological element in overrulings, and the continued rejection of some precedents by justices who initially opposed them make it clear that precedent does not exert an overwhelming effect on the justices' choices. But this does not mean that precedents have no impact at all. The set of precedents that exists in any area of law helps to channel the justices' judgments about cases in that area. This is especially true of analytic frameworks that were established by past decisions. By laying out standards to apply to individual cases, these frameworks help to determine what conditions are important in answering questions such as whether a particular form of speech is protected under the First Amendment or whether a specific police search is illegal.[55]

The Law's Significance in Decisions

As a nominee for chief justice in 2005, John Roberts told the Senate Judiciary Committee that "judges and justices are servants of the law, not the other way around. Judges are like umpires. Umpires don't make the rules; they apply them."[56] His statement received considerable attention because it presented a vivid image, but nominees to the Court and sitting justices often describe their work in similar ways. In doing so, they offer a simple explanation of the justices' choices as decision makers: justices reach their judgments on the basis of evidence about the meaning of the legal provisions they interpret.

This depiction of the justices' work may be attractive, but its limitations as an explanation of their choices are clear. For one thing, as umpires themselves have pointed out, application of even the seemingly rigid rules of baseball can involve considerable discretion.[57] And as the discussion so far should underline, the legal rules that the Court applies seldom lead to an unambiguous result: the cases in which the state of the law does dictate a ruling for one side or the other seldom get on the Court's agenda.

A second limitation to this depiction is the reality that justices care about more than the law. Most important, like other people in law and politics, they develop views about which government policies are most desirable. When they decide cases involving issues such as affirmative action, abortion, or the role of government in health care, they will be happier if their position in a case and the Court's collective decision are consistent with their conception of good policy on those issues.

Because of this reality, some observers of the Court take a position directly opposite to the one that justices usually express, arguing that the state of the law has essentially no impact on justices' choices.[58] This position can be defended, but there is good reason to conclude that legal considerations do have a meaningful effect on justices' choices. Even when decisions on either side of a case could be justified under the law, the law often provides more support for one side than for the other. If justices care about making good law, they will be drawn toward the side that seems to have a stronger legal argument.

Surely, most if not all justices do care about making good law. They have been trained in a tradition that emphasizes the law as a basis for judicial decisions. They are evaluated informally by a peer group of judges and legal scholars who assess their ability to reach well-founded interpretations of the law. Perhaps most important, they work in the language of the law. The arguments they receive in written briefs and oral arguments are primarily about the law, and so are the arguments they make to each other in draft opinions and memoranda.[59]

Indeed, some aspects of justices' behavior indicate that the state of the law affects their choices in meaningful ways.[60] They sometimes take positions that conflict with their conceptions of good policy. And occasionally, the justices in the majority are sufficiently unhappy with the effects of their interpretation of a statute that their opinion asks Congress to consider rewriting the statute to override their decision—that is, to establish a policy that the justices feel powerless to adopt themselves because of their reading of the law.

It seems likely that the state of the law has greater impact in some cases than in others. One reason is that the law sometimes leans in favor of one side but sometimes is too ambiguous to lean in either direction. Another reason is that other considerations in the justices' minds are stronger in some cases than in others. In cases in which their policy preferences are not very relevant, justices may enjoy using their intellectual skills to reach what they see as the best interpretation of the law. Because such cases tend to be less exciting than many others that the Court decides, those who focus on the Court's most visible decisions may underestimate the role of the law in the justices' choices.

JUSTICES' VALUES

Because legal considerations provide only a partial explanation of the justices' choices, the positions of individual justices and of the Court as a whole must have other bases as well. Of those other bases for choice, the one that has the greatest impact is the justices' own values. And as suggested already, justices' policy preferences are clearly the most powerful of those values, because justices typically hold strong views about most of the policy issues that are bound up in cases. The impact of policy preferences on decisions is widely recognized. That recognition is reflected in the close attention that participants in the selection of justices give to the policy views of potential and actual nominees to the Court. It is also reflected in commentaries on the Court, which regularly emphasize the justices' conceptions of good policy as a basis for their votes and opinions.

In part, the connection between justices' policy preferences and their votes and opinions is conscious. Justices sometimes act deliberately to advance the policies they favor on specific issues, and some justices seem to have broader policy agendas. But like other people, justices sometimes act on motivations that are not entirely conscious. They may believe that they are trying only to interpret the law accurately even as they move toward the interpretations that are most consistent with their policy preferences. One of Justice Felix Frankfurter's law clerks described that process well in talking about Frankfurter:

> He felt very intensely about lots of things, and sometimes he didn't realize that his feelings and his deeply felt values were pushing him as a judge relentlessly in one direction rather than another. I'm sure that you can put these things aside consciously, but what's underneath the consciousness you can't control.[61]

The impact of justices' policy preferences is most visible when justices disagree with each other about the outcome for the litigants, the legal rules to adopt, or both. The patterns of disagreement among justices strongly suggest that their differing conceptions of good policy are the primary basis for this disagreement. But explanation of differences among the justices in responding to the same cases is not the same thing as explanation of everything that justices do. Other considerations, including the state of the law, may move all the justices in the same direction in particular cases. If so, the impact of these considerations is substantial but not nearly as visible as the impact of policy preferences.

The Influence of Policy Preferences

It is difficult to measure the effect of justices' policy preferences on their behavior as decision makers, simply because their preferences cannot be observed directly. But some evidence strongly suggests that these preferences exert a powerful influence on justices' choices. When future justices take positions on policy issues, those positions are usually reflected in their votes and opinions as justices. Similarly, justices who speak about their personal views of issues when they are away from the Court generally take positions that are consistent with those views in the cases they decide. Both kinds of evidence are abundant for Ruth Bader Ginsburg, to take one example. She was a leading advocate for women's legal rights before she became a judge, and her opinions in sex discrimination cases were consistent with that advocacy. As a justice she increasingly expressed liberal views on issues in interviews and speeches, and her votes and opinions generally were consistent with those expressions.

Justices' attitudes on policy issues result from the same array of influences that shape political attitudes generally, including family socialization, religious training, and career experience. Justice John Paul Stevens acknowledged the impact of his military experience in World War II on his dissents in the cases in which the Court struck down prohibitions of flag desecration. He also said that his father's criminal conviction for embezzlement, later overturned by the Illinois Supreme Court, gave him "firsthand knowledge of the criminal justice system's fallibility" that affected his judgments about the death penalty.[62] Justice Stevens was more aware of those influences than some other justices, but all of them have perspectives that were shaped by their experiences.

As suggested earlier, justices' policy preferences could affect their decision making in two different ways. Justices might simply take positions in cases that accord with their views of good policy. Alternatively, they might act strategically, departing from the positions they most prefer when doing so could advance the policies they favor. It is not clear to what extent justices behave strategically and what forms their strategies take.[63] But it appears that strategic considerations generally do not move justices very far from the positions they most prefer. For this reason, the impact of justices' policy preferences can be considered initially without taking strategy into account. In the two sections that follow, I will consider strategy aimed at other justices and at the Court's political environment.

The Ideological Dimension

To a considerable degree, the policy preferences of people in politics and government are structured by ideology, in that most of these people take either a preponderance of positions that are defined as conservative or a preponderance of liberal positions. Thus, the relationship between policy preferences and the positions that government officials adopt in their decisions can be understood largely in ideological terms.

In applying that perspective to the Supreme Court, some cautions are necessary. First, some cases that come before the Court, such as disputes over state boundaries, have little or no relationship with ideology. Some other cases are ideologically ambiguous, in that it is unclear which side should be considered conservative. Second, justices do not always line up from liberal to conservative in the same ways on different issues.[64] But with these cautions, ideology provides a good way to summarize the policy preferences that are reflected in the justices' choices as decision makers.

Defining Liberal and Conservative Positions

On most of the issues that the Court addresses, the conservative and liberal labels have fairly clear meanings. In civil liberties, with some exceptions such as gun rights, the position more favorable to legal protection for liberties is considered liberal. Thus, the liberal position gives relatively heavy weight to people's right to equal treatment by government and private institutions, to procedural rights of criminal defendants and others who interact with government, and to substantive rights such as privacy. In contrast, the conservative position gives relatively great weight to values that compete with these rights, such as national security and effective law enforcement.

Liberal and conservative positions on economic issues are less clearly defined. But the liberal position is basically more favorable to economic "underdogs" and to government policies that are intended to benefit underdogs. In contrast, the conservative position is more favorable to businesses in conflicts with labor unions and consumers and less favorable to government regulation of business practices.

People often think of conservative and liberal positions as a product of people's reasoning from general values to specific issues, but this is not entirely true. To a degree, the labeling of policy positions as conservative or liberal results from a consensus that develops among people who are interested in politics and policy rather than simply logic. Further, ideological definitions of positions reflect the attitudes of conservatives and liberals toward various social and political groups rather than values alone. One result is that definitions can change over time. For instance, in American society as a whole and in the Supreme Court, support for broad protection of freedom of expression was long considered to be a liberal position, but ideological lines on this issue have become much less clear in the past few decades.[65]

Ideology and the Justices' Positions

At the broadest level, the justices' votes for one side or the other in cases may be summarized in terms of the frequency with which they support liberal or conservative positions. Figure 4-2 shows the ideological patterns of votes on case outcomes for the justices in the 2018 and 2019 terms, in cases in which the two sides clearly represented conservative and liberal positions. The figure shows that there was a substantial gap between the two ideological groupings of justices, about 34 percentage points between Justice Kagan and Justice Gorsuch. The difference between the justice with the most liberal record (Sotomayor) and the justice with the most conservative record (Thomas) was very large. But if we included cases in which the two sides were not so clearly defined ideologically, the differences between the conservative and liberal justices would not be as dramatic.

The relative positions of the justices on a conservative-to-liberal scale tend to remain fairly stable over time. It would be difficult to explain those stable differences except as a result of differences in the justices' policy preferences. In turn, those differences in preferences primarily reflect ideological positions. Thus, to take

Figure 4-2 Percentages of Liberal Votes Cast by Justices, 2018 and 2019 Terms

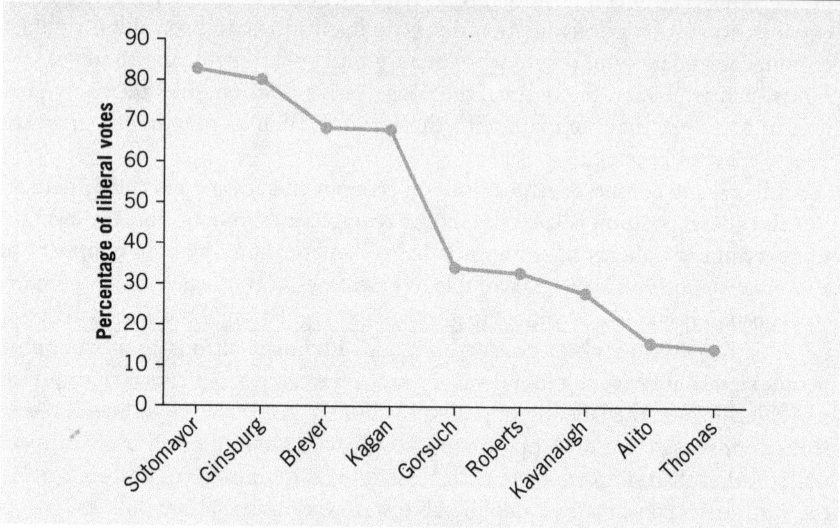

Source: Analysis of data in *The Supreme Court Database*, http://scdb.wustl.edu.

Note: Cases are included if they were decided after oral argument and if votes could be classified as liberal or conservative with little or no ambiguity. To make the percentages for different justices comparable in this figure and in Table 4-2, cases heard at the beginning of the 2018 term before Justice Kavanaugh joined the Court are excluded.

one example, it seems clear that Justice Alito is distinctly more conservative than Justice Sotomayor.

Justices' relative ideological positions are reflected in the frequency with which they vote for the same side in a case, shown for the Court's 2018 and 2019 terms in Table 4-2. Perhaps most striking is the high overall rate of agreement among justices: every pair of justices voted together more than 45 percent of the time. Still, there was considerable variation in agreement rates, variation that followed ideological lines. The mean rate of voting agreement among the four most liberal justices was 88 percent; for the four most conservative justices, the mean rate was 81 percent. In contrast, the mean rate of agreement between the four most liberal justices and the five most conservative justices was 62 percent. Rates of agreement on opinions may reflect self-conscious alliances or personal relationships to a small degree, but they are primarily the result of similar or differing policy preferences.

Divisions among the justices in individual cases have some tendency to fall along ideological lines. When the justices divide 5–4, the majority could include any of more than 100 combinations of five justices. But in the 2018 and 2019 terms, nearly half the 5–4 decisions found the five conservatives in the majority. On the other hand, this means that in more than half of the 5–4 decisions, the majority included both conservative and liberal justices.[66]

Table 4-2 Percentages of Cases in Which Pairs of Justices Voted for the Same Side, 2018 and 2019 Terms

	Gi	Br	Kag	Ro	Kav	Go	Al	Th
Sotomayor	91	85	88	68	65	64	52	48
Ginsburg (Gi)		87	87	67	65	63	55	50
Breyer (Br)			88	73	71	60	60	52
Kagan (Kag)				74	71	66	60	56
Roberts (Ro)					93	75	83	73
Kavanaugh (Kav)						79	85	79
Gorsuch (Go)							76	80
Alito (Al)								88
Thomas (Th)								

Sources: Adam Feldman, "Final Stat Pack for October Term 2018," SCOTUSblog, June 28, 2019, https://www.scotusblog.com/2019/06/final-stat-pack-for-october-term-2018/; Adam Feldman, "Final Stat Pack for October Term 2019," SCOTUSblog, July 10, 2020, https://www.scotusblog.com/2020/07/final-stat-pack-for-october-term-2019/.

Sometimes, divisions on the Court diverge quite substantially from ideological lines. In *Virginia House of Delegates v. Bethune-Hill* (2019), decided by a 5–4 vote, the majority included the two justices with the most liberal voting records that term as well as the two with the most conservative voting records. The existence of such divisions, like the frequency of unanimous decisions, makes it clear that justices do not respond to cases simply on the basis of their ideological tendencies.[67]

One reason for disagreements that do not follow ideological lines was noted earlier: some justices take more liberal or more conservative positions in certain areas of policy than they do in most others. Justice Thomas, for instance, takes highly conservative positions on most issues but is relatively favorable to some types of legal claims by criminal defendants. Another reason is that some cases do not relate directly to justices' policy preferences, so the justices disagree with each other on the basis of their approaches to legal interpretation or as a result of idiosyncratic responses to the issues in those cases. Some nonideological divisions may reflect disagreement among the justices about how to go about dividing authority between decision makers such as trial judges and juries.[68]

Observers of the Court regularly label justices not just relative to each other but in absolute terms as well. Justice Alito is called a conservative, Justice Sotomayor a liberal. This conclusion does not follow directly from the justices' votes and opinions. For one thing, their positions in cases are not solely the product of their policy preferences. In addition, the proportions of liberal and conservative votes that a justice casts in a particular period reflect the mix of cases that the Court decides in that period. A justice with a strongly liberal voting record might not have had as liberal a record in a different era.

Still, justices' policy preferences play a big enough role in their votes and opinions that the ideological labels assigned to them by observers of the Court are generally appropriate. A justice who casts a preponderance of votes that can be characterized as conservative almost surely holds conservative views on most issues. Indeed, most justices who were perceived as strongly liberal or strongly conservative at the time of their appointment establish records on the Court that are consistent with those perceptions.[69]

Justices' Preferences and Policy Change

If the positions of individual justices reflect their policy preferences, the collective decisions of the Court must also reflect the mix of preferences among the justices. When most justices are conservative, for instance, the Court will tend to make conservative decisions and move legal doctrine in a conservative direction.

The proportions of liberal and conservative decisions fluctuate from term to term, and that is even more true of the Court's most visible decisions. Commentators often treat this fluctuation as a sign that the Court has changed, but it usually reflects the particular mix of cases that the Court decides each term rather than a shift in the Court's ideological position. Sometimes, however, the Court's position on a particular issue or its overall ideological position does change, in the sense that the Court decides cases differently from the way it would have decided those cases at an earlier time. Such changes are especially clear when the Court directly overrules its precedents.

If the Court's collective positions reflect the policy preferences of its justices more than anything else, the primary source of changes in Court policies must be a shift in the preferences of the justices as a group. These shifts could come from change in the preferences of one or more justices or from change in the Court's membership. Both sources are significant, but the second is more important.

Changes in Justices' Preferences

Not surprisingly, individual justices tend to take stable positions on the issues that arise in the areas of legal policy that the Court addresses. Thus the views that a justice expressed in past cases about when police officers can search cars or when mergers of companies violate the antitrust laws are a good guide to the justice's stance in a future case on those issues. And on more specific legal questions that the Court resolves with its decisions, one legal scholar has suggested, justices tend to adhere to "personal precedent."[70] In turn, the Court's collective position on an issue generally remains stable as long as its membership remains unchanged.

But this stability is not an absolute rule. Over time, justices are exposed to new influences and confront issues in new forms. The result may be a change in their positions on specific legal questions or broader issues. Justice Thomas announced a change in his views of one legal question in 2018 and another in 2020, each time quoting from a 1950 opinion that said "it is never too late" to adopt "a better considered position."[71]

It is difficult to ascertain whether individual justices have shifted in their overall ideological positions over time, but it is clear that most justices retain the same basic positions throughout their career. Still, some justices do seem to move at least marginally, and Justice Harry Blackmun's positions shifted quite substantially.

Blackmun was appointed to the Court in 1970 by Republican Richard Nixon, and early in his tenure he aligned himself chiefly with the other conservative justices. He and Chief Justice Warren Burger, boyhood friends from Minnesota, were dubbed the "Minnesota Twins." In the 1973 term, Blackmun joined the same opinion as Burger in 84 percent of the Court's decisions but joined with the liberal William Brennan in only 49 percent.[72] After that, Blackmun gradually moved in a leftward direction. By 1985, Burger's last term, Blackmun's agreement rate with Brennan was 30 percentage points higher than his agreement with Burger. In the last few terms before his 1994 retirement, Blackmun was one of the two most liberal justices on the Court. Although the reasons for this change are uncertain, it appears that his experiences in dealing with cases that came to the Court—especially *Roe v. Wade*, in which he wrote the Court's opinion—were important.[73]

Perhaps more common than individual shifts are changes in the collective positions of the justices in a particular issue area. These changes typically result from developments in American society that affect the views of the general public and of people in government. The liberal Warren Court gave unprecedented support to the goal of equality under the law, but it did not strike down legal rules that treated women and men differently. In contrast, the more conservative Burger Court handed down a series of decisions promoting legal equality for men and women. The most fundamental cause of this change was the direct and indirect effect of the feminist movement on justices' views about women's social roles. To take another example, in 1972 the Burger Court summarily dismissed a challenge to the Minnesota prohibition of same-sex marriage. But in 2015 the more conservative Roberts Court directly overturned the 1972 decision by striking down state prohibitions of same-sex marriage, albeit by a 5–4 vote.[74] That difference can be explained by the impact of the gay rights movement and related changes in society on justices' attitudes.

Membership Change

A year after Anthony Kennedy announced his retirement from the Court in 2018, his colleague Ruth Bader Ginsburg said that this was "the event of greatest consequence for the current term, and perhaps for many terms ahead."[75] Ginsburg's statement underlined the most powerful source of change in the Court's policies: replacement of one justice by another shifts its collective views on matters that the Court addresses.

A change in the Court's membership sometimes alters its positions on specific issues. That effect was underlined in 2006, when Sandra Day O'Connor retired in the middle of the Court's term. She had voted with the majority in three prospective 5–4 rulings that were not finalized before her retirement. The cases were reargued with her successor Samuel Alito on the Court, and in all three cases he provided the decisive vote in 5–4 decisions that went in the opposite direction from the Court's earlier votes.[76] In 2019 a federal district judge rejected the argument that a public employees' union should have anticipated the 2018 Supreme Court decision overturning a precedent that a more liberal Court had established in 1977. The judge pointed out that if the 2016 presidential election had come out differently, "the composition of the Supreme Court that decided the case may well have been different, leading to a different result."[77]

More broadly, shifts in the Court's overall ideological position through new appointments typically lead to change in the general content of its policies. I will consider that process of change in Chapter 5.

Partisan Preferences

Supreme Court justices care about politics as well as policy. Like other people who are interested in politics and government, most if not all justices identify with a political party and hope it is successful. In an era of strong political polarization, undoubtedly some justices also have negative feelings toward the other party and its leaders. Occasionally the justices' feelings surface, as they did when

Ruth Bader Ginsburg denounced Donald Trump during his 2016 campaign for president and when Brett Kavanaugh denounced Democrats at one of his Senate confirmation hearings in 2018. The justices' life terms limit their personal stakes in political outcomes, but their partial insulation from politics does not extinguish their rooting interests in those outcomes.

These rooting interests might affect the justices' positions in cases that affect the electoral prospects of the parties and the success of their elected officials. Indeed, some observers of the Court have pointed to what they see as partisan behavior by the justices. In the last decade the justices have split along party lines in cases that affected the parties' interests on federal preapproval of election law changes in the South, federal court power to review partisan gerrymandering of legislative districts, and the ability of public employee unions to charge nonunion members for representing them in collective bargaining.[78] In *Department of Commerce v. New York* (2019), all the justices except for Chief Justice Roberts voted along party lines when the Court blocked the addition to the census of a question about citizenship that was thought to facilitate the drawing of legislative districts to favor Republican candidates.

The census case also involved a challenge to a Trump administration policy. The justices have divided along party lines in other challenges to presidential policies. When the Court upheld a key provision of President Obama's health care plan in 2012, all the Democratic justices were in the majority and all the Republicans—except, again, Chief Justice Roberts—dissented.[79] The justices voted along party lines in *Trump v. Hawaii* (2018), when the Court upheld President Trump's order limiting entry to the United States of citizens of certain countries. And the same split has occurred in several cases in which the Court has granted the federal government stays of lower-court decisions. When Justice Sotomayor complained in one of those cases that "the Court's recent behavior on stay applications has benefited one litigant over all others," she spoke of the federal government. But she was referring indirectly to the Trump administration, as the president himself noted.[80]

These partisan divisions do not necessarily mean that the justices are acting on a partisan basis, even unconsciously. Because the Court's ideological lines have coincided with party lines since 2010, some party-line votes in cases with partisan elements reflect policy preferences more than partisan preferences. Moreover, justices do not always vote in favor of their parties' interests. In *Evenwel v. Abbott* (2016), for instance, the Court unanimously ruled that the Constitution allows legislative districts to be based on total population rather than eligible voters or registered voters, thereby rejecting a position that would have benefited Republican candidates. Chief Justice Roberts's decisive votes in the health care and census cases are another example. The most striking example is the pair of 2020 decisions on subpoenas for President Trump's financial records, in which the Court's four liberals and three of its conservatives (including Roberts, who wrote the majority opinions) united in supporting rulings that favored the president in some respects but not in others.[81]

Bettmann/Getty Images

▶ **Photo 4-3** Governor George W. Bush (right) and Senator Al Gore at one of the 2000 presidential debates. In *Bush v. Gore*, the decision that resolved the election in favor of Bush, the justices divided 5-4 along ideological lines.

Even so, justices' attitudes toward the political parties undoubtedly have some impact on their thinking when the fortunes of the parties and their leaders are at stake. The classic example is *Bush v. Gore* (2000), in which the Court's 5–4 decision ensured the election of George W. Bush as president. The case had no discernible ideological element. But when the Court's five conservative Republicans were on the majority side and the four Democrats and liberal Republicans dissented, it seemed likely that all nine justices had cast votes in favor of the candidate whose election they favored.

The justices' partisan preferences have a far more limited impact than their policy preferences, largely because partisan considerations are relevant to only a small portion of the Court's cases. But partisan attitudes may have a decisive impact in some important cases. And in an era in which partisan battles increasingly make their way to the Court, such cases have become more common.

Role Values

Policy and party preferences are not the only values that can affect the Court's decisions. Justices may also act on their role values—their views about what constitutes appropriate behavior for the Supreme Court and its members. In any government body, whether it is a court or a legislature, members' conceptions of how they should carry out their jobs structure what they do.

A variety of role values might shape justices' behavior, including their views about the importance of consensus and about the legitimacy of "lobbying" colleagues on decisions. But the role values with the greatest potential impact are justices' beliefs about the considerations they should take into account in reaching their decisions and about the desirability of intervening in the making of public policy.

It is clear that multiple considerations affect justices' votes and opinions. The relative weight of these considerations depends in part on what justices think about how appropriate they are. In particular, justices have to balance their strong policy preferences on many issues against the expectation of others (and themselves) that they will seek to interpret the law accurately.

Some evidence suggests that justices differ in the relative weights they give to these legal and policy considerations.[82] However, these differences are not as sharp as they sometimes appear. For example, at any given time, some justices vote more often than others to uproot some of the Court's precedents. To a degree, this difference reflects differing judgments about the weight that should be given to precedents, such as Justice Thomas's belief the Court should readily overrule precedents that embody faulty interpretations of the law. But more important are justices' attitudes toward the policies embodied in particular precedents, attitudes that tend to fall along ideological lines. In *Obergefell v. Hodges* (2015), the five most liberal justices voted to overrule a 1972 precedent in the process of holding that states could not prohibit same-sex marriage. In *Franchise Tax Board v. Hyatt* (2019), in contrast, it was the five most conservative justices who voted to overrule a 1979 precedent by holding that states could not be sued by private parties in the courts of other states without their consent.

The Court's intervention in policy making, beyond what is unavoidable, is often viewed negatively. Justices who seem eager to engage in that intervention are criticized as "activists," and those who seem less prone to do so are praised as "restrained." But activism, like the treatment of precedent, does not seem to differ much among justices.

The most visible form of active intervention in policy making is striking down federal statutes. The historical patterns are illuminating. During the 1920s and early 1930s the laws that the Court struck down were primarily government regulations of business practices. Conservative justices were the most willing to strike down such laws, and liberals on the Court and elsewhere argued for judicial restraint. In contrast, in the 1960s and 1970s the Court struck down primarily laws that conflicted with civil liberties. Liberals were most likely to find these laws invalid and conservatives to call for judicial restraint.

Since the 1980s the Court has overturned a wide variety of federal laws. No justice has stood out for a willingness or unwillingness to strike down laws. In part, this is because the statutes that the Court has invalidated were ideologically mixed, and on the whole justices have voted to uphold laws that are consistent with their own conceptions of good policy and to strike down laws that conflict with those views. The same is true of decisions in which the Court strikes down state laws on constitutional grounds.[83] In this respect, the justices' judgments about whether to declare laws unconstitutional are similar to their judgments about whether to overrule precedents.

All this is not to say that justices' role values have no impact on their behavior. Undoubtedly, such values help to structure the ways in which justices decide cases. But justices' conceptions of good public policy have a more fundamental impact on their choices.

GROUP INTERACTION

In discussing legal and policy considerations in decision making, I have focused on justices as individuals. But when justices make choices, they do so as part of a court that makes collective decisions and as part of American government and society. Justices who seek to make good policy might act strategically by taking their colleagues and other institutions into account when they cast votes and write or join opinions. Whether or not justices act strategically, they can be influenced in a variety of ways by other justices and by their political and social environment. This section examines the justices as a decision-making group, and the next section considers the Court's environment.

The Collective Element in Decision Making

Descriptions of the Supreme Court as a group offer two competing depictions. In one depiction, the justices work together closely to reach decisions, and their positions in cases frequently shift as arguments made by some justices change colleagues' minds and as they negotiate over the language of opinions. In the other depiction, justices make up their own minds about cases, and their judgments are affected little by those colleagues' views. The reality lies somewhere between these two depictions. There are significant limitations on the influence of justices over each other, but there are also strong bases for influence.

The most fundamental limitation on influence among the justices is their strongly held views on many issues of law and policy. When they apply their general positions on an issue to a specific case, the resulting judgment about that case is often too firm for colleagues to sway. As Justice William Rehnquist wrote, when justices "assemble around the conference table on Friday morning to decide an important case presenting constitutional questions that they have all debated and written about before, the outcome may be a foregone conclusion."[84]

The justices' work styles also limit influence. Justices do most of their work in their own chambers, interacting with their law clerks far more than with their colleagues. And most justices are reluctant to lobby their colleagues directly. After completing his thirty-five-year tenure on the Court, John Paul Stevens recalled only one case "in which I visited another justice for the purpose of trying to persuade him or her to join one of my opinions."[85]

Balanced against these limitations are two powerful incentives for justices to try to influence their colleagues and to accept influence from them. One incentive is institutional: justices want to achieve opinions that at least five members endorse so that the Court can lay down authoritative legal rules. And to give more weight to the Court's decisions, they generally would like to reach even greater consensus. Justices may operate on this incentive simply because they think that legal clarity is good in itself, but the desire to maximize the impact of the Court's legal policies also plays a part.

A second incentive is more personal: justices' interest in winning majority support for their positions. Justices want the Court to adopt the legal rules they prefer, and most justices get satisfaction from being on the winning side. As Justice Breyer put it, "Would I prefer to be in the majority? Yeah. Would I prefer that people agree with me all the time? Of course. So would you. So would anyone."[86] Thus, justices have good reason to engage in efforts at persuasion. They also have reason to be flexible in the positions they take in cases because flexibility can help them win colleagues' support for legal rules that are close to the ones they prefer.

One way to gauge the extent of influence among the justices is by comparing the tentative votes they cast on case outcomes with their final votes in the same cases. Information in justices' papers allows that comparison for the Burger Court (1969–1986). During that time, 7.5 percent of the justices' individual votes to reverse or affirm switched from one side to the other, and at least one switch occurred in 37 percent of the cases.

Most vote switches increase the size of the majority, as the Court works toward consensus. During the Burger Court, the justices who initially voted with the majority switched their votes 5 percent of the time, but those who initially voted with the minority switched 18 percent of the time.[87] Occasionally, however, shifts of position turn an initial minority into a majority. This occurred in about 7 percent of the cases decided by the Burger Court.[88] It might be, however, that such flexibility has declined as ideological lines on the Court have hardened. Justice Ginsburg said that the majority will shift after the conference vote "maybe twice a term."[89] According to one report, one of those shifts occurred in *Department of Commerce v. New York* (2019), the case in which the Court determined whether the Trump administration had followed proper procedures in its effort to add a question on citizenship to the 2020 Census: Chief Justice Roberts was originally part of a 5–4 majority upholding the administration, but he switched sides and wrote the opinion for a new 5–4 majority ruling against the administration.[90]

Whether or not votes on the outcome of a case change, justices' shifts in position can have a powerful impact on the law. The Court largely reaffirmed *Roe v. Wade* rather than overruling it in *Planned Parenthood v. Casey* (1992) because discussions with two colleagues led Anthony Kennedy to abandon his original judgment that *Roe* should be overturned.[91]

Of course, not all vote switches result from influence by other justices. For that matter, a justice's initial vote may be shaped by what colleagues say at oral argument or in conference. Thus, it is impossible to ascertain the impact of justices on each other's votes from vote switches alone. But the frequency of those switches does suggest that justices influence colleagues' votes at least occasionally.

It is common for the content of the Court's opinion to change as a result of reactions to draft majority opinions.[92] A study of Harry Blackmun's draft opinions showed that he almost always made changes requested by other justices who had voted on the majority side in conference. Because of this responsiveness, the colleagues who requested changes in the original draft usually joined Blackmun's final opinion; they wrote concurring opinions in only about 20 percent of those cases. Not surprisingly, Blackmun became much less willing to accommodate colleagues when he had already secured majority support for his opinion.[93]

It is not just the opinion writer who compromises during this process; so do some justices who sign on to majority opinions. As Samuel Alito said, "I don't think any of us would actually sign on to something that we don't believe in. But we are often required to sign on to something that is not exactly what we would prefer."[94] Sometimes justices satisfy their concerns by signing on to most but not all of the majority opinion. In *Babb v. Wilkie* (2020), Justice Ginsburg joined the majority opinion except for one lengthy footnote.

Whether or not colleagues request changes in opinions for the Court, those opinions frequently are revised during the decision process. In the Burger Court, the author of the Court's opinion circulated at least three drafts of the opinion in slightly more than half of all cases.[95] Although successive drafts usually differ only in minor ways, they occasionally proclaim quite different legal rules. Moreover, the first draft of a majority opinion often reflects the writer's efforts to take into account the views that colleagues expressed in conference, so those colleagues influence the opinion even if they fully accept that first draft.

The extent to which justices seek and accept influence varies among cases. Justice Kagan has contrasted cases in which justices "just see the law differently" with those "where you can persuade each other."[96] On the whole, justices are more open to influence when they lack strong feelings about the issues in a case. On the other hand, they may make greater efforts at persuasion in cases they care most about, and more negotiation and compromise may be necessary in those cases to achieve a majority opinion.

The interplay among justices that occurs during the decision process has a large element of strategy, in that justices are trying to secure a decision that reflects their judgment about which side should win and an opinion for the Court that is as close as possible to their view about what the opinion should say. Strategy is not always carried out by individual justices: it is common for like-minded justices to work together to win the results they seek. Justice Ginsburg reported that after *Bush v. Gore* (2000), in which each of the four liberal dissenters wrote a separate opinion, those justices resolved to try to agree on a single opinion in future cases in which they voted together, whether they were in the majority or in dissent. To a considerable degree, the Court's liberals have been successful in that effort.[97]

Strategy within the Court can be oriented toward the future. For instance, the justice who writes the Court's opinion may include language in the opinion that can be used as a basis for reaching a desired decision in the future. Chief Justice Roberts appears to have taken that approach in opinions on enforcement of voting rights and government financial assistance to religious institutions, in each instance building on one opinion for the Court in a later one that he also wrote.[98] And when Roberts provided the fifth vote to strike down a Louisiana regulation of abortion clinics in *June Medical Services v. Russo* (2020), some language in his opinion provided him—and thus the Court—with a basis for allowing more state restrictions on abortion in the future.

Patterns of Influence

To the extent that justices actually influence their colleagues' choices, inevitably some are more influential than others. Justices' influence depends in part on how much they seek to exert influence rather than simply making their own individual judgments. To the extent that they do seek to influence their colleagues, justices' success in those efforts depends on their intellectual and interpersonal skills. Justices can also exert influence without directly seeking it because what they write in opinions and say in memos and conferences is persuasive.

It is very difficult to gauge justices' influence over each other from outside the Court, though scholars have used indicators such as joining of opinions and citation of colleagues' opinions in later cases as measures of influence.[99] But as information about the Court in past eras accumulates, a picture of some justices emerges. William O. Douglas, who served from 1939 to 1975, had relatively little influence with other justices because he made only limited efforts to achieve it. Douglas's longtime colleague Felix Frankfurter actively sought influence over his colleagues, and his eminence as a legal scholar should have enabled him to shape other justices' thinking about cases. But Frankfurter's personal traits, especially his inability to hide his lack of respect for colleagues, worked against him. William Brennan, who served from 1956 to 1990, was far more skilled in working with colleagues. This skill helped Brennan in his efforts to forge a liberal majority for the expansion of civil liberties in the Warren Court and perhaps helped him to limit the Court's conservative shift in the Burger Court.

It is more difficult to assess the influence of justices who have served more recently. One example is Antonin Scalia, who served from 1986 to 2016. Some observers of the Court think that Scalia's frequent strong criticism of colleagues in his opinions alienated some of them and thus weakened his capacity for persuasion. But Elena Kagan has noted that Scalia seemed to have considerable impact on the ways that justices and lower-court judges interpret statutes.[100] Kagan herself is viewed as influential by some observers because of her willingness to compromise with the Court's conservatives in order to reach decisions that are relatively satisfactory from her perspective.[101] But the accuracy of that judgment is uncertain.

One source of influence is a justice's position on the Court's ideological spectrum. The vote of a "swing" justice at the ideological center of the Court often will determine which side wins in cases that closely divide the Court along ideological lines. In itself, this does not mean that the swing justice is influential, because every justice in a 5–4 majority contributes to that result with one vote. Swing justices have some extra influence, however, because their positions are seen as relatively unpredictable and their support is seen as crucial to the outcome of some cases. Lawyers try to devise arguments that appeal to the swing justice, and colleagues work to win the support of that justice.

Anthony Kennedy was the swing justice in his last dozen years on the Court (2006–2018), because four justices were well to his ideological left and the other four were to his right. On a series of major decisions on issues such as abortion and the death penalty, he created liberal or conservative majorities with his vote. As a result, lawyers and colleagues showed considerable deference to him, and he likely exercised disproportionate influence.

But neither Kennedy nor any other justice could come close to dominating the Court. To the extent that the justices do affect each other's positions in cases, every justice has considerable influence as one of only nine members of the Court.

The Chief Justice

Compared with other justices, the chief justice has both advantages and disadvantages in achieving influence over colleagues. The disadvantage is administrative duties, which reduce the time that the chief can spend on cases. William Rehnquist, who served as an associate justice before his 1986 promotion to chief, said at the time that in accepting the promotion he was giving up some potential for influence over decisions.[102]

The primary advantage is a set of formal powers. The chief presides over the Court in oral argument and in conference. In conference, the chief speaks first on cases; by doing so the chief can direct discussion and frame alternatives. Aided by clerks, the chief makes up the initial version of the discuss list from the petitions for certiorari. This task gives the chief the largest role in determining which cases are set aside without group discussion. Another power, over opinion assignment, merits more extensive consideration.

Opinion Assignment

The chief justice is usually in the majority in conference votes on decisions and thus assigns the Court's opinion in the preponderance of cases. In making assignments, chiefs balance different considerations.[103]

Administrative considerations relate to spreading the workload and opportunities among the justices. Chief justices generally try to make sure that each colleague gets about the same number of majority opinions over a Court term. Chiefs may also take into account the workload of opinion writing that a justice already faces at a given time.

Other considerations relate to the substance of the Court's decisions. Because opinion writers have to take their colleagues' views into account, scholars disagree about how much difference it makes which justice is assigned the Court's opinion.[104] But justices perceive that the opinion writer has disproportionate influence over the content of the majority opinion. As a result, chief justices tend to favor themselves and colleagues who are close to them ideologically when assigning opinions in the cases they care about most. According to one study, in his first ten terms Chief Justice Roberts assigned opinions to himself in important cases more often than to any other justice. The Court's liberals generally received such assignments at a low rate, even taking into account the smaller numbers of cases in which they joined Roberts in the majority.[105]

The chief can also try to help the conference majority remain a majority. When there is a close vote at conference, the chief often assigns the opinion to a relatively moderate member of that majority. One reason is that a moderate may be in a good position to write an opinion that will maintain the majority and perhaps win over justices who were initially on the other side. Another reason is that if the swing justice gets the assignment, that justice will be more likely to remain on the majority side. That second reason probably helps to account for the frequency with which Justice Kennedy received assignments from Roberts in important cases.

Because chief justices favor ideological allies in assigning important opinions, in effect they reward the justices who vote with them the most often. They might also use the assignment power more directly to reward and punish colleagues. Roberts said in 2006 that "you can always give all the tax opinions to a justice, if you want to punish them."[106] He added that he had not yet taken that kind of action. But according to Justice Blackmun, Chief Justice Burger might assign one of the "crud" opinions "that nobody wants to write" to a justice who was "in the doghouse" with Burger.[107]

The associate justice who assigns the Court's opinion when the chief is in the minority is under fewer constraints than the chief, and the justice who assigns the primary dissenting opinion is even freer. This freedom is sometimes reflected in self-assignment of opinions. Justice Kennedy assigned himself opinions in several important cases when he was the most senior justice in the majority. As the most senior of the Court's liberals from 2010 to 2020, Justice Ginsburg assigned many dissenting opinions. She acknowledged that she probably took "more than a fair share of the dissenting opinions in the most-watched cases."[108]

Variation in Influence

Chief justices have differed considerably in their influence over the Court. These differences reflect the chief's interest in leading the Court, the chief's skill as a leader, and the willingness of the associate justices to be led.

Warren Burger sought to be a strong leader. He had some success in securing administrative changes in the federal courts and procedural changes in the Court itself. But he was not especially influential in the decision-making process.

Burger's limited impact on the Court's decisions stemmed largely from his own qualities and predilections. Colleagues chafed at what they considered a poor style of leadership in conference, and they disliked Burger's occasional practice of casting "false" votes so that he could assign the Court's opinion.[109] He was also accused of bullying his colleagues. One scholar concluded that Potter Stewart "loathed" Burger,[110] and other colleagues also disliked his leadership style.

William Rehnquist became chief justice in 1986 after serving on the Court for fifteen years. He brought important strengths to the position, especially his well-respected intellectual abilities and a pleasant manner of interaction with people. Having served in the Burger Court as an associate justice, Rehnquist learned—in one observer's words—"how *not* to be Chief Justice."[111] In any event, Rehnquist was an effective chief justice, and his leadership was widely praised even by justices who did not share his conservative views on most judicial issues.[112] Reflecting his preferences, the Court's discussions of cases at conference were shorter and tighter than they had been in the recent past. Rehnquist's leadership was one source of the sharp decline in the number of cases accepted by the Court. In decision making, he enhanced his influence by taking strong positions with an affable style.

Both colleagues and observers of the Court have attested to John Roberts's strengths as leader of the Court. John Paul Stevens, who served on the Court during Roberts' first five terms, said that "with regard to all of his special responsibilities" as chief justice, "John Roberts is an excellent chief justice."[113] But according to one reporter who talked with some justices more recently, there is some dissatisfaction with his leadership of the Court.[114] Certainly it is too early to reach anything like a definitive judgment about Roberts as chief justice.

Roberts himself has emphasized the limits on the power that he or any other chief justice holds. "I have the same vote as everybody else. I can't fire them if they disagree with me. I can't even dock their pay."[115] But the powers that the chief justice does possess, if used effectively, can give the chief disproportionate influence over the Court's decisions.

Harmony and Conflict

Some personal conflict among the justices is inevitable. Justices with differing points of view vie to achieve decisions that reflect their own views, and those who find themselves in the minority in cases that are important to them are likely to feel some bitterness toward colleagues on the winning side. In itself, the pressure to finalize decisions late in the Court's term can create tensions among the justices. By the end of the term, Justice Alito reported, "We tend to be kind of angry with each other."[116] The biting language in some dissenting opinions sometimes reflects those tensions, and it can exacerbate them as well. And when justices interact with each other in Court sessions and conferences, what they say can annoy their colleagues. Ruth Bader Ginsburg, a close friend of Antonin Scalia's, once told a reporter that "I love him, but sometimes I'd like to strangle him."[117]

Yet the justices have strong incentives to maintain good relations with their colleagues. Good relations can facilitate effective decision making, and they also make life more pleasant. "When you're charged with working together for most of the remainder of your life," said Sonia Sotomayor, "you have to create a relationship."[118]

Just as it is difficult to ascertain patterns of influence among the justices from outside the Court, it is also difficult to determine the balance between harmony and conflict in the Court. The justices themselves usually emphasize how well they get along with each other. In recent years they seem especially eager to demonstrate that the deep political conflicts elsewhere in government—including battles over confirmation of justices—are absent from the Court. Yet there are also signs of interpersonal conflict among the justices. One thing does seem clear: the current Court is more harmonious than several past Courts, in which some pairs of justices were actually unable to work with each other. Undoubtedly, the absence of such deep conflicts improves the functioning of the Court.

THE COURT'S ENVIRONMENT

The Supreme Court depends on litigants to bring cases from which the justices can choose. In the cases that the Court considers and the subset that it hears, lawyers for litigants and amici advocate for their positions in briefs and oral argument. Outside the formal litigation process, law reviews, legal blogs, and other outlets provide additional arguments for the justices to consider. On a different level, developments in American society and in the political world can shape the justices' thinking. Through all these vehicles, what justices do can be influenced by the world outside the Court.

Beyond this inevitable influence, the extent to which the Court's social and political environment shapes justices' choices is uncertain. Some attributes of the Court give it greater isolation and insulation from the outside world than Congress and the president have. The isolation is reflected in the relatively limited contact between the justices and other participants in politics, such as members of Congress and representatives of interest groups. The primary source of insulation is the justices' life terms, which free them from pressures that elected officials feel.

But all this does not rule out influence from the Court's environment. Justices might take the political world into account for strategic reasons, acting to avoid negative responses to their decisions that would endanger the policies they favor or even damage the Court itself. Strategic considerations aside, justices might simply like to be viewed positively by people outside the Court. For both reasons, the Court's environment could affect the justices' choices as decision makers.

Congress and the President

The other branches of the federal government cannot easily remove the justices from office, and they cannot reduce the justices' salaries. But they can and do take other actions that affect the Court itself and the impact of its policies. Because of this effect, justices may take those policy makers into account when they reach decisions.

Congress

Congressional powers over the Court range from overriding the Court's interpretations of statutes to deciding on salary increases for the justices. Because of this array of powers, justices have reason to consider congressional reactions to their decisions. Relations with Congress can affect the justices' prestige and their comfort. And justices who care about the impact of the Court's policies want to avoid congressional actions that undercut those policies.

If justices do act strategically toward Congress for these reasons, one potential form of strategy involves decisions that interpret federal statutes. These decisions are more vulnerable than the Court's interpretations of the Constitution because Congress and the president can override them simply by enacting a new statute. Indeed, Congress considers such overrides quite frequently, and it enacts them into law fairly often.

For this reason, justices might try to calculate whether their preferred interpretation of a statute would be sufficiently unpopular in Congress to produce an override. If so, justices could modify their interpretation to make it more acceptable to members of Congress and thereby avoid an override. It may be, however, that most justices are not bothered much when Congress overrides their statutory decisions. And justices might find it so difficult to predict overrides that little could be gained by trying to make those predictions.

It is not clear how often justices pursue this strategic approach. One possibility is that they do so selectively, when they perceive that a decision on an issue that is important to them is a very good candidate for an override. One corollary is that when party control of Congress and the presidency is divided, as it was most of the time between 2011 and 2020, justices might feel great freedom to interpret statutes as they wish on issues on which the parties disagree with each other.

When Court decisions interpret the Constitution rather than statutes, those decisions are considerably more difficult to overturn directly. But constitutional decisions also have the potential to arouse strong negative reactions from Congress when the Court overturns major government policies. Justices may have reason to avoid arousing such reactions and to reduce conflict with Congress when it arises.

Justices seem to have taken this approach in a few historical periods. In the early nineteenth century, Chief Justice John Marshall's Court faced congressional attacks because of its policies. As the Court's dominant member, Marshall was careful to limit the frequency of decisions that would further anger the Court's opponents. In the late 1930s the Court's shift from opposition to support of major New Deal legislation may have reflected an effort by one or two justices to end a serious confrontation with the other branches. In the late 1950s members of Congress reacted to the Court's expansions of civil liberties by trying to override some of its policies and limit its jurisdiction. A few justices then shifted their stances on some contentious issues. As a result, the Court reversed some of its collective policy positions and thereby helped to quiet congressional attacks on the Court.

Strong criticism of the Court from congressional conservatives has continued since the 1950s. This criticism was triggered by the civil libertarian policies of the Warren Court in the 1960s and by major liberal decisions from the Court in later decades, on issues ranging from abortion to flag burning. On a range of issues, conservative members have introduced bills to overturn the Court's decisions, to limit its jurisdiction over the issue, or both. There have also been proposals to attack the Court more broadly, such as constitutional amendments that would limit the justices' tenure to a set number of years. More recently, liberal members have criticized the Roberts Court for its overall conservatism and some specific decisions. Liberals also have made proposals to overturn decisions and to change the Court itself, primarily by increasing the number of justices when a Democrat is next elected president.

There have been no clear signs of retreat by the Court in the face of these actions over the last several decades, and the Court has maintained many of the policies that aroused congressional criticism. Indeed, visible retreats have been rare over the Court's whole history. Yet it may be that threats of negative congressional action and even the ideological composition of Congress have a subtle effect on the justices' inclination to strike down statutes that is difficult to ascertain.[119] Such an effect might help to explain the relatively small numbers of federal statutes that the Court has declared unconstitutional, and justices may be more willing to strike down statutes when Congress becomes less favorable to those statutes over time.[120]

The President

The president has far more impact on the Supreme Court's decisions than anyone else outside the Court. The power to appoint justices gives presidents considerable ability to determine the Court's general direction. The justices' willingness to accept a high proportion of the cases that the solicitor general asks the Court to hear is another source of influence for the president, who appoints the solicitor general and sometimes intervenes to shape the federal government's positions in litigation. And there is considerable evidence that the solicitor general's support for one side as amicus curiae enhances the probability of victory for that side.

Presidents might also influence justices' choices more directly. Certainly presidents would like to have such influence. Presidents occasionally speak about Supreme Court cases before they are decided.[121] When they announce their interest in the outcome of a pending case—as Barack Obama and Donald Trump have done—they probably hope to affect the thinking of at least some justices. In one instance, President Dwight Eisenhower went considerably further. While the Court was considering *Brown v. Board of Education* (1954), Eisenhower invited his appointee Chief Justice Earl Warren to a White House dinner. Warren arrived to discover that another guest was John W. Davis, an esteemed lawyer who had argued in *Brown* on behalf of one of the states seeking to maintain racial segregation in its schools. After dinner Eisenhower told Warren of his own sympathy for white southerners who opposed desegregation.[122]

Justices might be inclined to favor the positions and interests of the president who appointed them, but such an inclination is likely to be weak. Warren was in a vulnerable position when he went to the Eisenhower dinner, because the president had given him what is called a recess appointment when the Senate was out of session and he had not yet been confirmed by the Senate. Even so, Warren found the president's intervention inappropriate rather than persuasive, and three months later he announced the Court's unanimous decision striking down segregated school systems. Of course, justices' opinions of the president that are based on policy or partisan considerations may work to the president's advantage or disadvantage in relevant cases, but that is not a product of presidential influence in itself.

Presidents do have more meaningful sources of influence. Their role in setting the congressional agenda and their veto power mean that they shape legislative action affecting the Court. Presidents occasionally initiate action to attack the Court or overturn its decisions, and sometimes they help to block such action. As chief executive, the president also can shape how the Court's decisions are put into effect. And like members of Congress, the president sometimes criticizes a decision in an effort to put the Court in a bad light.

Thus justices may have more reason to take the president into account than they do with Congress. In any event, justices almost surely are influenced by presidents from time to time. In the conflicts between the Court and the other branches that occurred in the Marshall Court and New Deal eras, the attacks on the Court by Presidents Jefferson and Franklin Roosevelt may have affected some justices' choices in major cases. But it also seems clear that these are rare circumstances. Ordinarily, any direct presidential influence on the Court's rulings is marginal at most.

The General Public

Supreme Court justices might seem to be immune to influence from the general public. The public has no direct power over the Court, and the great majority of the Court's decisions are essentially invisible to the public. Yet many observers of the Court believe that the justices pay attention to public opinion. The primary reason, as they see it, is that the Court's ability to maintain its institutional position depends on its legitimacy with the public—the belief that the Court is "worthy of respect and obedience."[123] In this view, the Court's success in getting its decisions carried out and in avoiding attacks on its powers and autonomy depends on retaining what is sometimes called diffuse public support.

It is not clear that justices need to worry about maintaining public support when they reach decisions. The Court is viewed more positively by the public than are the other branches of government. Further, it is uncertain whether the Court's legitimacy is damaged significantly by reaching unpopular decisions.[124] And even if public support for the Court declines, such a decline may not have much effect on the Court as an institution.

But more important than the reality is justices' perceptions of that reality, and there is considerable evidence that justices in the current era think and worry about the Court's legitimacy. References to the Court's legitimacy in justices' opinions have been fairly common since the 1950s, and justices often refer to that legitimacy or make efforts to bolster it in talks outside the Court.[125] Thus justices may see it as important to protect the Court's legitimacy by taking the public into account when they reach decisions. Legitimacy aside, justices might simply feel more comfortable when the public approves of what the Court does and views its members favorably.

If the justices do take public opinion into account when they decide cases, one effect might be to draw them to support the majority view among the public on issues that many people know and care about. Some observers argue that the justices collectively do fall in step with public opinion on major issues. Yet the Court sometimes makes highly unpopular decisions, even when reactions to earlier decisions on similar issues have made it clear that a decision will arouse strong disapproval. Two examples were its rulings on flag burning in 1989 and 1990 and on religious observances in public schools over four decades.[126]

Even so, public opinion may set bounds on the legal policies that justices consider seriously. The dramatic growth in public support for same-sex marriage did not guarantee that the Court would strike down state prohibitions of such marriages in *Obergefell v. Hodges* (2015). But the justices probably would have feared a strong negative reaction to such a decision during the long period when there was overwhelming public opposition to same-sex marriage. Of course, during that period such a decision probably would have been unthinkable to the justices themselves: the attitudes of some justices changed in the same way that the attitudes of people outside the Court changed.

Another possible effect of concern with public opinion is more subtle but also more pervasive. It might be that as the general public moves left or right on the ideological spectrum, the Court moves along with it to avoid straying too far from public opinion in its decisions as a whole. Indeed, studies generally find a tendency for the Court and the public to move in the same ideological direction over time.[127] But even if that tendency exists, it is uncertain whether the justices are being pulled along by the public or whether the justices and the public are responding to the same developments in government and society.

In recent years the justices have had a new source of concern about public attitudes toward the Court. Outside the Court, heated battles over the selection of justices since 2016 have weakened perceptions that the Court is disconnected from partisan politics. Since 2010, for the first time in the Court's history, ideological and partisan lines on the Court have coincided: all the justices appointed by Republican presidents are more conservative than all the Democratic appointees. As a result, decisions that divide the Court because of ideological disagreements can look partisan. Meanwhile, the Court has been hearing more cases that have major stakes for the political parties. When the Court divides along party lines in such cases, observers of the Court might get the impression that, as Justice Breyer put it when speaking more broadly about the Court, "our decisions are nothing but politics, that we're junior varsity politicians."[128]

In reaction, justices have made an effort to show that the Court is immune from the partisan animus that exists in the other branches of government. They could also look for opportunities to show that they do not simply follow ideological and partisan leanings, and in Brett Kavanaugh's first two terms on the Court it appeared that Kavanaugh and Neil Gorsuch did so.

In this respect, John Roberts is in a unique position as chief justice. He clearly feels special responsibility for the Court's image, which reflects on his own image in the short and long term. Perhaps this concern helps to explain an apparent small movement toward the ideological center during his tenure on the Court. Roberts has joined the Court's four liberals to create 5–4 majorities in a few major cases, including 2020 decisions on deportation of people who came to the United States as children and on regulation of abortion clinics.[129] His votes in these cases may have been aimed in part at countering the impression that the Court was carrying out the political agenda of its conservative majority. For Roberts personally, those liberal votes could help to foster a reputation for independence from ideological orthodoxy and partisanship, though at the cost of strong criticism from some conservatives.

Overall, the impact of the general public on the justices is uncertain. At least some justices might be drawn toward positions that the public supports by their concern for the Court's standing or their personal interest in public approval. But under most circumstances, the justices seem fairly free to act without taking public opinion into account. And the justices surely have greater independence from the public than do elected officials in the other branches and in state courts.

The Justices' Reference Groups

Beyond the other branches of government and the general public, justices can be influenced by sets of people with whom they have more personal links—those with whom they identify and whose approval is important to them.[130] One set of relevant people is the justices' personal friends and acquaintances. Other reference groups for justices are professional colleagues and people in political groups with which they identify. None of these people have direct power over justices, but a desire to foster and maintain their approval may influence justices' responses to the cases they decide. The news media that cover the Court may have influence as well, because they communicate information about the justices' work to their reference groups and to the general public. Justices have indicated that they pay attention to how they and the Court are depicted in the media.

How might these reference groups help to shape the justices' choices as decision makers? One hypothesis has been suggested by some conservative observers of the Court. Several of the justices who were appointed by Republican presidents between 1953 and 1990 developed more liberal records on the Court than would have been expected, and some seemed to shift in a liberal direction after they joined the Court. In the view of these conservatives, the justices with unexpectedly moderate or liberal records were influenced by their desire for the approval of left-leaning groups in the Court's environment, including social circles in Washington, elite segments of the legal profession, and the news media that cover the Court.

The validity of this hypothesis is quite uncertain. But from the 1960s until at least the 1980s, groups such as elite lawyers and the reporters who covered the Court did have a liberal leaning. Thus it is plausible that these groups had some impact on the thinking and decision making of some justices.

The world around the Court has changed in the past few decades. There are now distinct liberal and conservative segments of the legal profession, the news media, and other groups that the justices care about. Beginning with Clarence Thomas in 1991, justices appointed by Republican presidents have had deep roots in the conservative world. For instance, most developed ties with the Federalist Society, the dominant association of conservative lawyers, and most had worked in Republican administrations.

As a result, conservative justices today can get approval from like-minded people in the legal profession, in politics, in the news media, and in Washington social circles. Like their liberal counterparts, they are supported in their ideological leanings by some of their reference groups. Those groups may also reinforce the justices' leanings; one legal scholar has said that "each Justice emulates or seeks the approval of his or her own ideologically polarized in-group."[131] Thus, the justices' personal audiences may contribute marginally to the substantial difference in voting patterns between conservative Republicans and liberal Democrats that is a key feature of the current Court. On the other hand, the justices' desire to avoid being seen by some of their reference groups as acting "politically" may work to limit the strength of ideological and partisan divisions in the Court. If so, this would be another form of influence for the justices' reference groups.

CONCLUSION

The considerations that shape Supreme Court decisions can vary in their importance from justice to justice. It is possible that some justices give greater weight to legal considerations than do others, and justices differ in their willingness to compromise their positions in order to achieve agreement with their colleagues. It appears that some justices are subject to greater influence than others from particular sets of people and institutions outside the Court.

The determinants of the Court's decisions also may vary across cases. Most important, the relative weight of legal and policy considerations seems likely to vary. The justices have much stronger views about some policy issues than others, and the application of the law to a particular case varies in how clear or ambiguous it is. The justices' conceptions of good policy probably have greater impact relative to the state of the law when the justices' policy preferences are strong and the law is quite ambiguous.

This variation requires caution in generalizing about the importance of the various factors that shape Supreme Court decisions, but some generalization is still possible. Of all the considerations that influence the Supreme Court's decisions, the justices' policy preferences appear to be the most important. The application of the law to the Court's cases is usually ambiguous, and constraints from the Court's environment are generally weak. As a result, justices have considerable freedom to take positions that accord with their own conceptions of good policy. For this reason, the Court's membership has strong effects on the Court's direction.

If justices' policy preferences explain a great deal, they do not explain everything. The law and the political environment rule out some possible options for the Court, and they influence the justices' choices among the options that remain. The group life of the Court affects the choices of individual justices and the Court's collective decisions. In particular, justices frequently adjust their positions in cases to win support from colleagues and help build majorities. Factors other than policy preferences are reflected in results that might seem surprising—strikingly liberal decisions from conservative Courts and the maintenance of precedents even when most justices no longer favor the policies they embody.

Thus, what the Court does is a product of multiple, intertwined forces. These forces operate together in complicated ways to shape the Court's decisions. Efforts to understand why the Court does what it does must take into account the complexity of the process by which the justices make their choices.

NOTES

1. Quoted in Tony Mauro, "Supreme Court's Style Manual Is Private No More," *National Law Journal*, March 28, 2016.
2. Tonja Jacobi and Matthew Sag, "The New Oral Argument: Justices as Advocates," *Notre Dame Law Review* 94 (January 2019): 1161–1253.
3. Tonja Jacobi, Timothy R. Johnson, Eve Ringsmuth, and Matthew Sag, "Look Who's Talking Less: Supreme Court Justices," *Washington Post*, November 1, 2019.
4. Tonja Jacobi, "Gendered Interruptions at the Court," *SCOTUS OA*, August 2, 2018, https://scotusoa.com/gendered-interruptions-at-the-court/.
5. RonNell Andersen Jones and Aaron Nielson, "Pandemic Proves Justice Thomas Does Have Something to Say," *The Hill*, May 7, 2020.
6. Jess Bravin, "Justice Kennedy on Choosing Cases, 'Empathy,' and Diversity," *Wall Street Journal* Law Blog, October 10, 2013.
7. Margaret Talbot, "The Pivotal Justice," *The New Yorker*, November 18, 2019, 41.
8. Jacobi and Sag, "The New Oral Argument: Justices as Advocates."
9. Ryan C. Black, Sarah A. Treul, Timothy R. Johnson, and Jerry Goldman, "Emotions, Oral Arguments, and Supreme Court Decision Making," *Journal of Politics* 73 (April 2011): 572–581; Bryce J. Dietrich, Ryan D. Enos, and Maya Sen, "Emotional Arousal Predicts Voting on the U.S. Supreme Court," *Political Analysis* 27 (April 2019): 237–243.
10. Joan Biskupic, "This Justice Began the Supreme Court's Conservative Transformation," *CNN*, December 8, 2018.

11. *Flowers v. Mississippi*, 17-9572, oral argument, March 20, 2019, 57–58. Oral argument transcripts are archived at https://www.supremecourt.gov/oral_arguments/argument_ transcript/2019.

12. Barry Sullivan and Megan Canty, "Interruptions in Search of a Purpose: Oral Argument in the Supreme Court, October Terms 1958–60 and 2010–12," *Utah Law Review* 2015 (2015): 1037.

13. Tonja Jacobi and Matthew Sag, "Taking Laughter Seriously at the Supreme Court," *Vanderbilt Law Review* 72 (October 2019): 1423–1496.

14. Amy Howe, "Courtroom Access: Where Do We Go from Here?" *SCOTUSblog*, May 13, 2020.

15. "A Conversation with U.S. Supreme Court Justice Elena Kagan on Her Love of Law and Landing 'The Dream Job'," *Harvard Law Today*, September 17, 2017, https://today.law .harvard.edu/conversation-u-s-supreme-court-justice-elena-kagans-love-law-landing- dream-job/.

16. Adam G. Unikowsky, "My First Supreme Court Argument . . . and Then What Happened," *Journal of Appellate Practice and Process* 19 (Spring 2018): 49.

17. Eve M. Ringsmuth, Amanda C. Bryan, and Timothy R. Johnson, "Voting Fluidity and Oral Argument on the U.S. Supreme Court," *Political Research Quarterly* 66 (June 2013): 429–440.

18. Bill Kristol, "Conversation with Samuel Alito," *Conversations with Bill Kristol*, July 10, 2015, http://conversationswithbillkristol.org/transcript/samuel-alito-transcript/.

19. Brian Lamb, Susan Swain, and Mark Farkas, eds., *The Supreme Court: A C-Span Book Featuring the Justices in Their Own Words* (New York: PublicAffairs, 2010), 63.

20. Adam Liptak, "Justice Antonin Scalia Questions Logic Behind Gay Rights Protections," *New York Times, First Draft*, November 16, 2015.

21. Tom McParland, "As Justices Change, 'Court Works as an Institution,' Kagan Tells NY State Bar Leaders," *New York Law Journal*, January 31, 2020.

22. The process of responding to draft majority opinions is described in Forrest Maltzman, James F. Spriggs II, and Paul J. Wahlbeck, *Crafting Law on the Supreme Court: The Collegial Game* (New York: Cambridge University Press, 2000), 62–72.

23. Kevin Merida and Michael A. Fletcher, "*Thomas v. Blackmun*: Late Jurist's Papers Puncture Colleague's Portrait of a Genteel Court," *Washington Post*, October 10, 2004, A15.

24. Clare Cushman, *Courtwatchers: Eyewitness Accounts in Supreme Court History* (Lanham, Md.: Rowman & Littlefield, 2011), 198–199.

25. Dan Berman, "Ginsburg Suggests She Has at Least Five More Years on the Supreme Court," *CNN*, July 29, 2018.

26. *Reed v. Town of Gilbert*, 192 L. Ed. 2d 236, 259 (2015).

27. *Holguin-Hernandez v. United States*, 206 L. Ed. 2d 95, 101 (2020).

28. *Iancu v. Brunetti*, 204 L. Ed. 2d 714, 723 (2019).

29. Matthew Walther, "Sam Alito: A Civil Man," *The American Spectator* 47 (May 2014): 30.

30. *Rucho v. Common Cause*, 204 L. Ed. 2d 931, 966 (2019).

31. *Washington State Department of Licensing v. Cougar Den, Inc.*, 203 L. Ed. 2d 301, 325 (2019).

32. *SCA Hygiene Products Aktiebolag v. First Quality Baby Products*, 197 L. Ed. 2d 292, 308 (2017).

33. Allison Orr Larsen, "Confronting Supreme Court Fact Finding," *Virginia Law Review* 98 (October 2012): 1255–1312; Allison Orr Larsen, "The Trouble with Amicus Facts," *Virginia Law Review* 100 (December 2014), 1757–1818; Ryan Gabrielson, "It's a Fact: Supreme Court Errors Aren't Hard to Find," ProPublica, October 17, 2017.

34. Greg Moran, "No Retirement Plans for Justice Ginsburg," *San Diego Union Tribune*, February 8, 2013.

35. Mark Walsh, "A 'View' from the Courtroom: The 'Court of History' Is in Session," *SCOTUSblog*, June 26, 2018.

36. The lengths of time from oral argument to decision are from Adam Feldman, "Final Stat Pack for October Term 2018," *SCOTUSblog*, June 28, 2019.

37. See Richard L. Pacelle Jr., Brett W. Curry, and Bryan W. Marshall, *Decision Making by the Modern Supreme Court* (New York: Cambridge University Press, 2011).

38. Matthew E. K. Hall, *What Justices Want: Goals and Personality on the U.S. Supreme Court* (New York: Cambridge University Press, 2018); Ryan C. Black, Ryan J. Owens, Justin Wedeking, and Patrick C. Wohlfarth, *The Conscientious Justice: How Supreme Court Justices' Personalities Influence the Law, the High Court, and the Constitution* (New York: Cambridge University Press, 2020).

39. Jeffrey A. Segal and Alan J. Champlin, "The Attitudinal Model," in *Routledge Handbook of Judicial Behavior*, ed. Robert M. Howard and Kirk A. Randazzo (New York: Routledge, 2018), 17–33.

40. Neil M. Gorsuch with Jane Nitze and David Feder, *A Republic, If You Can Keep It* (New York: Crown Forum, 2019), 108–127.

41. *Gitlow v. New York* (1925); *Cantwell v. Connecticut* (1940).

42. *Bolling v. Sharpe* (1954).

43. *Hans v. Louisiana* (1890).

44. Robert A. Katzmann, *Judging Statutes* (New York: Oxford University Press, 2014).

45. Chris Wallace, "Justice Antonin Scalia on Issues Facing SCOTUS and the Country," *Fox News Sunday*, July 29, 2012, https://www.foxnews.com/transcript/justice-antonin-scalia-on-issues-facing-scotus-and-the-country.

46. Robert Barnes, "Powerful Group Lauds Approach to Stocking Courts with Conservative Judges," *Washington Post*, November 19, 2017, A6.

47. Criteria for overrulings used in that source are described at https://constitution.congress.gov/browse/essay/appx_1/#ALDD_00000479.

48. These decisions were *Citizens United v. Federal Election Commission* (2010), *Obergefell v. Hodges* (2015), and *Rucho v. Common Cause* (2019), respectively.

49. *Kimble v. Marvel Entertainment*, 192 L. Ed. 2d 463, 472 (2015).

50. J. Gordon Hylton, "Why Baseball's Antitrust Exemption Still Survives," *Marquette Sports Law Journal* 9 (Spring 1999): 391–402.

51. Harold J. Spaeth and Jeffrey A. Segal, *Majority Rule or Minority Will: Adherence to Precedent on the U.S. Supreme Court* (New York: Cambridge University Press, 1999); Allison Orr Larsen, "Perpetual Dissents," *George Mason Law Review* 15 (Winter 2008): 447–478.

52. *Gamble v. United States*, 204 L. Ed. 2d 322, 349 (2019).

53. These opinions were, in order, in *Collins v. Virginia* (2018), questioning *Mapp v. Ohio* (1961); *McKee v. Cosby* (2019), questioning *New York Times v. Sullivan* (1964); and *Garza v. Idaho* (2019), questioning *Gideon v. Wainwright* (1963).

54. *Franchise Tax Board v. Hyatt*, 203 L. Ed. 2d 768, 790 (2019) (Breyer); *Knick v. Township of Scott*, 204 L. Ed. 2d 558, 593 (2019) (Kagan).

55. Mark J. Richards and Herbert M. Kritzer, "Jurisprudential Regimes in Supreme Court Decision Making," *American Political Science Review* 96 (June 2002): 305–320; Herbert M. Kritzer and Mark J. Richards, "The Role of Law in the Supreme Court's Search and Seizure Jurisprudence," *American Politics Research* 33 (January 2005): 33–55. See Brandon L. Bartels and Andrew J. O'Geen, "The Nature of Legal Change on the U.S. Supreme Court:

Jurisprudential Regimes Theory and Its Alternatives," *American Journal of Political Science* 59 (October 2015): 880–895.

56. U.S. Senate, Confirmation Hearing on the Nomination of John G. Roberts Jr. to be Chief Justice of the United States, 109th Cong., 1st sess., 2005, 55.

57. Jim Evans, "Sorry Judges, We Umpires Do More than Call Balls and Strikes," *Washington Post*, September 8, 2018.

58. Jeffrey A. Segal and Harold J. Spaeth, *The Supreme Court and the Attitudinal Model Revisited* (New York: Cambridge University Press, 2002), chap. 2; Richard A. Posner, "What Is Eminently Wrong with the Federal Judiciary, Yet Eminently Curable, Part II," *The Green Bag* 19 (Spring 2016): 263–266.

59. Walter Murphy, *Elements of Judicial Strategy* (Chicago: University of Chicago Press, 1964), 44n. See Jack Knight and Lee Epstein, "The Norm of Stare Decisis," *American Journal of Political Science* 40 (November 1996): 1018–1035.

60. Evidence of the impact of law is discussed and presented in Stefanie A. Lindquist and David E. Klein, "The Influence of Jurisprudential Considerations on Supreme Court Decision Making: A Study of Conflict Cases," *Law & Society Review* 40 (2006): 135–161; and Michael A. Bailey and Forrest Maltzman, *The Constrained Court: Law, Politics, and the Decisions Justices Make* (Princeton, N.J.: Princeton University Press, 2011), chaps. 4–5.

61. Norman I. Silber, *With All Deliberate Speed: The Life of Philip Elman* (Ann Arbor: University of Michigan Press, 2004), 51.

62. John Paul Stevens, *The Making of a Justice: Reflections on My First 94 Years* (New York: Little, Brown, 2019), 236, 25. The quotation is from p. 25.

63. For two differing positions, see Lee Epstein and Jack Knight, *The Choices Justices Make* (Washington, D.C.: CQ Press, 1998); and Saul Brenner and Joseph M. Whitmeyer, *Strategy on the United States Supreme Court* (New York: Cambridge University Press, 2009).

64. Tom S. Clark, *The Supreme Court: An Analytic History of Constitutional Decision Making* (New York: Cambridge University Press, 2019).

65. Lawrence Baum, *Ideology in the Supreme Court* (Princeton, N.J.: Princeton University Press, 2017).

66. Percentages were calculated from data in Adam Feldman, "Final Stat Pack for October Term 2018," *SCOTUSblog*, June 28, 2019, https://www.scotusblog.com/2019/06/final-stat-pack-for-october-term-2018/; Adam Feldman, "Final Stat Pack for October Term 2019," *SCOTUSblog*, July 10, 2020, https://www.scotusblog.com/2020/07/final-stat-pack-for-october-term-2019/.

67. Paul H. Edelman, David E. Klein, and Stefanie A. Lindquist, "Consensus, Disorder, and Ideology on the Supreme Court," *Journal of Empirical Legal Studies* 9 (March 2012): 129–148.

68. Joshua B. Fischman, "Politics and Authority in the U.S. Supreme Court," *Cornell Law Review* 104 (2019): 1513–1592.

69. Jeffrey A. Segal, Lee Epstein, Charles M. Cameron, and Harold J. Spaeth, "Ideological Values and the Votes of Justices Revisited," *Journal of Politics* 57 (August 1995): 812–823.

70. Richard M. Re, "Personal Precedent in *Bay Mills*," *Re's Judicata*, June 4, 2014, http://richardresjudicata.wordpress.com/2014/06/04/personal-precedent-in-bay-mills.

71. *South Dakota v. Wayfair, Inc.*, 201 L. Ed. 2d 403, 427 (2018); *Baldwin v. United States*, 206 L. Ed. 2d 231, 231-232 (2020).

72. Figures on agreement between Blackmun and his colleagues are taken from the annual statistics on the Supreme Court term in the November issues of *Harvard Law Review*,

vols. 85–100 (1972–1987). See also "The Changing Social Vision of Justice Blackmun," *Harvard Law Review* 96 (1983): 717–736.

73. See Linda Greenhouse, *Becoming Justice Blackmun: Harry Blackmun's Supreme Court Journey* (New York: Times Books, 2005).

74. *Baker v. Nelson* (1972); *Obergefell v. Hodges* (2015).

75. Adam Liptak, "Ginsburg Gives Hints of Sharp Divisions," *New York Times*, June 11, 2019, A17.

76. Stevens, *The Making of a Justice*, 456.

77. *Janus v. AFSCME*, 2019 U.S. Dist. LEXIS 43152, at 8 (N.D. Ill. 2019).

78. These cases were, in order, *Shelby County v. Holder* (2013), *Janus v. AFSCME* (2018), and *Rucho v. Common Cause* (2019).

79. *National Federation of Independent Business v. Sebelius* (2012).

80. *Wolf v. Cook County*, 206 L. Ed. 2d 142, 145 (2020); Peter Baker, "Presidents Wants 2 Liberal Justices Off His Cases," *New York Times*, February 26, 2020, A1.

81. *Trump v. Vance* (2020); *Trump v. Mazars USA* (2020).

82. Bailey and Maltzman, *The Constrained Court*, chaps. 4–5.

83. Lee Epstein and Andrew D. Martin, "Is the Roberts Court Especially Activist? A Study of Invalidating (and Upholding) Federal, State, and Local Laws," *Emory Law Journal* 61 (2012): 737–758.

84. William H. Rehnquist, "Chief Justices I Never Knew," *Hastings Constitutional Law Quarterly* 3 (Summer 1976): 647.

85. John Paul Stevens, *The Making of a Justice*, 205.

86. Robert Barnes, "Breyer: Fears of Foreign Law Don't Resonate," *Washington Post*, September 13, 2015, A3.

87. Forrest Maltzman and Paul J. Wahlbeck, "Strategic Policy Considerations and Voting Fluidity on the Burger Court," *American Political Science Review* 90 (September 1996): 587.

88. Segal and Spaeth, *The Supreme Court and the Attitudinal Model Revisited*, 286.

89. Jeffrey Rosen, *Conversations with RBG: Ruth Bader Ginsburg on Life, Love, Liberty, and Law* (New York: Henry Holt, 2019), 125. It is uncertain when Ginsburg made that statement, but the context suggests that it was in 2014.

90. Joan Biskupic, "Exclusive: How John Roberts Killed the Census Citizenship Question," *CNN*, September 12, 2019.

91. Evan Thomas, *First: Sandra Day O'Connor* (New York: Random House, 2019), 279–280.

92. See Maltzman, Spriggs, and Wahlbeck, *Crafting Law on the Supreme Court*.

93. Pamela C. Corley, "Bargaining and Accommodation on the United States Supreme Court: Insight from Justice Blackmun," *Judicature* 90 (January–February 2007): 157–165.

94. Kristol, "Conversation with Samuel Alito."

95. Maltzman, Spriggs, and Wahlbeck, *Crafting Law on the Supreme Court*, 116.

96. Tal Kopan, "Elena Kagan Talks Diversity and (Dis)agreement on the Supreme Court," *Under the Radar* Blog, Politico, December 14, 2012.

97. Nina Totenberg, "Ginsburg: Liberal Justices Make a Point to Speak with One Voice," National Public Radio, July 10, 2015; Samantha Lachman and Ashley Alman, "Ruth Bader Ginsburg Reflects on a Polarizing Term One Month Out," *Huffington Post*, July 29, 2015.

98. The opinions on voting rights were in *Northwest Austin Municipal Utility District v. Holder* (2009) and *Shelby County v. Holder* (2013). The opinions on religious institutions were in *Trinity Lutheran Church v. Comer* (2017) and *Espinoza v. Montana Department of Revenue* (2020).

99. Tom Pryor, "Using Citations to Measure Influence on the Supreme Court," *American Politics Research* 45 (May 2017): 366–402.

100. Jonathan Adler, "Kagan Discusses Statutory Interpretation at Law School," *Harvard Crimson*, November 18, 2015, http://www.thecrimson.com/article/2015/11/18/kagan-talk-law-school/.

101. Margaret Talbot, "The Pivotal Justice," *The New Yorker*, November 18, 2019, 44–45.

102. Joan Biskupic, *The Chief: The Life and Turbulent Times of Chief Justice John Roberts* (New York: Basic Books, 2019), 177.

103. This discussion of criteria for opinion assignment draws from several studies, including Forrest Maltzman and Paul J. Wahlbeck, "May It Please the Chief? Opinion Assignments in the Rehnquist Court," *American Journal of Political Science* 40 (May 1996): 421–443; Richard J. Lazarus, "Back to 'Business' at the Supreme Court: The 'Administrative Side' of Chief Justice Roberts," *Harvard Law Review Forum* 129 (2015): 33–93; and Paul J. Wahlbeck, Alyx Mark, Ryan Krog, and Phillip J. Wininger, "Forecasting Opinion Assignment on the U.S. Supreme Court," in *The Chief Justice: Appointment and Influence*, ed. David J. Danelski and Artemus Ward (Ann Arbor: University of Michigan Press, 2016), 174–201.

104. See Jeffrey R. Lax and Kelly Rader, "Bargaining Power in the Supreme Court: Evidence from Opinion Assignment and Vote Switching," *Journal of Politics* 77 (July 2015): 648–663; and James Khun, Matthew E. K. Hall, and Kristen Macher, "Holding versus Dicta: Divided Control of Opinion Content on the U.S. Supreme Court," *Political Research Quarterly* 70 (June 2017): 257–268.

105. Lazarus, "Back to 'Business,'" 84.

106. Jan Crawford Greenburg, "Interview with Chief Justice Roberts," *ABC News*, November 28, 2006.

107. Ruth Marcus, "Alumni Brennan, Blackmun Greet Harvard Law Freshmen," *Washington Post*, September 6, 1986, 2.

108. Jeffrey Rosen, "RBG Presides," *New Republic*, October 13, 2014, 21.

109. See Timothy R. Johnson, James F. Spriggs II, and Paul J. Wahlbeck, "Passing and Strategic Voting on the U.S. Supreme Court," *Law & Society Review* 39 (June 2005): 349–377.

110. David J. Garrow, *Liberty and Sexuality: The Right to Privacy and the Making of Roe v. Wade* (New York: Macmillan, 1994), 558.

111. Linda Greenhouse, "How Not to Be Chief Justice: The Apprenticeship of William H. Rehnquist," *University of Pennsylvania Law Review* 154 (June 2006): 1367 (emphasis in original).

112. Jeffrey Rosen, "Rehnquist the Great?" *Atlantic Monthly*, April 2005, 79–80.

113. John Paul Stevens, *Five Chiefs: A Supreme Court Memoir* (New York: Little, Brown, 2011), 210.

114. Biskupic, *The Chief*, 278–279.

115. Adam Liptak, "Roberts Uses Predecessor to Discuss Changing Face of Court," *New York Times*, November 24, 2015, A17.

116. "Supreme Court Justice Visits UK, Interviews Himself," *Kentucky Kernel*, September 24, 2015.

117. Joan Biskupic, "Supreme Court Still Feeling the Impact of Antonin Scalia's Death," *CNN*, February 13, 2018.

118. Kevin Daley, "Justice Sotomayor Reveals How She Greeted Brett Kavanaugh After His Confirmation," *The Daily Caller*, November 18, 2018, https://dailycaller.com/2018/11/18/sonia-sotomayor-brett-kavanaugh/.

119. Tom S. Clark, *The Limits of Judicial Independence* (New York: Cambridge University Press, 2011); Anna Harvey, *A Mere Machine: The Supreme Court, Congress, and American Democracy* (New Haven, Conn.: Yale University Press, 2013).

120. Matthew E. K. Hall and Joseph Daniel Ura, "Judicial Majoritarianism," *Journal of Politics* 77 (July 2015): 818–832.

121. Paul M. Collins, Jr., and Matthew Eshbaugh-Sosa, *The President and the Supreme Court: Going Public on Judicial Decisions from Washington to Trump* (New York: Cambridge University Press, 2020), 20–23.

122. James F. Simon, *Eisenhower vs. Warren: The Battle for Civil Rights and Liberties* (New York: W.W. Norton, 2018), 179–181.

123. Tara Leigh Grove, "The Supreme Court's Legitimacy Dilemma," *Harvard Law Review* 132 (June 2019): 2244. The article was referring to "the legal system and its institutions" generally.

124. For opposing views on this question, see Brandon L. Bartels and Christopher D. Johnston, "On the Ideological Foundations of Supreme Court Legitimacy in the American Public," *American Journal of Political Science* 57 (January 2013): 184–199; and James L. Gibson and Michael J. Nelson, "Is the U.S. Supreme Court's Legitimacy Grounded in Performance Satisfaction and Ideology?" *American Journal of Political Science* 59 (January 2015): 162–174.

125. Dion Farganis, "Do Reasons Matter? The Impact of Opinion Content on Supreme Court Legitimacy," *Political Research Quarterly* 65 (March 2012): 207; Colin Glennon and Logan Strother, "The Maintenance of Institutional Legitimacy in Supreme Court Justices' Public Rhetoric," *Journal of Law and Courts* 7 (Fall 2019): 241–261.

126. The flag burning decision was *United States v. Eichman* (1990). The school religion decisions include *Abington School District v. Schempp* (1963), *Wallace v. Jaffree* (1985), and *Santa Fe Independent School District v. Doe* (2000).

127. See Matthew E. K. Hall, "The Semiconstrained Court: Public Opinion, the Separation of Powers, and the U.S. Supreme Court's Fear of Nonimplementation," *American Journal of Political Science* 58 (April 2014): 352–366.

128. John Newsom, "Justice Stephen Breyer Gives a Bryan Series Audience a Peek Inside the Supreme Court," *Greensboro News & Record*, October 3, 2019.

129. *Department of Homeland Security v. Regents of University of California* (2020); *June Medical Services v. Russo* (2020).

130. The discussion in this section draws from Neal Devins and Lawrence Baum, *The Company They Keep: How Partisan Divisions Came to the Supreme Court* (New York: Oxford University Press, 2019), chaps. 3–4.

131. Suzanna Sherry, "Our Kardashian Court (and How to Fix It)," Vanderbilt Law Research Paper No. 19-30, July 24, 2019, 9.

CHAPTER FIVE

POLICY OUTPUTS

Chapters 3 and 4 examined the processes that shape the Supreme Court's agenda and its decisions on the cases it hears. In this chapter, I consider the Court's work from a broader perspective by focusing on the policies that have resulted from these processes, both historically and in the current era.

These policies have multiple facets, each discussed in one of the sections that follow. The first is the content of the Court's agenda, the mix of issues that the Court addresses. The second is the Court's activism, the extent to which it intervenes in the policies that policy makers in the other branches of government have adopted. The last is the substance of the Court's policies, which can be analyzed in terms of their ideological content and the sectors of American society that they benefit.

The final section of the chapter focuses on explanation of the historical patterns that were described in the preceding sections. What are the sources of the paths that the Court's policies have taken?

AREAS OF ACTIVITY: WHAT THE COURT ADDRESSES

The Supreme Court addresses issues in fields as different as antitrust, criminal law, and freedom of speech. In this sense, the Court's agenda is highly diverse. But the Court devotes most of its efforts to a few types of policy. To a considerable degree, then, the Court is a specialist.

The Court's Current Activity

The shape of the Court's agenda in the current era can be illustrated with the cases that it heard in the 2019 term. It is useful to begin by describing the issues in a fairly representative sample of cases decided during that term.

1. Did the U.S. Forest Service have the authority to grant the right to build a natural gas pipeline across land that was administered by the National Park Service? (*U.S. Forest Service v. Cowpasture River Preservation Association*, 2020)

▶ **Photo 5-1** Colorado members of the electoral college in 2016. One of the Supreme Court's 2020 decisions dealt with penalties that Colorado and Washington State imposed on electors who violated their pledge to vote for the candidate who received the most votes in their state.

2. Does the right to a jury trial, applied to state cases by the Fourteenth Amendment, require a unanimous jury vote in order to convict defendants of serious offenses? (*Ramos v. Louisiana*, 2020)

3. Does the Constitution allow a state to penalize members of the electoral college who violate their pledge to vote for the presidential and vice presidential candidates who received the most votes in the state? (*Chiafalo v. Washington*, 2020)

4. Under the requirement in the Employee Retirement Income Security Act (ERISA) that plaintiffs must sue for a breach of fiduciary duties within three years of the time they gain "actual knowledge" of that breach, do they automatically have actual knowledge of information contained in materials that they received from the administrators who had fiduciary duties? (*Intel Corp. Investment Policy Committee v. Sulyma*, 2020)

5. Under the Federal Rules of Criminal Procedure, does a defendant's argument in district court for a specific sentence preserve the defendant's right to argue on appeal that the sentence imposed was unreasonably long? (*Holguin-Hernandez v. United States*, 2020)

6. Did a provision of the Affordable Care Act obligate the federal government to pay health insurance companies for certain losses in online insurance marketplaces during the first three years of those marketplaces? (*Maine Community Health Options v. United States*, 2020)

7. In a lawsuit for infringement of a trademark, are plaintiffs required to show that defendants willfully infringed their trademarks in order to be awarded the profits that defendants gained? (*Romag Fasteners Inc. v. Fossil Inc.*, 2020)

8. Can criminal defendants be found in violation of two federal fraud statutes if they did not seek to obtain government money or property? (*Kelly v. United States*, 2020)

9. Does employment discrimination based on sexual orientation or transgender status constitute sex discrimination that is prohibited by Title VII of the Civil Rights Act of 1964? (*Bostock v. Clayton County*, 2020)

10. As applied to one person's situation, does a statute that allows expedited deportation of certain applicants for asylum violate either of the constitutional provisions that prohibit suspension of habeas corpus and require due process of law? (*Department of Homeland Security v. Thuraissigiam*, 2020)

Table 5-1 provides a more systematic picture of the Court's agenda in the 2019 term by summarizing the characteristics of the fifty-three cases decided with oral argument and signed opinions in that term. While the content of the Court's agenda differs from term to term, the 2019 agenda was fairly typical of the current era in most respects.

First, the Court's decisions were closely connected with the other branches of government. The federal government or one of its agencies was a party in about half of all cases. State governments were also frequent participants in cases, so that three-quarters of all cases had at least one government party. Moreover, most of the disputes between private parties were based directly on government policy in fields such as pensions and bankruptcy.

Second, decisions that were based on provisions of the Constitution constituted a distinct minority of the agenda, only about one-third. The Court's interpretations of the Constitution tend to receive the most attention, but the justices devote most of their work to other forms of law—primarily federal statutes, but also federal rules of court procedure.

Third, the Court gave considerable attention, about one-fifth of all its decisions, to criminal cases. The great majority of criminal cases that the Court hears fall into two categories. The first is interpretations of federal statutes that define crimes and set rules for sentencing. The second is interpretation of constitutional protections of defendants' procedural rights.

Finally, the Court concentrated on two areas of policy. About one-third of the Court's decisions concerned civil liberties. As in earlier discussions, the term *civil liberties* refers here to three general types of rights that are protected by the Constitution and federal statutes: the right to fair procedure in dealings with government, the right to equal treatment by government and by private institutions,

Table 5-1 Characteristics of Decisions with Oral Argument and Signed Opinions, 2019 Term

Characteristic	Percentage
Litigants	
Federal government party[a]	49
State or local government party[a]	26
No government party	25
Constitutional issue decided[b]	32
Criminal case[c]	21
Civil liberties issue present[d]	34
Economic issue present	45

Note: Consolidated cases decided with one set of opinions were counted once.

Source: Cases in the table were those listed at the Supreme Court's website, https://www.supreme court.gov/opinions/slipopinion/19.

a. Cases with both a federal government party and another government party were listed as federal government. Government as party includes agencies and individual government officials.

b. Cases involving federal preemption of state laws are not treated as having a constitutional issue.

c. This category includes actions brought by prisoners to challenge the legality of their convictions but excludes cases concerning rights of prisoners.

d. This category includes cases in which the Court did not decide the civil liberties issue directly. A few cases were counted in both the civil liberties and economic categories because their issues overlapped the two categories.

and certain substantive rights protected against government violations such as freedom of expression and freedom of religion. By the broader definitions that some scholars use, about half the Court's cases involved civil liberties.[1] It is striking how large a share of the agenda is devoted to that field.

Economics also occupied a large share of the Court's 2019 agenda, with 45 percent of all cases. The Court dealt with a wide range of issues arising from relationships between participants in economic activity and from government regulation of that activity. Economic issues were especially prominent in the Court's statutory decisions.

Change in the Court's Agenda

The Court's agenda is not static. Even over a few terms, the Court's attention to specific categories of cases sometimes increases or decreases considerably.

The shape of its agenda as a whole has changed more slowly, but the changes have been fundamental.[2]

Changes in Specific Portions of the Agenda

Sometimes an issue that has occupied a very small place on the Court's agenda, or no place at all, becomes more prominent. Often, this change comes from new federal legislation. Enactment of the Employee Retirement Income Security Act of 1974 (ERISA) led to a continuing string of legal questions about employee pension plans that the courts had to address, and the Supreme Court has heard more than sixty cases interpreting ERISA. The major environmental laws of the 1970s had a similar effect.

The Court itself opens up new areas on its agenda with decisions that create legal rights or that make major changes in legal rules. *Strickland v. Washington* (1984) set up new standards to determine whether a criminal defendant was effectively denied the right to counsel by a lawyer's poor performance. Since that time, the Court has given full consideration to three dozen cases about interpretation of the *Strickland* standards, and it has reached a substantial number of additional decisions about *Strickland* without oral argument.

Just as issues can rise on the Court's agenda, they can also recede. Often, a new statute or Court decision raises a series of issues that the Court resolves during a particular period, but after that wave of cases the Court can move away from that field. In *Benton v. Maryland* (1969), the Court ruled that the constitutional protection against double jeopardy for criminal offenses applied to the states. This decision opened the way for state cases with double jeopardy issues to reach the Court, and the Court decided more than fifty cases in that field in the 1970s and 1980s. But with so many issues resolved, the Court has heard only occasional double jeopardy cases since then.

Changes in the Agenda as a Whole

Beyond changes in specific areas, the overall pattern of the Court's agenda may change over a period of several decades. The current agenda reflects a fundamental change that occurred between the 1930s and 1960s. In the half century up to the 1930s, the largest part of the Court's agenda was devoted to economic issues. Also important but clearly secondary were cases about federalism. Issues of procedural due process constituted a small proportion of the agenda, and relatively few cases concerned other civil liberties of individuals.

Over the next three decades, the Court evolved into an institution that gave most of its attention to individual liberties. The proportion of decisions dealing with civil liberties as defined broadly grew from 8 percent of the agenda in the 1933–1937 terms to 59 percent in the 1968–1972 terms.[3] Cases about the rights of criminal defendants became far more numerous, and other civil liberties issues such as racial equality took a large share of the agenda. At the same time, some kinds of economic cases declined precipitously. In the 1933–1937 terms, one of every three cases involved federal taxation or economic disputes between private parties. By the 1968–1972 terms, those two areas accounted for only 6 percent of the Court's agenda. Federalism also took a reduced share of the agenda, falling from 14 percent in 1933–1937 to 5 percent in 1968–1972.

Many forces contributed to this change, from public opinion to federal legislation. Interest groups that supported civil liberties cases played a key role by bringing relevant cases to the Court. But actions by the Court itself had the most direct effect. Perhaps most important, the justices became more interested in protecting civil liberties and thus in hearing claims that government policies infringed on liberties. Partly because they had to make room for civil liberties cases, the justices gave more limited attention to other fields. They continued to hear a good many cases involving economic issues, but economics declined considerably as part of the Court's work.

The Court's agenda has changed marginally since the 1960s, but its general form has remained fairly stable. Thus, the Court's work still reflects the changes in its agenda that occurred between the 1930s and the 1960s.

A Broader View of the Agenda

The Supreme Court's current agenda distinguishes the Court from other policy makers. In some respects, the Court's agenda resembles the agendas of other appellate courts, especially state supreme courts and federal courts of appeals. Where the Court stands out is in the prominence of civil liberties issues on its agenda. Except for the rights of criminal defendants, most other appellate courts hear few cases about civil liberties.

Congress is a generalist that spreads its attention across a very broad set of issues. As a result, the congressional agenda covers virtually all the types of policy that the Supreme Court deals with as well as others that the Court barely touches. Presidents are also generalists, but they give primary attention to foreign policy and management of the economy. Both the executive and legislative branches address civil liberties issues, but those issues have a much lower priority than they do in the Court.

These comparisons provide some perspective on the Court's role by underlining the limited range of its work. Its jurisdiction is broad, but the bulk of its decisions are made in only a few policy areas. By deciding as many civil liberties cases as it does, the Court can do much to shape law and policy in this area. In contrast, the Court's more limited activity in some major areas severely narrows its potential impact in those fields. That is especially true of foreign policy.

Even in the areas in which it is most active, the Court addresses only certain types of issues. In criminal justice, for instance, the Court does much to define the rights of criminal defendants and the scope of federal criminal statutes. But its decisions do not affect the funding of criminal justice agencies, and they have little direct impact on prosecutors' decisions whether to bring cases against defendants.

The Court's relatively narrow focus means that it does not deal with most of the issues that are high on the agendas of government and the public. U.S. military action in Iraq, Afghanistan, and other countries in the early twenty-first century has proceeded with essentially no involvement by the Court. Although the Court is active in the economic field, its decisions do not often address government policies that have broad effects on the economy. In this respect, its rulings on the Affordable Care Act sponsored by President Obama were exceptional. In contrast, the Court seems unlikely to play a significant role in shaping federal policies that address the economic effects of the coronavirus pandemic.

These realities should caution against exaggerating the Supreme Court's power as a policy maker. Although the importance of its role can be debated, the relatively narrow range of the Court's activities inevitably limits its power. The Court could not possibly be dominant as a policy maker except in civil liberties and some limited areas of economic policy. For reasons that are discussed later in this chapter and in Chapter 6, even in those areas the Court is far from dominant.

THE COURT'S ACTIVISM

The shares of the Supreme Court's agenda that are devoted to particular areas of policy help determine in which areas it plays a significant role, but its impact also depends on what it actually decides in those areas. One important element of those decisions is the extent of the Court's activism.

The term *judicial activism* has multiple meanings, and people most often use the term simply as a negative label for decisions they dislike. What I mean by activism is that a court makes significant changes in public policy, especially in policies established by the other branches. The most visible form of activism is the use of judicial review, the power to overturn acts of other policy makers on the ground that they violate the Constitution.

Overturning Acts of Congress

The most familiar use of judicial review comes in Supreme Court rulings that federal statutes are unconstitutional. Such a ruling represents a clear assertion of power by the Court because it directly negates a decision by another branch of the federal government.

The numbers of federal laws that the Court has overturned can be counted in different ways. According to one count, shown in Table 5-2, by the end of 2019 the Court had overturned 185 federal laws completely or in part.[4] (When different provisions of a statute were struck down in different decisions, each decision is counted once.) This number in itself is noteworthy. On the one hand, it indicates that the Court has made considerable use of its review power. On the other hand, the laws struck down by the Court constitute a very small fraction of the laws that Congress has adopted. And when the Court rules on whether a federal statute is unconstitutional, the great majority of the time it upholds the statute.[5]

Table 5-2 Number of Federal Statutes and State and Local Statutes Held Unconstitutional by the Supreme Court, 1790–2019

Period	Federal statutes	State and local statutes
1790–1799	0	0
1800–1809	1	1
1810–1819	0	7
1820–1829	0	6
1830–1839	0	2
1840–1849	0	7
1850–1859	1	7
1860–1869	4	15
1870–1879	7	36
1880–1889	4	43
1890–1899	5	33
1900–1909	9	39
1910–1919	6	93
1920–1929	15	119
1930–1939	13	77
1940–1949	2	48
1950–1959	4	47
1960–1969	18	125
1970–1979	19	174
1980–1989	16	116
1990–1999	24	49
2000–2009	16	27
2010–2019	21	37
Total	185	1,108

Source: Congressional Research Service, The Constitution of the United States of America: Analysis and Interpretation (Washington, D.C.: Government Printing Office, 2017), 2327–2619, updated to 2019.

Note: State and local laws do not include those that the Supreme Court held to be preempted by federal statutes.

A closer look at the decisions striking down federal laws provides a better sense of how the Court has used judicial review.[6] One question is the importance of the statutes that the Court overturns. The Court has struck down some statutes of major importance. One example was the Missouri Compromise of 1820, limiting slavery in federal territories, which the Court declared unconstitutional in *Scott v. Sandford* (the Dred Scott case, decided in 1857). Another was the New Deal economic legislation that the Court overturned in several decisions in 1935 and 1936.[7] In contrast, many of the Court's decisions declaring statutes invalid were unimportant to the policy goals of Congress and the president, either because the statutes were minor or because they were struck down only as they applied to particular circumstances.

A related question is the timing of judicial review. The Court's decisions striking down federal statutes fall into three groups of nearly equal size: those that came within four calendar years of a statute's enactment, those that came five to twelve years after enactment, and those that occurred more than twelve years later—in one instance, more than a hundred years later.[8] Often, few members of Congress care much when an older law is overturned because the statute has become less relevant over time or because Congress collectively has become less favorable to the provision that was struck down.

For these reasons, the Court's fairly frequent use of its power to invalidate congressional acts is somewhat misleading. Any decision that strikes down a federal statute might seem likely to produce major conflict between the Court and Congress, but that is not necessarily the case. Conflict is most likely when the Court invalidates an important congressional policy within a few years of its enactment, but most decisions striking down statutes do not meet both those criteria. Some decisions overturning legislation receive little attention, and some others are actually welcomed by presidents and members of Congress.[9]

As Table 5-2 shows, the Court has not overturned federal statutes at a constant rate. According to the count used for the table, the Court struck down only two statutes before 1865. It then began to exercise its judicial review power more frequently, overturning thirty-five federal laws between 1865 and 1918. Two more increases, even more dramatic, followed: the Court struck down fifteen federal laws during the 1920s and twelve from 1934 through 1936.

The period between 1918 and 1936 featured the highest level of conflict between the Court and Congress. The Court overturned twenty-nine federal laws, many of them quite significant. Between 1918 and 1928, the Court invalidated two child labor laws and a minimum wage law, along with several less important statutes. Then, between 1933 and 1936, a majority of the Court engaged in a broad attack on the New Deal program, an attack that ended with the Court's 1937 shift to a broader interpretation of federal power.

The Court used its judicial review power sparingly in the quarter-century after 1936, but it then overturned 114 federal statutes in the forty-seven years from 1963 through 2019. That number is far greater than in any previous period of the same length, and it constitutes three-fifths of the total for the Court's entire history.

Most of the statutes that the Court struck down in this period were of limited significance, but some were quite important. For instance, *Buckley v. Valeo* (1976), *Citizens United v. Federal Election Commission* (2010), and other decisions invalidated major provisions of federal laws regulating the funding of political campaigns. *Immigration and Naturalization Service v. Chadha* (1983) disallowed statutory provisions under which Congress could veto actions by administrative agencies without enacting new legislation, and *Clinton v. City of New York* (1998) invalidated the statute that allowed presidents to veto individual items in budget bills. Decisions in the last two decades have overturned the system of mandatory sentencing guidelines for federal cases, a provision that states would lose their federal Medicaid money if they did not broaden the coverage of their Medicaid programs, and the prohibition on federal recognition of same-sex marriages.[10]

Overturning State and Local Laws

The Supreme Court's exercise of judicial review over state and local laws has less of an activist element than its use of that power over federal laws. When the Court strikes down a state law, it does not put itself in conflict with the other branches of the federal government. Indeed, it may be supporting their powers over those of the states. Still, the Court is invalidating the action of another policy maker. For that reason, this form of judicial review is significant.

From 1790 to 2019, by one count, the Court overturned 1,108 state statutes and local ordinances as unconstitutional. As Table 5-2 shows, that number is about six times the number for federal statutes. The disparity is even greater than that figure suggests, because many decisions that overturned specific state and local laws also applied to similar laws in other locations.

As with federal laws, the rate at which the Court overturns state and local laws has tended to increase over time, and it was far higher in the twentieth century than in the nineteenth. The rate of invalidations per year was very high between 1909 and 1937, and the rate was even higher from the 1960s through the 1980s. In that period, the Court struck down an average of fourteen state and local laws per year. The rate of invalidations has been much lower since 1990, as low as it was in the late nineteenth century.

Although the Court struck down relatively few state laws before 1860, its decisions during that period were important because they limited state powers under the Constitution. For example, under Chief Justice John Marshall (1801–1835) the Court weakened the states with decisions such as *McCulloch v. Maryland* (1819), which held that states could not tax federal agencies, and *Gibbons v. Ogden* (1824), which reduced state power to regulate commerce. During the late nineteenth century and the first one-third of the twentieth, the Court struck down a great deal of state economic legislation, including many laws regulating business practices and labor relations. The net effect was to slow a major tide of public policy.

Some of the Court's decisions since the mid-1950s have also impinged on major elements of state policy. A series of rulings helped to break down the legal bases of racial segregation and discrimination in the southern states. In *Roe v. Wade* (1973), the Court overturned the broad prohibitions of abortion that existed in the great majority of states, thereby requiring a general legalization of abortion. Decisions from 1976 to 2020 struck down several post-*Roe* laws regulating abortion and indirectly invalidated many others. In *Obergefell v. Hodges* (2015), the Court ruled that state prohibitions of same-sex marriage were unconstitutional. And through a long series of decisions, the Court has limited state power to regulate the economy in areas that Congress has preempted under its constitutional supremacy. To a degree, however, the impact of those decisions has been balanced by the Court's rulings since 1995 that struck down federal laws on the ground that they infringed on state powers.

Other Targets of Judicial Review

The Supreme Court can declare unconstitutional any government policy or practice, not just laws enacted by legislatures. In 2018 and 2019 the Court found violations of the Constitution in a police search, the selection of jurors in a criminal case, the appointment process for administrative law judges in a federal agency, and the decision of a state civil rights commission.[11] The Court is especially active in overseeing criminal procedure under the Constitution, and it frequently holds that actions by police officers or trial judges violate the rights of defendants. The number of nonstatutory policies and practices that the Court has struck down is probably much larger than the number of statutes it has overturned.

Of particular interest is the Court's review of presidential orders and policies. Decisions of presidents or officials acting on their behalf can be challenged on the grounds that they are unauthorized by the Constitution or that they violate a constitutional rule. It is impossible to specify how frequently the Court strikes down presidential actions as unconstitutional, because it is often unclear whether an action by the executive branch should be considered presidential. But such decisions by the Court seem to be relatively rare, though the Court arguably has become more willing to challenge presidential policies in the past few decades.[12]

Over its history, the Court has invalidated a few significant actions by presidents on constitutional grounds. In *Ex parte Milligan* (1866), it held that President Abraham Lincoln had lacked the power to suspend the writ of habeas corpus for military prisoners during the Civil War. In *Youngstown Sheet and Tube Co. v. Sawyer* (1952), it declared that President Harry Truman had gone beyond his constitutional powers during the Korean War when he ordered the federal government to seize and operate major steel mills because their workers were preparing to go on strike. In *New York Times v. United States* (1971), the Court ruled that an effort by the Nixon administration to prevent publication of the "Pentagon Papers," an internal Defense Department report about the conduct of the Vietnam War, violated the First Amendment. More recently, the Court ruled in 2014 that some "recess appointments" of executive branch officials by President Obama were invalid under the constitutional provision that allows such appointments when the Senate is not in session, though the Court's interpretation of the recess appointment power was favorable to presidents in some important ways.[13]

Legal scholar David Rudenstine argued that the Court has been highly deferential to the president and the executive branch on issues relating to national security since the onset of the Cold War in the late 1940s.[14] His argument is supported by rulings such as the Court's decision in *Trump v. Hawaii* (2018), which upheld President Trump's proclamation limiting entry into the United States by citizens of eight countries. The steel seizure and Pentagon Papers cases make it clear that this deference is not total. But the Court generally has ruled against legal challenges to actions undertaken or directed by presidents that implicate national security.

Statutory Interpretation

Although the Court's interpretations of the Constitution generally receive the most attention, until the late 1940s constitutional decisions constituted only a small portion of the Court's work. Even today, a majority of the Court's decisions—in most terms, a substantial majority—involve interpretation of federal statutes rather than provisions of the Constitution.

Statutory interpretation may seem routine, but it can involve activism by the Court. For one thing, statutory decisions often determine whether an administrative agency interpreted a statute correctly when it wrote rules filling in the gaps that Congress left or when it applied the statute to specific situations. If the Court concludes that an agency has erred, it strikes down the agency's action as contrary to the statute. Further, the Court's interpretation of a statute can have considerable impact on the operation of that statute.

Interpretations of the procedural requirements for action by administrative agencies in the Administrative Procedure Act (APA) can also be consequential. Decisions based on the APA in 2019 and 2020 blocked the Trump administration's effort to include a question about citizenship on the 2020 Census and its initial effort to end the DACA program, under which certain people who arrived in the United States as children were protected from deportation and made eligible for some benefits for a period of time.[15]

More broadly, the Court often puts its own stamp on a statute through its interpretations of that statute over the years. The antitrust statutes that prohibit monopolistic practices are written in very general terms, and the Court's decisions interpreting those statutes over more than a century have effectively created most of the law of antitrust. The Court's decisions have also had major effects on the operation of statutes that regulate labor–management relations and environmental protection.

This role is exemplified by Title VII of the Civil Rights Act of 1964, the most important of the federal statutes that prohibit employment discrimination. As with many other statutes, Congress laid out the broad outlines of the law and left it to the other branches to fill in the gaps. Most important, Title VII did not define what kinds of actions constituted discrimination by race, sex, or other categories covered by the law.

▶ **Photo 5-2** A form for the 2020 U.S. census. In Department of Commerce v. New York (2019), the Court ruled that the Commerce Department had not offered proper justification for its decision to include a question on citizenship in the census.

After the Equal Employment Opportunity Commission and the lower federal courts began the process of interpreting Title VII, the Court heard its first case under the statute in 1971. It has now decided about 100 cases involving the meaning of Title VII, and in doing so it has resolved many major issues. For example, it has established and revised the guidelines that trial courts use to determine whether an employer has engaged in discrimination. It ruled that a company's policies could violate Title VII on the basis of their impact, even if the employer did not intend to discriminate.[16] It held that sexual harassment may constitute sex discrimination under Title VII and set up rules to determine when an employer is legally responsible for harassment.[17] It limited the use of class action lawsuits to challenge a company's employment practices.[18] And it ruled in 2020 that discrimination in firing based on sexual orientation or transgender status constitutes sex discrimination and thus is prohibited by Title VII.[19] Through these and other rulings, the Court has powerfully shaped federal policy on employment discrimination.

THE CONTENT OF POLICY

So far, I have examined the Supreme Court's agenda and its activism. A third aspect of the Court's role as a policy maker is the content of its policies. This content can best be understood in terms of the ideological direction of the Court's policies and the segments of society they benefit. Dividing the Court's history into eras is arbitrary. But it is useful to think of the period since the late nineteenth century as containing three eras, each with its own themes in the content of the Court's policies.

The 1890s to the 1930s

The Court's overall positions on the broad issues it addresses are very likely to change during a period of several decades. Such changes certainly occurred in the period that began in the 1890s and ended in the 1930s. But throughout that period, the Court was predominantly conservative in ideological terms.

Scrutinizing Economic Regulation

In 1915 the Court decided *South Covington & Cincinnati Street Railway Co. v. City of Covington*. The company, which ran streetcars between Covington, Kentucky, and Cincinnati, challenged several provisions of a Covington ordinance regulating its operations. The Court struck down some provisions on the ground that they constituted a burden on interstate commerce between Ohio and Kentucky. The Court also declared invalid a regulation stipulating that the temperature in the cars never be permitted to go below 50 degrees Fahrenheit—"We therefore think . . . this feature of the ordinance is unreasonable and cannot be sustained"—apparently on the ground that the regulation violated the Fourteenth Amendment by depriving the company of its property without due process of law.[20]

The *South Covington* case illustrates some important attributes of the Court's decisions from the 1890s to the late 1930s. During that period, the Court dealt primarily with economic issues. Most important, it frequently addressed challenges to the growing body of government regulations of business practices. From 1872 through 1910, according to one count, the Court heard 312 challenges to state policies that corporations had brought under the Fourteenth Amendment; in contrast, it heard only twenty-eight Fourteenth Amendment cases that involved racial discrimination, the concern that had led to adoption of the Fourteenth Amendment.[21]

The Court ruled against most constitutional challenges to federal and state policies, and it gave broad interpretations to some government powers.[22] But it also limited government regulatory powers in important respects, and its limits on regulation tightened over time. This development is reflected in the number of laws involving economic policy that the Court struck down each decade: forty-three from 1900 to 1909, 114 from 1910 to 1919, and 133 from 1920 to 1929.[23] The Court's attacks on government regulation peaked in the mid-1930s, when it struck down most of the major statutes in President Franklin Roosevelt's New Deal program to deal with the Great Depression.

The theme of limiting government regulatory powers was reflected in the Court's constitutional doctrines. At the national level, the Court gave narrow interpretations to congressional powers to tax and to regulate interstate commerce. In contrast, the Court gave a broad reading to the general limitation on federal power in the Tenth Amendment, using that provision to prohibit some federal actions on the ground that they interfered with state prerogatives. At the same time, the Court limited state powers in the economic sphere. It ruled in 1886 that corporations were "persons" with rights protected by the Fourteenth Amendment.[24] It also interpreted the Fourteenth Amendment requirement that state governments provide due process of law as an absolute prohibition of regulations that interfered unduly with the liberty and property rights of businesses. The Court's ruling against the streetcar temperature regulation was one of many such decisions.

Civil Liberties: A Limited Concern

Some of the Court's decisions limiting government regulation of business were based on constitutional protections of civil liberties. The Court decided relatively few cases involving the liberties of individuals in that era, but it gave some attention to that field.[25] Overall, the justices provided less protection for individual liberties than for the economic rights of businesses. The Court's limited support for racial equality was exemplified by *Plessy v. Ferguson* (1896), in which it promoted racial segregation by ruling that state governments could mandate "separate but equal" facilities for different racial groups. The Court reached some decisions that favored the rights of criminal defendants, but it held that only a few of the procedural rights for criminal defendants in the Bill of Rights were incorporated into the due process clause of the Fourteenth Amendment and thus were applicable to proceedings in state courts.[26] Late in that era, the Court ruled that the due process clause protected freedom of speech and freedom of the press from state violations. But in a series of decisions, it held that the federal government could prosecute people whose expressions arguably endangered military recruitment and other national security interests.[27]

The Court's Beneficiaries

The Court's mixed record in economic cases meant that there was no dominant beneficiary of its decisions. But to the extent that the Court limited government regulatory powers, the business community—especially large businesses—benefited from the Court's policies during this period. Of the regulatory legislation that the Court overturned or limited, much was aimed at the activities of large businesses. The railroads were the most prominent example. Although the Court allowed a good deal of government control over railroads, it also struck down a large body of railroad regulation.[28] In the decade from 1910 to 1919, the Court overturned forty-one state laws in challenges to government policies by railroad companies. Large corporations such as railroads might be considered the primary clientele of the Court from the 1890s to the 1930s.

A Long-Standing Position

The Court's conservatism during that period was not new; the dominant themes of the Court's work in earlier periods were also conservative. The Court provided considerable support for the rights of property holders and much less support for civil liberties outside the economic sphere.

Because of this history, some observers of the Supreme Court in the New Deal period concluded that the Court was a fundamentally conservative body. The historian Henry Steele Commager argued in 1943 that, with one possible exception, the Court had never intervened on behalf of the underprivileged; in fact, it frequently had blocked efforts by Congress to protect the underprivileged.[29] Two years earlier, Attorney General Robert Jackson, a future Supreme Court justice, reached this stark conclusion: "Never in its entire history can the Supreme Court be said to have for a single hour been representative of anything except the relatively conservative forces of its day."[30] Jackson may have exaggerated for effect, but he captured an important theme in the Court's history.

1937 to 1969

Even before Commager and Jackson described this record of conservatism, however, the Court was beginning a shift in its direction, which one historian called "the Constitutional Revolution of 1937." That revolution, he said,

> altered fundamentally the character of the Court's business, the nature of its decisions, and the alignment of its friends and foes. From the Marshall Court to the Hughes Court, the judiciary had been largely concerned with questions of property rights. After 1937 the most significant matters on the docket were civil liberties and other personal rights. . . . While from 1800 to 1937 the principal critics of the Supreme Court were social reformers and the main supporters people of means who were the principal beneficiaries of the Court's decisions, after 1937 roles were reversed, with liberals commending and conservatives censuring the Court.[31]

Acceptance of Government Economic Policy

In the first stage of the revolution, the Court abandoned the limits it had placed on government intervention in the economy. That step came quickly. In a series of decisions beginning in 1937, majorities accepted the constitutional power of government—especially the federal government—to regulate and manage the economy. This shift culminated in *Wickard v. Filburn* (1942), in which the Court held that federal power to regulate interstate commerce extended so far that it applied to a farmer who grew wheat for his own livestock.

This collective change of heart proved to be long lasting. The Court consistently upheld major economic legislation against constitutional challenges, striking down only one minor provision of the federal laws regulating business from the 1940s through the 1960s.[32] Supporting federal supremacy in economic matters, the Court invalidated many state laws on the ground that they impinged on the constitutional powers of the federal government or that they were preempted by federal statutes. But in other respects, it gave state governments more freedom to make economic policy.

The Court continued to address economic issues involving interpretations of federal statutes, including the set of laws enacted by Congress as part of President Franklin Roosevelt's New Deal program. In those decisions the Court generally followed the broad themes of the New Deal, such as support for labor unions in their contention with employers. In this respect too, the Court reinforced rather than challenged the policies of the other branches.

Support for Civil Liberties

In a 1938 decision, *United States v. Carolene Products Co.*, the Court signaled that there might be a second stage of the revolution. The case was one of many in which the Court upheld federal economic policies. But in what became known simply as "footnote 4," Justice Harlan Fiske Stone's opinion for the Court argued that the Court was justified in taking a tolerant view of government economic policies while it gave "more exacting judicial scrutiny" to policies that infringed on civil liberties.

This second stage took a long time to develop. The Court gave more support to civil liberties in the 1940s and 1950s than it had in earlier eras, but it did not make a strong and consistent commitment to the expansion of individual liberties. This stage of the revolution finally came to full fruition in the 1960s. Civil liberties issues dominated the Court's agenda for the first time. The Court's decisions expanded liberties in many areas, from civil rights of racial minority groups to procedural rights of criminal defendants to freedom of expression.

As in the preceding era, the Court's policy position was reflected in the constitutional doctrines it adopted. Departing from its earlier view, the Court of the 1960s ruled that nearly all the rights of criminal defendants in the Bill of Rights were incorporated into the Fourteenth Amendment and therefore applied to state proceedings. In interpreting the equal protection clause of the Fourteenth Amendment, the Court held that it would give government policies "strict scrutiny" if the groups that the policies disfavored were especially vulnerable or if the rights involved were especially important.

The Court's sympathies for civil liberties were symbolized by *Griswold v. Connecticut* (1965), which established a new constitutional right to privacy. A majority of the justices discovered that right in provisions of the Bill of Rights nearly two centuries after those provisions were written.

The Court's direction after 1937 is illustrated by the pattern of decisions declaring laws unconstitutional. Figure 5-1 shows the number of economic statutes and statutes limiting civil liberties that the Court overturned in each decade of the twentieth century and the first two decades of the twenty-first century. The number of economic laws the Court struck down declined precipitously between the 1920s and the 1940s and fell even lower in the 1960s. In contrast, the number of statutes struck down on civil liberties grounds became substantial in the 1940s and 1950s and rose sharply in the 1960s. The reversal of these trends in the 1980s is also noteworthy, and I will discuss its implications later in this section.

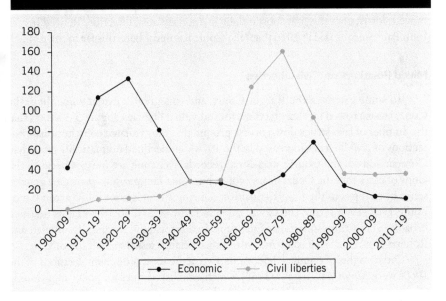

Figure 5-1 Number of Laws (Federal, State, and Local) Struck Down by the Supreme Court, in Economic and Civil Liberties Categories, by Decade, 1900–2019

Source: Calculated from information in Congressional Research Service, *The Constitution of the United States of America: Analysis and Interpretation* (Washington, D.C.: Government Printing Office, 2017), 2317–2619, updated to 2019.

Notes: The civil liberties category does not include laws supportive of civil liberties; laws in neither category are excluded.

The Court's Beneficiaries

The groups that the Court's policies benefited most were those that gained from expansions of legal protections for civil liberties. Among them were socially and economically disadvantaged groups, criminal defendants, and people who took unpopular political stands. In 1967, during the Court's most liberal period, an unsympathetic editorial cartoonist depicted the Court as a Santa Claus whose list of gift recipients included communists, pornographers, extremists, drug pushers, criminals, and perverts.[33] Whatever may be the accuracy of that characterization, it underlines the change in the Court.

The segment of the population that the Court supported most strongly was African Americans, especially in the fields of education and voting rights. The Court also made efforts to protect the civil rights movement when southern states attacked it in the late 1950s and 1960s. These beneficiaries were very different from the Court's primary beneficiaries in the late nineteenth and early twentieth centuries.

The Era Since 1969

It is even more difficult to characterize the Supreme Court's policies in a current era than in more distant eras, and that certainly is true of the period since the end of the Warren Court in 1969. Probably the best description is that the Court has moved slowly, unevenly, but substantially in a conservative direction. Retired Justice John Paul Stevens said in 2016 that "the Court has never been this far to the right."[34]

Mixed Positions on Civil Liberties

To some extent in the Burger Court, and to a greater extent since then, the Court has narrowed legal protections for individual liberties. Figure 5-1 shows that the number of laws struck down on the ground that they violated constitutional protections of civil liberties increased in the 1970s but declined dramatically after that. Comparisons of the Court's decisional records over time are inexact because the kinds of cases that the Court hears evolve, but those comparisons provide a general sense of changes in the Court's position. During the height of the Warren Court in the 1962–1968 terms, the Court ruled in favor of civil liberties claims (defined broadly) about three-quarters of the time; in contrast, the Burger, Rehnquist, and Roberts Courts have all ruled in favor of those claims less than half the time.[35]

On the rights of criminal defendants, two of the most prominent decisions of the 1960s were *Miranda v. Arizona* (1966), which established rules for police questioning of suspects, and *Mapp v. Ohio* (1961), which disallowed the use of evidence obtained through illegal searches in state prosecutions. The Court began to narrow both the *Miranda* and *Mapp* rules in the early 1970s and continued to do so in later years. The Court's policies on capital punishment have been complicated: it struck down existing death penalty laws in *Furman v. Georgia* (1972), it upheld a new set of laws in *Gregg v. Georgia* (1976), and since then it has had a mixed record on rules about the circumstances under which the death penalty can be imposed. In conjunction with Congress, the Court limited the use of habeas corpus petitions as a means for criminal defendants to challenge their convictions after their original appeals ran out.

On issues of equality, the Court moved in a conservative direction more slowly and unevenly. The Burger Court was the first to rule that laws discriminating against women violated the equal protection clause. It also held that northern-style school segregation, in which schools were not explicitly segregated by law, could violate equal protection. It generally gave broad interpretations to federal laws against discrimination but ruled against constitutional challenges to discrimination by private institutions that are connected to government.

The Rehnquist and Roberts Courts have interpreted federal antidiscrimination laws more narrowly. The Rehnquist Court approved the termination of court orders that maintained racial integration of public schools and limited the power of the federal government to enforce antidiscrimination laws against state governments. The Roberts Court effectively ended the supervision of state election laws under the Voting Rights Act, upheld state voter identification requirements, and ruled that gerrymandering of legislative districts to benefit one political party could not be challenged in federal court.[36] However, the Rehnquist Court continued to strengthen legal protections against sex discrimination in some important respects, and the Rehnquist and Roberts Courts were the first to strike down laws on the ground that they discriminated on the basis of sexual orientation.

The Court has had a complicated record on freedom of expression. The most prominent theme of decisions by the Rehnquist and Roberts Courts has been their protection for types of speech that attract the sympathies of conservatives rather than those of liberals. One example is the decisions striking down restrictions on spending in political campaigns. In contrast, the Court has given narrow interpretations to the speech rights of government employees, except for those who challenge requirements that they pay fees to labor unions for representing them in contract negotiations.[37]

The Burger Court and its successors have established rules that make it more difficult to win lawsuits for monetary damages against public officials for violations of rights.[38] In a series of cases, most of them involving the criminal justice system, the Court has used reversals of lower-court decisions to protect officials from such lawsuits.[39]

Conservatism on Economic Issues

Since 1969 the Court has not reversed its earlier expansion of government powers to regulate the economy, though it has narrowed federal power to regulate interstate commerce in some respects. Most recently, in *National Federation of Independent Business v. Sebelius* (2012), five justices agreed that the commerce power did not extend to a mandate that some people buy health insurance, though the Court upheld that mandate under the federal power to levy taxes.

In the current era, decisions based on the Constitution constitute only a small proportion of the Court's economic decisions, and the Court shapes economic policy primarily by interpreting federal statutes and procedural rules. Overall, it has taken positions that are increasingly conservative in the sense that they favor groups with relatively high economic status over competing groups with lower status. The proportion of economic decisions that were classified as liberal by one set of criteria was 71 percent in the 1962–1968 terms. That proportion dropped to 53 percent in the Burger Court (1969–1985 terms), 49 percent in the Rehnquist Court (1986–2004 terms), and 43 percent in the first fourteen terms of the Roberts Court.[40]

This decrease has been accompanied by policy changes in several economic fields. Since 1969, the Court has narrowed the application of antitrust laws to business practices, and it has given more support to employers in labor law. In environmental law, the Court has moved from an era in which it "seemed to embrace the mood" of the environmental movement to one in which it "adopted a more neutral and often even skeptical stance in its environmental decisions."[41]

The Court's economic conservatism is also reflected in rules that determine what kinds of legal claims can be brought to court.[42] In one set of decisions, it has interpreted a 1925 federal statute to allow enforcement of contract provisions that require employees and consumers to take their disputes against companies to arbitration rather than going to court.[43] The Court has also limited the circumstances under which consumers and employees can bring class action suits against businesses rather than suing as individuals.[44] And a pair of Roberts Court decisions that established more stringent requirements for carrying civil cases forward to trial have the greatest impact on individuals who sue companies and other defendants.[45]

The Court's Beneficiaries

By definition, the Court's economic conservatism in the current era has favored the interests of the business community where they conflict with the interests of employees and consumers. Since the 1990s the business community has also benefited from the Court's decisions in some fields of civil liberties. Some of the Court's expansions of protection for freedom of expression have come in cases brought by businesses, and corporations have been major beneficiaries of the Court's decisions limiting government regulation of electoral campaign funding. And just as the campaign funding decisions reinforced the Court's position that corporations have free speech rights, its decision in *Burwell v. Hobby Lobby Stores* (2014) established that at least some corporations have the right to religious freedom under the federal Religious Freedom Restoration Act.

Some commentators argue that the Roberts Court has a strong inclination to rule in favor of business, while others argue that the Court's recent pro-business tendencies are not especially strong.[46] Those differing judgments reflect the complexity of the Court's record in cases that affect business interests, a complexity that exists

▶ **Photo 5-3** Headquarters of the U.S. Chamber of Commerce. The Roberts Court has generally been favorable to the positions that the Chamber takes in cases on behalf of the business community.

for any broad area of the Court's work in any era. But the business community has enjoyed a high level of success in significant cases: according to one analysis, the Court took the side advocated by the U.S. Chamber of Commerce in amicus briefs 56 percent of the time in the last dozen years of the Rehnquist Court and 70 percent in the first fourteen years of the Roberts Court.[47] And overall, the Court's decisions and legal doctrines since 1969 are more supportive of the business community than they are of any other segment of society. Indeed, the breadth of the Court's support for the business community may exceed that of the late nineteenth and early twentieth centuries.

EXPLAINING THE COURT'S POLICIES

In the preceding sections, I described the Supreme Court's agenda, the extent of its activism, and the content of its policies in three historical periods. Each is summarized in Table 5-3.

The substantial changes in these aspects of the Court's policies over time underline the need to explain them. What forces can account for patterns in Supreme Court policies, especially their ideological content? Elaborating on ideas presented earlier in this chapter and in the book as a whole, I will suggest some explanations for those patterns.

The Court's Environment

Freedom from External Pressures

The life terms of Supreme Court justices give them considerable freedom from the rest of the government and the general public, a freedom that distinguishes the Court from the other branches of government. The Court's freedom is reflected in

Table 5-3	Summary of the Supreme Court's Policies during Three Historical Periods		
Period	**Predominant area on agenda**	**Extent of activism**	**Content of policy**
1890s–1937	Economic issues	Variable, increasing over time	Mixed, primarily conservative
1937–1969	Economic issues, then civil liberties	Initially low, then increasing; very high in 1960s	Generally liberal, very liberal in the 1960s
1969–2020	Civil liberties	High, declining in some respects after the 1970s	Initially moderate, then increasingly conservative

Note: Characterizations of each period are approximate and subject to disagreement. The extent of activism is gauged primarily by the striking down of government policies.

some of the positions that it takes in individual decisions. Political realities would not allow a legislature to support the right to burn the American flag as a form of political protest or to prohibit student-led prayers at football games. But the Court did make those decisions.[48]

More important, the Court has adopted some broad lines of policy that conflicted with the majority view in the general public and elsewhere in government. In the era from the 1890s to the 1930s, the Court was less favorable to regulations of business than the legislatures that adopted these regulations—regulations that had a good deal of public support as well. The Court of the 1960s was more favorable to individual liberties than the public and the other branches of government. Perhaps most striking were the Court's major expansions of the procedural rights of criminal defendants in the 1960s, when most of these expansions had only limited support outside the Court.

Influence from the Other Branches

The Court is not entirely free from external pressure. For one thing, Congress and the president have substantial powers over the Court and its decisions. The other branches frequently act to override Court decisions or to limit their impact. They seldom take action against the Court itself, but threats of such action—especially bills to limit the Court's jurisdiction—are common. The existence and use of these powers give the justices some incentive to avoid or minimize conflicts with the other branches.

It is difficult to ascertain the effect of this incentive on the Court's policies. On the whole, it appears, the justices have felt free to go their own way. But there are some specific episodes in which the other branches appeared to influence the course of Court policy. Examples include the Court's retreat from some of its expansions of civil liberties in the late 1950s and its refusal to decide whether American participation in the Vietnam War was unconstitutional.

More broadly, the Court has shown some caution about using judicial review to strike down significant national policies that enjoyed strong support in the other branches. It is noteworthy that the Court has struck down far more state laws than federal laws. The activism of the Warren Court in civil liberties was directed primarily at the states, and on the whole, that Court was sympathetic to the federal government.[49] Justices in the Rehnquist Court may have felt free to adopt new limitations on federal power because members of Congress during that period were largely sympathetic to those limitations.[50]

Societal Influence

It may be that the state of public opinion on particular issues exerts a subtle impact on justices. More important, however, are broader developments in society. Those developments affect justices' attitudes toward issues such as women's rights and terrorism, just as they affect the attitudes of the public as a whole. They can also exert a direct influence on the Court.

One form of influence involves what can be called a requirement of minimum support: the Court is unlikely to take a sustained policy position that lacks significant support outside the Court, especially support from the segments of society whose judgment is most important to its members. Justices may perceive that taking such positions would damage the Court's institutional position. More fundamentally, they may see positions that have little support as unreasonable in themselves. Further, the Court acts on the cases that litigants bring to it, and litigants are often supported by interest groups. In turn, the kinds of cases that litigants and groups bring to the Court reflect the state of society.

These influences are reflected in the two most distinctive patterns in the Court's policies during the twentieth century. The Court's resistance to government regulation of the economy before 1937 may have conflicted with the majority view in society, but most of the business community and much of the legal community strongly approved that position. The Court's expansions of civil liberties from the 1940s to the 1970s also benefited from social support. If these expansions were not always popular, they had significant support within society as a whole and within political and legal elite groups that were especially relevant to the justices.[51]

The most direct link between society and the Court is the litigation campaigns that bring cases to the Court and help to shape the justices' thinking. In the late nineteenth and early twentieth centuries, the corporate community employed much of the best legal talent in the United States to challenge the validity of regulatory statutes.[52] Litigation by corporations gave the Court frequent opportunities to strike down regulations of businesses. The effective advocacy of attorneys for corporations contributed to the successes that the business community achieved in the Court. Similarly, the Court's support for civil liberties in the era that followed was facilitated by the litigation campaigns of groups such as the NAACP Legal Defense Fund on issues related to race and the ACLU on a broad range of civil liberties issues. The efforts of these groups were especially important because many of the issues they litigated could not have reached the Court without their logistic and financial support.[53]

Changing public attitudes on some issues may help to account for the Court's increased conservatism since the 1970s. But more important has been the development of a stronger movement to provide intellectual and financial support for conservative positions on legal issues. Conservative legal groups have engaged in litigation campaigns on both economic and civil liberties issues. Their efforts have given the Court opportunities to move legal doctrine in a conservative direction.

Policy Preferences and the Appointment Power

Whether the Court makes use of such opportunities depends heavily on who the justices are. The justices' high level of autonomy gives them considerable freedom to make their own judgments about the issues they face. Those judgments are based in part on the justices' assessments of the legal merits of cases. But because the questions before the Court seldom have clear legal answers, justices' policy preferences are the primary basis for the positions they take.

The importance of policy preferences suggests that a great deal about the Court's policies can be explained simply and directly: during any given period in the Court's history, its policies have largely reflected the collective preferences of its members. Most of the justices who served from the 1890s through the early 1930s were political conservatives who questioned the desirability of government regulation of business enterprises. In contrast, the justices who came to the Court from the late 1930s through the mid-1960s were predominantly liberals who supported government management of the economy and, in most instances, broader protections of civil liberties.

Collectively, the justices joining the Court since 1969 have been more conservative on civil liberties and economic issues than the justices of the preceding period. In 2007, Justice John Paul Stevens underlined how much the Court's membership had changed in ideological terms: "Including myself, every judge who's been appointed to the Court since Lewis Powell [selected in 1971] has been more conservative than his or her predecessor. Except maybe Justice Ginsburg. That's bound to have an effect on the court."[54]

An explanation of the Court's direction that focuses on the justices' policy preferences is not entirely satisfying, because it does not show why certain preferences predominated in the Court during particular periods. One reason is that some values were dominant in the nation during the periods in which justices were developing their attitudes. Another is that the justices came from backgrounds that instilled particular values in them. Most important, the higher-status backgrounds that predominated during most of the Court's history fostered sympathy for the views and interests of higher-status segments of society. Further, the prevailing ideology in elite segments of the legal profession shapes the views of its members, including future Supreme Court justices.

The most direct source of the Court's collective preferences, however, is the decisions that presidents make in appointing justices.[55] The predominant pattern of Supreme Court policy at any given time tends to reflect the identities of the presidents who selected the justices. If a series of appointments is made by conservative presidents, the Court is likely to become a conservative body. And because vacancies occur in the Court fairly often—historically, about every two years on average—most presidents can affect the Court's direction significantly.

Robert Dahl argued that for this reason, "the policy views dominant on the Court are never for long out of line with the policy views dominant among the lawmaking majorities of the United States."[56] In Dahl's judgment, the president's power to make appointments, with Senate confirmation of nominees, limits the frequency with which the Court overturns major federal statutes: justices generally have the same views about policy as the president and members of Congress, so they seldom upset the policies of these branches. I think there is much to Dahl's argument. But because of several complicating factors, the appointment power produces only imperfect control by "lawmaking majorities."

One factor is time lag. Most justices serve for many years, and this is especially true in the current era. As a result, the Court usually reflects the views of past presidents and Senates more than those of the current president and Senate. The lag varies in length, chiefly because presidents have differing opportunities to make appointments. Richard Nixon selected four justices during his six years in office, but Bill Clinton, George W. Bush, and Barack Obama each chose only two justices in eight years. Jimmy Carter did even worse. The absence of vacancies during his single term made him the only president to serve at least four years without appointing any justices. As a result, every appointment to the Court between 1969 and 1992 was made by a Republican president.

Further, a president's influence on the Court depends in part on its ideological configuration and on which members leave it. Both vacancies that Obama filled resulted from the retirement of a liberal justice, so his two appointments had little impact on the Court's overall ideological position.

Another complicating factor is deviation of justices from presidential expectations. Presidents usually get most of what they want from their appointees, but that is not a certainty. The unprecedented liberalism of the Court in the 1960s resulted largely from Dwight Eisenhower's miscalculations in nominating Earl Warren and William Brennan. The Rehnquist Court was not as conservative as it could have been because Sandra Day O'Connor, Anthony Kennedy, and especially David Souter diverged from the expectations of the Republican presidents who chose them. Such unexpected results are far less likely today than in most past eras because of the ideological gulf between the two parties and the greater care that presidents take in choosing justices. But they are still possible.

The role of chance in shaping the Court's general direction should be underlined. Chance plays a part in the timing of Court vacancies and in the performance of justices relative to their appointers' expectations. For that matter, the identity of the president who fills vacancies in the Court sometimes reflects a considerable degree of chance. John Kennedy in 1960, Richard Nixon in 1968, and Donald Trump in 2016 all won by substantial margins in the electoral college, but Kennedy and Nixon had only narrow victories in the popular vote and Trump received fewer votes than his opponent. George W. Bush in 2000 had a narrow electoral college victory and lost in the popular vote. But all four presidents made appointments that significantly affected the Court's policies.

The policy orientations of the Supreme Court between the 1890s and the 1960s reflected the existence of strong lawmaking majorities during two periods: the conservative Republican governments that dominated much of the period from the Civil War to the Great Depression and the twelve-year tenure of Franklin Roosevelt that was accompanied by heavily Democratic Senates. These orientations also reflected patterns of resignations, retirements, and deaths; the unexpected policy stances of some justices; and other factors that were a good deal less systematic. And if these factors had operated differently in the era since 1969, the current Court might be less conservative—or even more so—than the one that actually exists. The forces that shape the Court's policy positions, like so much about the Court, operate in complex ways.

CONCLUSION

I have examined several issues relating to the Supreme Court's policy outputs in this chapter. A few conclusions merit emphasis.

First, in some periods the Court's policy making has had fairly clear themes. During the first part of the twentieth century, the dominant theme was scrutiny of government economic policies. Later in that century the primary theme was scrutiny of policies and practices that impinged on individual liberties. In each instance, the theme was evident in both the Court's agenda and the content of its decisions.

Second, these themes and the Court's work as a whole reflect both the justices' policy preferences and the influence of the Court's environment. The Court's policies are largely what its members would like them to be. But the Court is subject to some external influences that shape its policies in direct and indirect ways. And the president's appointment power creates a link between the justices' policy preferences and their political environment.

Finally, the Court's role as a policy maker, significant though it is, has major limitations. The Court gives considerable attention to some areas of policy but scarcely touches others. Some critical matters, such as foreign policy, are left almost entirely to the other branches of government. Even in the areas to which the Court gives the most attention, it seldom disturbs the basic features of national policy.

To a considerable degree, the significance of the Supreme Court as a policy maker depends on the impact of its decisions, the subject of Chapter 6. After examining the effects of the Court's decisions, I can assess the Court's role in the policy-making process more comprehensively.

NOTES

1. Under these definitions, to take two examples, all immigration cases and the great majority of criminal cases would fall into the civil liberties category.
2. The discussion of agenda change in this section is drawn in part from Richard L. Pacelle Jr., *The Transformation of the Supreme Court's Agenda: From the New Deal to the Reagan Administration* (Boulder, Colo.: Westview Press, 1991); Richard L. Pacelle Jr., "The Dynamics and Determinants of Agenda Change in the Rehnquist Court," in *Contemplating Courts*, ed. Lee Epstein (Washington, D.C.: CQ Press, 1995), 251–274; and Drew Noble Lanier, *Of Time and Judicial Behavior: United States Supreme Court Agenda-Setting and Decision-Making, 1888–1997* (Selinsgrove, Pa.: Susquehanna University Press, 2003), chap. 3. Numbers of cases in broad policy areas and involving particular issues were calculated from data collected and presented by Pacelle in his publications and from data in the Supreme Court Database at http://scdb.wustl.edu. The Pacelle studies included cases if the Court issued an opinion of more than one page in length; cases from the Database were counted if the Court issued a decision after oral argument.

3. These and other data in this paragraph are taken from Pacelle, *The Transformation of the Supreme Court's Agenda*, 56–57. The civil liberties category includes cases classified by Pacelle as due process, substantive rights, and equality.
4. This number and other numbers of laws struck down in this chapter are based on data in Congressional Research Service, *The Constitution of the United States of America: Analysis and Interpretation, 2017 Edition* (Washington, D.C.: Government Printing Office, 2017), 2327–2619, updated through 2019. There are some errors and inconsistencies in the Congressional Research Service data, and that organization is currently revising its count. Keith Whittington's careful count of cases, which includes decisions interpreting a statute narrowly to avoid constitutional problems, identified nearly twice as many laws struck down by 2017 (a total of 345). Keith E. Whittington, *Repugnant Laws: Judicial Review of Acts of Congress from the Founding to the Present* (Lawrence: University Press of Kansas, 2019), 318–319. However, the trends over time in the two counts are quite similar.
5. Linda Camp Keith, *The U.S. Supreme Court and the Judicial Review of Congress* (New York: Peter Lang, 2008), 26; Whittington, *Repugnant Laws*, 318–319.
6. The distinctions made in the paragraphs that follow are drawn chiefly from Robert A. Dahl, "Decision-Making in a Democracy: The Supreme Court as a National Policy-Maker," *Journal of Public Law* 6 (Fall 1957): 279–295.
7. Among these decisions were *United States v. Butler* (1936) and *Schechter Poultry Corp. v. United States* (1935).
8. *Bolger v. Youngs Drug Products Corp.* (1983).
9. See Keith E. Whittington, *Political Foundations of Judicial Supremacy: The Supreme Court and Constitutional Leadership in U.S. History* (Princeton, N.J.: Princeton University Press, 2007).
10. These decisions were, in order, *United States v. Booker* (2005), *National Federation of Independent Business v. Sebelius* (2012), and *United States v. Windsor* (2013).
11. The decisions were, in the order they were presented in the text, *Collins v. Virginia* (2018), *Flowers v. Mississippi* (2019), *Lucia v. Securities and Exchange Commission* (2018), and *Masterpiece Cakeshop v. Colorado Civil Rights Commission* (2018).
12. Robert Scigliano, "The Presidency and the Judiciary," in *The Presidency and the Political System*, 3rd ed., ed. Michael Nelson (Washington, D.C.: CQ Press, 1990), 471–499; David A. Yalof, "The Presidency and the Judiciary," in *The Presidency and the Political System*, 9th ed., ed. Michael Nelson (Washington, D.C.: CQ Press, 2010), 456–459.
13. *National Labor Relations Board v. Noel Canning* (2014).
14. David Rudenstine, *The Age of Deference: The Supreme Court, National Security, and the Constitutional Order* (New York: Oxford University Press, 2016).
15. The decisions were *Department of Commerce v. New York* (2019) and *Department of Homeland Security v. Regents of the University of California* (2020).
16. *Griggs v. Duke Power Co.* (1971).
17. *Meritor Savings Bank v. Vinson* (1986); *Burlington Industries v. Ellerth* (1998).
18. *Wal-Mart Stores, Inc. v. Dukes* (2011).
19. *Bostock v. Clayton County* (2020).
20. *South Covington & Cincinnati Street Railway Co. v. City of Covington*, 235 U.S. 537, 549 (1915).
21. Charles Wallace Collins, *The Fourteenth Amendment and the States* (Boston: Little, Brown, 1912), 138.
22. Collins, *The Fourteenth Amendment and the States*, 82, 138; William G. Ross, *A Muted Fury: Populists, Progressives, and Labor Unions Confront the Courts, 1890–1937* (Princeton, N.J.: Princeton University Press, 1994).

23. To obtain these figures and others that are presented later in the chapter, I categorized decisions that struck down laws according to whether they pertained to economics, civil liberties, or other subjects. The criteria that I used were necessarily arbitrary; other criteria would have resulted in somewhat different totals, though the general patterns would not have changed.

24. *Santa Clara County v. Southern Pacific Railroad Co.* (1886).

25. This discussion draws from John Braeman, *Before the Civil Rights Revolution: The Old Court and Individual Rights* (Westport, Conn.: Greenwood Press, 1988).

26. *Twining v. New Jersey* (1908).

27. See, for example, *Schenck v. United States* (1917). See also David Rabban, *Free Speech in Its Forgotten Years* (New York: Cambridge University Press, 1997).

28. James W. Ely Jr., *Railroads and American Law* (Lawrence: University Press of Kansas, 2001); Richard C. Cortner, *The Iron Horse and the Constitution: The Railroads and the Transformation of the Fourteenth Amendment* (Westport, Conn.: Greenwood Press, 1993).

29. Henry Steele Commager, "Judicial Review and Democracy," *Virginia Quarterly Review* 19 (Summer 1943): 428. The possible exception was *Wing v. United States* (1896).

30. Robert H. Jackson, *The Struggle for Judicial Supremacy* (New York: Knopf, 1941), 187.

31. William E. Leuchtenburg, *The Supreme Court Reborn: The Constitutional Revolution in the Age of Roosevelt* (New York: Oxford University Press, 1995), 235.

32. *United States v. Cardiff* (1952).

33. Ken Alexander, *San Francisco Examiner*, December 14, 1967, 42.

34. Evan Thomas, *First: Sandra Day O'Connor* (New York: Random House, 2019), 380.

35. These proportions are calculated from data in the Supreme Court Database, with cases included if they were decided after oral argument and if they fell in issue areas 1–5.

36. The Voting Rights Act decision was *Shelby County v. Holder* (2013); the voter registration decisions were *Crawford v. Marion County Election Board* (2008) and *Husted v. A. Philip Randolph Institute* (2018); the gerrymandering decision was *Rucho v. Common Cause* (2019).

37. *Garcetti v. Ceballos* (2006); *Janus v. American Federation of State, County, and Municipal Employees* (2018).

38. Sarah Staszak, *No Day in Court: Access to Justice and the Politics of Judicial Retrenchment* (New York: Oxford University Press, 2015), chap. 6; William Baude, "Is Qualified Immunity Unlawful?" *California Law Review* 106 (February 2018): 45–90.

39. Recent examples include *District of Columbia v. Wesby* (2018), *Kisela v. Hughes* (2018), and *City of Escondido v. Emmons* (2019).

40. Economic cases were defined as those in issue areas 7 and 8 in the Supreme Court Database. See note 35.

41. Jonathan Z. Cannon, *Environment in the Balance: The Green Movement and the Supreme Court* (Cambridge, Mass.: Harvard University Press, 2015), 2.

42. Stephen B. Burbank and Sean Farhang, *Rights and Retrenchment: The Counterrevolution Against Federal Litigation* (New York: Cambridge University Press, 2017), chap. 4.

43. Among these decisions are *Circuit City Stores, Inc. v. Adams* (2001) and *Kindred Nursing Centers v. Clark* (2017).

44. These decisions, some of which also relate to arbitration agreements, include *AT&T Mobility LLC v. Concepcion* (2011), *Wal-Mart Stores, Inc. v. Dukes* (2011), *Epic Systems Corp. v. Lewis* (2018), and *Lamps Plus, Inc. v. Varela* (2019).

45. The decisions were *Bell Atlantic v. Twombly* (2007) and *Ashcroft v. Iqbal* (2009).

46. Jonathan H. Adler, ed., *Business and the Roberts Court* (New York: Oxford University Press, 2016); "Symposium: Business in the Roberts Court," *Case Western Reserve Law Review* 67 (Spring 2017): 681–896.

47. Brian R. Frazelle, "Corporations and the Supreme Court: A Muted Term Belies a Supreme Court Deeply Polarized on Corporate Power," Constitutional Accountability Center, September 2019, 3, https://www.theusconstitution.org/think_tank/corporations-and-the-supreme-court-a-muted-term-belies-a-supreme-court-deeply-polarized-on-corporate-power-2018-2019-term/.

48. *Texas v. Johnson* (1989); *Santa Fe Independent School District v. Doe* (2000).

49. Lucas A. Powe Jr., *The Warren Court and American Politics* (Cambridge, Mass.: Harvard University Press, 2000).

50. See Keith E. Whittington, "Taking What They Give Us: Explaining the Court's Federalism Offensive," *Duke Law Journal* 51 (2001): 477–520.

51. See Powe, *The Warren Court and American Politics*.

52. Benjamin Twiss, *Lawyers and the Constitution* (Princeton, N.J.: Princeton University Press, 1942).

53. Charles R. Epp, *The Rights Revolution: Lawyers, Activists, and Supreme Courts in Comparative Perspective* (Chicago: University of Chicago Press, 1998), chaps. 3–4.

54. Jeffrey Rosen, "The Dissenter," *New York Times Magazine*, September 23, 2007, 52–53.

55. See David Cottrell, Charles R. Shipan, and Richard J. Anderson, "The Power to Appoint: Presidential Nominations and Change on the Supreme Court," *Journal of Politics* 81 (July 2019): 1057–1068.

56. Dahl, "Decision-Making in a Democracy," 285.

CHAPTER SIX

THE COURT'S IMPACT

When the Supreme Court rules on a controversial issue such as abortion or affirmative action, its decision has symbolic importance: it constitutes a victory for one side on the issue and a defeat for the other side. But even more important are the practical effects of the Court's decisions on government policy and on society as a whole.

Most observers of the Court believe that its decisions have quite substantial effects. That belief helps to explain the intense interest in appointments to the Court and the litigation campaigns that are aimed at shaping the Court's decisions. But there is considerable debate about the validity of that belief among scholars. Focusing on social change, political scientist Gerald Rosenberg argued that the Court has only a limited impact on conditions such as racial equality. In response, some other scholars have contended that the Court has considerable capacity to shape policy and society.[1]

This chapter probes the impact of Supreme Court decisions and the forces that shape their impact. I begin by examining what happens to litigants after the Court decides their cases. In the remainder of the chapter, I discuss the broader effects of the Court's policies: their implementation by judges and administrators, responses to them from legislatures and chief executives, and their effects on society as a whole. After considering the evidence about those broader effects, I offer some conclusions about the Court's impact on public policy and the lives of people in the United States.

OUTCOMES FOR THE LITIGANTS

Whatever else it does, a Supreme Court decision affects the parties in the case. But the Court's ruling does not always determine the final outcome for the two sides. Indeed, a great deal can happen to the parties after the Court rules in their case.

One type of response comes from the lower court whose ruling the Court had reviewed. If the Court reverses or vacates a ruling, most of the time it remands (sends back) the case to the lower court for "further proceedings consistent with this opinion" or similar language. When it remands a case, the Court sometimes gives the lower court little leeway on what to do. In that situation, the judges on that court almost always follow the Supreme Court's lead. To take one example, in 2019 a panel of the federal court of appeals for the Third Circuit in Philadelphia wrote a short opinion vacating its decision in a Fifth Amendment case in compliance with the Supreme Court's recent decision in the case.[2]

But often the lower court has considerable discretion about how to apply the Court's ruling on remand, and sometimes it rules in favor of the party that had lost in the Supreme Court. In 2017 the Fifth Circuit Court of Appeals in New Orleans held that the question of whether a dispute should be decided by a court or by an arbitrator under a contract between the two businesses in the case should be resolved in the courts. Two years later the Supreme Court overturned that judgment, ruling that the doctrine applied by the Fifth Circuit was inconsistent with a federal statute. But the Court left it up to the Fifth Circuit to determine whether the contract in this case did give an arbitrator power to determine whether a dispute should go to arbitration. The court of appeals ruled that it did not, so the company that had won in its earlier ruling and lost in the Supreme Court won once again.[3]

After such a reinstating decision, the losing party can ask the Supreme Court to consider the case once again, and occasionally the Court accepts that request.[4] One example was the question of whether a Texas man named Bobby James Moore had an intellectual disability that made him ineligible for the death penalty. The Texas Court of Criminal Appeals said that Moore did not have a disability, but in 2017 the Supreme Court found several errors in the Texas court's analysis of the case and remanded the case to that court for reconsideration. After the Supreme Court's remand in the case, the Texas court once again ruled that Moore did not have a disability. The Supreme Court heard the case again in 2019 and overruled the Texas court a second time—this time reaching a definitive ruling that Moore had a disability.[5]

The Court's interpretation of the constitutional protection against double jeopardy allows a criminal defendant to be retried after a conviction is appealed and overturned on procedural grounds. Prosecutors often do carry such a case forward, and the retrial sometimes produces a second conviction. To take one prominent example, Ernesto Miranda was convicted a second time after the Court reversed his conviction in *Miranda v. Arizona* (1966). Although his statements to the police could not be used in the retrial, other evidence was sufficient to produce a conviction.

The specific case that the Court decides is sometimes resolved outside the courts. For one thing, the Court's ruling can spur the two parties to settle the case between themselves. In *Lewis v. Clarke* (2017), the Court reached a ruling on the immunity of Native American tribes from lawsuits in a case that arose from an auto accident. Two years later, the two sides reached an out-of-court settlement in the case.[6]

In 2012 the Court ruled that it was unconstitutional for a statute to require a life sentence without the possibility of parole for someone convicted of murder as a juvenile. Four years later the Court held in *Montgomery v. Louisiana* (2016) that this ruling applied to prisoners whose convictions and sentences were final by 2012. Montgomery, who had been imprisoned in 1963, took the steps required to be eligible for parole and then applied. But the Louisiana parole board twice denied him parole in 2019, so he remained in prison.[7]

IMPLEMENTATION OF SUPREME COURT POLICIES

With occasional exceptions, the outcome of a case for the litigants is not nearly as important as the broader effects of the legal rules that the Court lays down in its opinions. Like statutes or presidential orders, these rules have to be implemented by administrators and judges. Judges are obliged to apply the Court's interpretations of the law whenever they are relevant to a case. When the Idaho Supreme Court in 2015 asserted that state courts did not have to accept the U.S. Supreme Court's interpretations of federal statutes under some circumstances, the Court issued a sharp rebuke of the Idaho court.[8] For their part, administrators at all levels of government, such as cabinet officers and police officers, are expected to follow Court-created rules that are relevant to their work.

The ways that judges and administrators actually apply the rules of law that the Court issues help to determine the ultimate impact of the Court's decisions. The responses of these officials range from complete rejection of the Court's rulings to enthusiastic acceptance and extension of those rulings. This range of responses can be described in terms of the effectiveness with which decisions are implemented. After discussing conditions that help determine the level of effectiveness, I will look more closely at three issues the Court has addressed and then consider the implications of the evidence on implementation of the Court's decisions.

Explaining the Effectiveness of Implementation

How well Supreme Court decisions are implemented depends on several conditions. The key conditions relate to communication of policies to relevant officials, the motivations of those officials to follow or resist the Court's policies, the Court's authority, and the sanctions it can use to deter noncompliance with its rulings.

Communication

Judges and administrators can carry out Supreme Court decisions well only if they know what the Court wants them to do. The communication process begins with the Court's opinions. Ideally, an opinion would state the Court's legal rules with sufficient precision and specificity that any official who reads the opinion knows how to apply those rules to any other case or situation. But it can be difficult to achieve that goal, and sometimes the Court deliberately leaves an issue open for lower courts to consider further.

The Court can reduce its ambiguity by deciding a series of cases that fills in needed detail. Sometimes, however, the Court does not follow up on an ambiguous decision. The Court ruled in 2008 that the Second Amendment protects individual possession and use of firearms,[9] but since then it has said very little about how that right applies to specific kinds of gun regulations. As a result, lower courts were left to review regulations without much guidance from the Court. When the Court does follow up a ruling with additional decisions, it sometimes fosters ambiguity rather than clarity by taking a position that conflicts with its original ruling in some respects. Such conflicts can result when the Court's membership changes and the new justices are unenthusiastic about the Court's original ruling.

Ambiguity does more than create uncertainty for judges and administrators; it also leaves them with more freedom to reach judgments that accord with their own views. If they disagree with a Supreme Court decision, they may use their freedom to limit the impact of that decision. Justice Clarence Thomas contended in a 2018 opinion that the Court's lack of clarity on the scope of gun rights was allowing lower-court judges to interpret those rights narrowly in ways that were inconsistent with the Court's 2008 decision.[10]

Whether the Court's position on an issue is clear or ambiguous, its decisions must be transmitted to relevant judges and administrators. That transmission is not guaranteed. Even judges are unlikely to monitor the Supreme Court's output to identify relevant decisions. Instead, decisions come to the attention of officials through other channels.

One channel is the mass media. But most decisions garner little or no coverage in the mass media, and what the media report is sometimes misleading.

Attorneys communicate decisions to some officials. Through their arguments in court proceedings and administrative hearings, lawyers bring precedents to the attention of judges and administrators. Staff lawyers in administrative agencies often inform agency personnel of relevant decisions. But administrators such as teachers usually lack that source of information.

Another channel of information is professional hierarchies. State trial judges often become aware of the Court's decisions when they are cited by state appellate courts. Police officers learn of decisions from superiors in their departments. There is considerable potential for misinformation in this process, especially when the communicator disagrees with a decision. State supreme courts and police officials sometimes convey negative views of court decisions that expand the rights of criminal defendants when they inform their subordinates of those decisions.

Awareness of Supreme Court decisions tends to fade over time. In 1989 and 1990 the Court struck down criminal laws that prohibited desecration of the American flag, laws aimed at flag burning in political protests. The decisions received enormous attention at the time. Despite those decisions, prosecutions are occasionally brought under old state flag-desecration laws. In a 2014 case that involved such a prosecution in Missouri, the arresting police officer and the prosecuting attorney said they had not known about the Court's decisions.[11]

Effective communication of decisions depends on the receivers as well as the channels of transmission. Legally trained officials are the most capable of understanding the Court's decisions and their implications. Police officers and other non-lawyers who work regularly with the law also have some advantage in interpreting decisions. On the whole, administrators who work outside the legal system have the greatest difficulty in interpreting what they learn about Supreme Court rulings.

These communication problems have an obvious impact. Policy makers who do not know of a decision cannot implement it, and those who misunderstand the Court's requirements will not follow them as intended. Successful implementation of the Court's policies requires both clarity in those policies and their effective transmission to the people responsible for carrying them out.

Policy Preferences and Self-Interest

If policy makers know of a Supreme Court ruling that is relevant to a choice they face, they must decide what to do about that ruling. Often, their decision is easy because there is good reason to carry out the Court's ruling faithfully: it is consistent with their own policy preferences and their self-interest. Thus, a great deal of compliance with the Court's interpretations of the law is easy in the sense that the Court asks people to do something they are happy to do. For instance, Cabinet departments in the Trump administration readily carried out decisions that favored government assistance to religious organizations and exemptions from certain legal requirements for those organizations, because these decisions were consistent with the views of department administrators.[12]

By the same token, when a Supreme Court ruling conflicts with officials' self-interest or their conceptions of good policy, resistance to that ruling becomes a possibility. Following the Supreme Court's lead seldom impinges directly on the self-interest of judges on appellate courts. When appellate judges do not implement decisions fully, the most common reason is a conflict between those decisions and their policy preferences. That conflict frequently follows ideological lines. For a long time, the Ninth Circuit Court of Appeals on the West Coast was the most liberal federal appellate court, distinctly more liberal than the Supreme Court. As a result, judges on the Ninth Circuit sometimes gave narrow interpretations to conservative decisions by the Court.

Trial judges and administrators may also disagree with decisions on policy grounds, as many teachers and school administrators do with the Court's rulings limiting religious observances in public schools. In contrast with appellate judges, however, their self-interest often comes into play as well. This is especially true when Supreme Court policies threaten officials' success in carrying out their missions. Police officers, for instance, tend to see rulings that create limits on searches and questioning of suspects as weakening their ability to investigate and solve crimes.

Another example arises from a series of decisions between 1983 and 2011 in which the Court established that criminal defendants could not be jailed if they were unable to pay fines or other fees. But local governments have increasingly imposed fees and fines on defendants as a means to raise money, and they use the threat of jail to pressure defendants to find a way to pay those costs. As part of local governments, trial judges are usually willing to cooperate with these efforts. As a result, a great many people with limited economic resources are jailed in violation of the Court's decisions.[13]

Elected judges and executive branch officials have an incentive not to carry out Supreme Court decisions that are highly unpopular with their constituents. This is true, for instance, when following the Court's rules would require ruling in favor of criminal defendants who are charged with serious crimes. Federal judges with life terms need not worry about keeping their positions, but they still may want to avoid incurring public wrath on highly visible issues.

The Court's Authority

When judges or administrators dislike a Supreme Court decision, they do not always rebel. Indeed, it is quite common for them to carry out such decisions. The primary reason is that they accept both the Supreme Court's authority to make conclusive judgments about the law and their own obligation to comply with the Court's decisions. This acceptance, broadly shared among judges and administrators, fosters faithful implementation of Supreme Court decisions.

The impact of the Court's authority is occasionally made explicit in lower-court opinions expressing their disagreement with Court decisions that they feel obliged to follow. One judge on a federal court of appeals in 2018 described his strong disagreement with the Supreme Court's rulings on state regulation of abortion but added that "I am not on the Supreme Court, and as a federal appellate judge, I am bound by my oath to follow all of the Supreme Court's precedents, whether I agree with them or not."[14] Another court of appeals judge wrote in 2019 of a similar disagreement with the Court's decisions limiting the legal liability of public officials for violations of rights. "That said," he added, "as a middle-management circuit judge, I take direction from the Supreme Court. . . . We must respect the Court's exacting instructions—even as it is proper, in my judgment, to respectfully voice unease with them."[15]

Those expressions symbolize the strength of the Court's authority for judges, who have been socialized to follow the lead of higher courts and who benefit themselves from acceptance of judicial authority. It is highly unusual for a judge to reject the Court's authority directly. This does not mean that lower courts always follow the Court's lead fully. Judges sometimes give narrow interpretations to Court decisions with which they disagree, thereby limiting the impact of those decisions while acknowledging the Court's authority.[16] In some instances, these narrow interpretations seem inconsistent with the Court's rulings. But because most judges fully accept their duty to follow the Court's lead, even that indirect noncompliance is the exception to the rule.

The Court's authority extends to administrators, and it helps to foster faithful implementation of decisions by administrative bodies. For instance, some public school officials have eliminated religious observances they would prefer to maintain because they accept their duty to follow Supreme Court rulings.[17] On the whole, however, the Court's authority is weaker for administrators than for judges. Administrative bodies are somewhat removed from the judicial system and its norm of obedience to higher courts, and relatively few administrators have had the law school training that supports this norm. As a result, administrative officials find it easier to justify deviation from Supreme Court policies than judges do.

The Court's authority tends to decline as organizational distance from the Court increases. State trial judges typically orient themselves more closely to appellate courts in their state than to the Supreme Court, which is several steps away from them in the judicial hierarchy. For administrators at the grassroots level, both state courts and administrative superiors may seem far more relevant to their policy choices than the Supreme Court does.

Sanctions for Disobedience

When its authority is not sufficient to secure positive responses to its rulings, the Court can employ sanctions to promote faithful implementation of those rulings. For judges, the most common sanction is reversal. If a court does not follow an applicable Supreme Court policy, the losing litigant may appeal the case and secure a reversal of the judge's decision. The Court sometimes uses reversals as a means to get compliance from lower courts, especially when it issues summary reversals of decisions without hearing oral argument. The Court's explicit or implicit message in most of the opinions that accompany summary reversals is that the lower court simply failed to follow clear commands in the Court's decisions. A 2018 opinion, for instance, said that a court of appeals opinion "does not comply" with a three-year-old decision by the Court.[18]

The threat of reversal does not always produce compliance. The primary reason is that reversal has limits as a sanction. Judges who feel strongly about an issue may be willing to accept reversals on that issue as the price for following their personal convictions. For that matter, failure to follow the Supreme Court's lead does not always lead to reversal. The Court reviews a very small proportion of the decisions by federal courts of appeals and state supreme courts. Further, the great majority of judges are reviewed by a court other than the Supreme Court, and the reviewing court may share their opposition to the Court's policies.

For administrators, the most common sanction is a court order that demands compliance with a decision. If an agency fails to follow an applicable Supreme Court policy, someone who is injured by its failure may bring a lawsuit to compel compliance. Administrative agencies find any lawsuit unwelcome because of the trouble and expense it entails. A successful lawsuit is even worse, because an order to comply with a Supreme Court rule puts an agency under judicial scrutiny and can embarrass agency officials. The agency may also be required to pay monetary damages to the person who brought the lawsuit.

But this sanction has weaknesses. Most important, it can be used only if people sue agencies, and often agency noncompliance does not lead to any lawsuits.

Most school religious observances that violate the Court's decisions are never challenged in court, either because nobody in the community disagrees with those observances or because the negative consequences of bringing a lawsuit—especially hostile reactions from people in the community—discourage such challenges. If a lawsuit is threatened or actually brought, whether on school religion or another issue, agencies can usually change their practices in time to avoid serious costs.

Still, to follow a policy that conflicts with a Supreme Court ruling carries risks that officials generally prefer to avoid. This preference helps to account for the frequency with which administrative organizations take the initiative to eliminate practices that the Court has prohibited.

Police practices in searches and seizures illustrate both the strengths and limitations of sanctions.[19] Under *Mapp v. Ohio* (1961), noncompliance with constitutional rules for searches generally prevents the use of the seized evidence in court. Largely for this reason, officers frequently comply with rules they would prefer to ignore. Indeed, decisions that restrict searches of particular types can have quite substantial effects on police practices.[20]

But the sanction of throwing out illegally seized evidence is imperfect. Officers seldom receive any personal sanctions for noncompliant practices that cause evidence to be thrown out, and they do not necessarily give a high priority to helping secure convictions of the people they arrest. "We don't care about what happens in court," one officer said. "We just care about getting the arrest."[21] Moreover, illegal searches may not prevent convictions. Most defendants plead guilty, and by doing so they generally waive their right to challenge the legality of searches. When searches are questioned in court, trial judges usually give the benefit of the doubt to police officers. And evidence that is ruled illegal may not be needed for a conviction. Thus, police officers have an incentive to avoid illegal searches but not so strong an incentive that they always try to follow the applicable rules.

The weakness of the sanctions that are available to the Court means that people who are determined to resist the Court's rulings often have considerable freedom to do so. When resistance is widespread, the Court may be dependent on the other branches of government to use their own powers on its behalf—help that does not always come.

This discussion points to two conditions that affect the implementation of the Court's decisions. First, organizations that have an incentive to challenge noncompliance are important to the enforcement of decisions. Businesses and business groups are usually in a good position to act in support of rulings that benefit them. Similarly, interest groups concerned with civil liberties often act on behalf of beneficiaries of decisions who lack the resources to challenge noncompliance on their own.

Second, the Court's decisions are easiest to enforce when the affected policy makers are small in number and highly visible. It is relatively simple for the Court to oversee the fifty state governments that are responsible for carrying out some decisions. It is far more difficult for the Court to oversee the day-to-day activities of all the police officers who carry out searches and question suspects.

Three Case Studies of Implementation

The implementation process can be illuminated with three case studies. School desegregation in the South, prosecutors' responsibility to disclose evidence, and same-sex marriage highlight the sources of effective and ineffective implementation of Supreme Court decisions.

School Desegregation

Before the Supreme Court's 1954 decision in *Brown v. Board of Education*, separate public schools for Black and white students existed throughout the South and in most districts of border states such as Oklahoma and Maryland. The Court's decision required that these dual school systems be eliminated. In the border states, compliance was slow and imperfect, but there was a gradual movement toward a degree of desegregation. In contrast, policies in the South changed very little in the first decade after *Brown*. As late as 1964–1965, there was no southern state in which even 10 percent of the Black students went to school with any white students, a minimal definition of desegregation.[22]

The difference between the two regions reflected differences in the level of commitment to segregated schools. Southern judges and school officials responded to *Brown* in an atmosphere that was quite hostile to desegregation. Most white citizens were strongly opposed to desegregation. The opinions of Black citizens had only a limited impact, in part because a large proportion of them were prevented from voting. For their part, high-ranking public officials encouraged resistance to the Supreme Court.

Because of this political atmosphere and their own opposition to *Brown*, most school administrators in the South did everything possible to preserve segregation. Those administrators who did want to comply with the Court's ruling were deterred from doing so by pressure from state officials and local citizens.

In places where the schools did not comply on their own, parents could file lawsuits in the federal district courts to challenge the continuation of segregated systems. There were many districts in which no suits were ever brought, in part because of fear of retaliation.

Even where suits were brought, their success was limited. In its second decision in *Brown* in 1955, the Supreme Court gave federal district judges great freedom to determine the appropriate schedule for desegregation in a school district. Many judges themselves disagreed with *Brown*, and all felt local pressure to maintain segregation. As a result, few judges demanded speedy desegregation of schools, and some actively resisted desegregation. Some judges did support the Court wholeheartedly, but they found it difficult to overcome delaying tactics by school administrators and elected officials. And with the exception of its decision in a 1958 case that arose in Little Rock, Arkansas, the Court itself did little to support *Brown* until the late 1960s.[23]

After a long period of resistance, officials in the southern states began to comply. In the second decade after *Brown*, most dual school systems in the South were finally dismantled. Although school segregation was not eliminated altogether, the proportion of Black students attending school with whites increased tremendously. Table 6-1 shows that change.

The impetus for the change came primarily from Congress rather than the Court. The Civil Rights Act of 1964 allowed federal funds to be withheld from institutions that practiced racial discrimination. In carrying out that provision, President Lyndon Johnson's administration required that schools make a "good-faith start" toward desegregation to receive federal aid. Faced with a threat to important financial interests, school officials had an incentive to go along. The 1964 statute also allowed the Justice Department to bring desegregation suits where local residents were unable to do so. The Court later reinforced the congressional action with decisions in 1968 and 1969 that demanded effective desegregation without further delay.[24] As a result of all these actions, racial segregation of schools as official policy finally ended in the 1970s.

Prosecutors' Disclosure of Evidence

In *Brady v. Maryland* (1963), the Supreme Court ruled that "the suppression by the prosecution of evidence favorable to an accused upon request violates due process where the evidence is material either to guilt or punishment."[25] It is clear that prosecutors often comply with *Brady*, sometimes going beyond the requirements of that decision in providing evidence to defendants. It may be that the overall rate of compliance is high. But it is also clear that compliance has been far from complete. Over the years, defense lawyers and other people have identified a substantial

Table 6-1	Percentages of Black Elementary and Secondary Students Going to School with Any Whites, in Eleven Southern States, 1954–1973		
School year	**Percentage**	**School year**	**Percentage**
1954–1955	0.001	1964–1965	2.25
1956–1957	0.14	1966–1967	15.9
1958–1959	0.13	1968–1969	32.0
1960–1961	0.16	1970–1971	85.6
1962–1963	0.45	1972–1973	91.3

Sources: For 1954–1967, Southern Education Reporting Service, *A Statistical Summary, State by State, of School Segregation-Desegregation in the Southern and Border Area from 1954 to the Present* (Nashville, Tenn.: Southern Education Reporting Service, 1967); for 1968–1973, U.S. Bureau of the Census, *Statistical Abstract of the United States* (Washington, D.C.: Government Printing Office, 1971, 1975).

Note: The states are Alabama, Arkansas, Florida, Georgia, Louisiana, Mississippi, North Carolina, South Carolina, Tennessee, Texas, and Virginia.

number of cases in which defendants were convicted of serious crimes because prosecutors suppressed evidence indicating their innocence.[26] Undoubtedly, many other instances of noncompliance have gone undetected. And in some localities, it appears that prosecutors have engaged in numerous violations of *Brady*.[27]

What accounts for imperfect compliance with *Brady*? Most fundamentally, prosecutors have a personal and institutional interest in winning convictions. Although many prosecutors are willing to follow the *Brady* rule even when it jeopardizes their cases, others succumb to the temptation to withhold evidence that might prevent convictions.

That temptation is enhanced by the low probability of negative consequences when prosecutors do not turn over relevant evidence.[28] Quite frequently—almost surely, in the great majority of cases—suppressed evidence never comes to light. If such evidence does become known, prosecutors can argue that it was not "material" under *Brady*.

Noncompliance with *Brady* occasionally leads to sanctions such as firing or a criminal conviction, and in 2019 the New York legislature enacted a statute under which prosecutors could be censured or even removed from office for misconduct.[29] (The legislature also established new rules that required prosecutors to provide their evidence to defendants early in the court process.) But in general, prosecutors are quite unlikely to suffer negative consequences of any kind as a result of noncompliance.[30]

▶ **Photo 6-1** A Pennsylvania prosecutor at the Montgomery County courthouse. Prosecutors' responses to the requirement in Brady v. Maryland that they disclose certain evidence to the defense have varied a good deal.

As the Supreme Court collectively has become less committed to *Brady*, the Court has limited the reach of the decision and made it more difficult to enforce. The Court has narrowly defined the conditions under which evidence favorable to the defense is material to the outcome of a case, thus giving prosecutors more reason to think they are justified in withholding evidence.[31] In *Imbler v. Pachtman* (1976), the Court extended the long-standing immunity of prosecutors to lawsuits based on their prosecution of cases to civil rights suits under federal law. In *United States v. Ruiz* (2002), the Court held that prosecutors are not required to disclose relevant evidence to defendants prior to a plea bargain. As a result, defendants may be unaware of evidence that would work against conviction when they choose whether to plead guilty, as the great majority do.[32] And in *Connick v. Thompson* (2011), the Court made it more difficult to win lawsuits against a district attorney's office when prosecutors suppress evidence in violation of *Brady*. These decisions have reduced prosecutors' incentives to comply with the letter and spirit of *Brady*.

Same-Sex Marriage

When the Supreme Court ruled that states could not prohibit same-sex marriage in *Obergefell v. Hodges* (2015), its ruling gave clear responsibilities to state judges and administrators. Judges had to cease enforcing the prohibitions that had continued in some states, and court clerks had to provide marriage licenses to same-sex couples.

For judges and administrators who agreed with the ruling in *Obergefell*, it was easy to carry out the decision. For those who strongly disagreed, the decision created a conflict. Nonetheless, it appears that the great majority of those officials complied with the Court's ruling. One justice on the Louisiana Supreme Court, for instance, denounced *Obergefell*, referring to the decision as "an utter travesty." But he also said that "I am constrained to follow the rule of law set forth by a majority of the nine lawyers appointed to the United States Supreme Court."[33]

In contrast, some officials who strongly disagreed with the Court's ruling chose not to follow it. A federal district judge held that the ruling did not apply to Puerto Rico because it was a territory rather than a state.[34] Roy Moore, the chief justice of Alabama, issued an order that seemed to prohibit the state's trial judges from issuing marriage licenses to same-sex couples.[35] And some judges and court clerks across the country decided on their own not to issue licenses for same-sex marriages.

Those actions typically were overcome by higher authorities. The Puerto Rico district court decision was reversed by a federal court of appeals, which said that the decision "errs in so many respects that it is hard to know where to begin."[36] A Kentucky county clerk whose refusal to issue licenses to same-sex couples received national attention was jailed for five days and ultimately agreed to issue the licenses.[37] And Alabama's judicial disciplinary body suspended Chief Justice Moore for the remainder of his term for violating a rule of judicial ethics with his action.[38]

Two state legislatures accommodated the views of officials who did not want to accept same-sex marriages while ensuring that such marriages could take place.

In 2016 the Kentucky legislature enacted a law that removed the names of clerks from the forms for marriage licenses.[39] In 2019 the Alabama legislature went further. After some Alabama judges who opposed same-sex marriage stopped issuing marriage licenses to any couple, the legislature eliminated marriage licenses altogether and simply required couples to submit a notarized form.[40]

The *Obergefell* decision had implications for issues such as adoptions and government benefits for married couples. The Supreme Court underlined one implication in *Pavan v. Smith* (2017). The Arkansas Supreme Court had held that the state did not have to issue birth certificates that included the name of a female spouse of a woman who gave birth, even though birth certificates in the state included the name of a male spouse who was not the father. The Court summarily reversed the Arkansas decision, though with three justices in dissent. A few days after the *Pavan* decision, the Texas Supreme Court reached a decision in a case involving government benefits to married couples that indicated no more than lukewarm support for the implications of *Obergefell*.[41] But lower courts typically have followed those implications by ruling that same-sex married couples have the same legal rights and responsibilities as opposite-sex couples.[42]

Summing Up: The Effectiveness of Implementation

We know far too little to make confident judgments about how effectively judges and administrators carry out Supreme Court decisions, even if that question is simplified to the question of compliance and noncompliance. Still, a few generalizations are possible.

When judges and administrators address issues on which the Supreme Court has ruled, most of the time they readily apply the Court's ruling. They often do so even when that requires them to depart from positions on legal policy they had adopted before the Court's decision. These actions typically get little attention because they accord with most people's assumption that judges and administrators will follow the Court's lead and carry out its decisions fully.

Contrary to this assumption, however, implementation of the Court's policies is often quite imperfect, and the record is mixed. Some Court rulings are carried out more effectively than others, and specific decisions often are implemented better in some places or situations than in others.

Implementation of the Court's decisions is most successful in lower courts, especially appellate courts. When the Court announces a new rule of law, judges generally do their best to follow its lead. And when a series of decisions indicates that the Court has changed its position in a field of policy, lower courts tend to follow the new trend. For this reason, Court decisions that require only action by lower courts tend to be carried out more effectively than decisions that involve other policy makers.[43]

But even appellate judges sometimes diverge from the Court's rulings. Seldom do they explicitly refuse to follow the Court's decisions. More common is what might be called implicit noncompliance, in which a court purports to follow the Supreme Court's lead but actually evades the implications of the Court's ruling.

The greater frequency of implementation problems in the executive branch reflects several conditions. One condition is that administrators tend to feel less obligation to follow the Court's lead than do judges. Another is that carrying out the Court's decisions is more likely to create practical problems for administrators. Even so, the Court enjoys considerable success in getting compliance from administrative bodies.

Imperfect implementation is not unique to the Supreme Court. All policy makers whose rulings are carried out by other officials have mixed success in getting their policies carried out. It may be that courts have less success than legislatures and chief executives because of their limited powers to overcome noncompliance. But the existence and extent of that difference are uncertain on the basis of what we know about implementation processes.

RESPONSES BY LEGISLATURES AND CHIEF EXECUTIVES

Congress, the president, and their state counterparts frequently respond to Supreme Court decisions. Their responses shape the impact of those decisions, and some responses by Congress and the president affect the Court itself.

Congress

Congressional responses to the Court's rulings take several forms. Within some limits, Congress can modify or override the Court's decisions. Congress also affects the implementation of decisions, and it can act against individual justices or the Court as a whole.

Statutory Interpretation

In the world of statutory law, Congress is legally supreme. When the Supreme Court interprets a federal statute, as it does in most of its decisions, Congress can override that interpretation simply by enacting a new statute, so long as the president signs the statute or Congress overrides a veto. Such action is not rare. One study identified 275 decisions that Congress overrode in the forty-five years from 1967 through 2011, an average of more than ten in each two-year Congress.[44] One study found that 11 percent of the Court's statutory decisions in the 1997–2012 period were the subjects of bills to override them by 2012, and 3 percent of those decisions were actually overridden—not counting the times that members of Congress were unaware that a new statute overrode a Court decision.[45]

Some overrides represent direct efforts to invalidate recent Supreme Court decisions that have aroused widespread disagreement in Congress. But statutes aimed at specific decisions are a distinct minority. More often, Congress updates the law in an area of policy with a new statute, and in the process, it consciously or inadvertently overrides one or more decisions.

Members of Congress themselves initiate some efforts to override decisions. But they frequently are responding to efforts by interest groups. Just as groups that are unsuccessful in Congress turn to the courts for relief, groups whose interests have been hurt by the Supreme Court can turn to Congress. Sometimes the initiative comes from the Court itself. A dissenting justice may urge Congress to negate the decision in question, as Justice Sonia Sotomayor did in a 2017 decision interpreting the Fair Debt Collection Practices Act.[46] And occasionally, the Court's majority opinion invites members of Congress to override the Court's decision if they think that the Court's decision created an undesirable result. In a 2019 decision interpreting the same debt collection act, Justice Stephen Breyer's opinion for the Court suggested that Congress could "expand the reach" of the statute if members shared the view of the losing litigant that "our opinion will open a loophole."[47]

Significant legislation is usually difficult to enact, and that is true of bills to override Supreme Court decisions. It can help if an override is attached to a broad bill that has strong support, but even that may not be enough. In 1950 the Court ruled that members of the military services could not sue the federal government under a federal statute for injuries that arose from their service. The decision aroused considerable criticism, which seemed to grow in the 2010s. But an effort to insert an override of this decision as it applied to medical malpractice into the defense authorization bill of 2020 failed. Congress instead enacted a provision that set up an administrative process by which injured service members could seek compensation for malpractice.[48]

Partisan control of the two houses and the presidency affects the prospects of overrides. On issues that have an ideological element, overrides are difficult to enact when control of government is divided between the two parties, as it was from 2011 through 2016 and again in 2019 and 2020. And the partisan polarization of the current era, which often makes it more difficult to enact controversial legislation of any type, helps to account for a reduction in the number of overrides since the 1990s.

Statutes that override the Court's decisions, like other statutes, are subject to the Court's interpretation in later cases. Sometimes the Court reads an override in a way that limits the impact of that override on the law. This has been the case with some of the congressional overrides of decisions that gave narrow interpretations to statutes prohibiting employment discrimination.[49] When that happens, Congress could enact another statute to clarify the law. But often there is not sufficient political support for such action.

Constitutional Interpretation

When the Supreme Court interprets the Constitution, its decisions can be overturned only by amending the Constitution. Members of Congress often introduce resolutions to overturn or blunt the effects of decisions with constitutional amendments. In the 116th Congress of 2019–2020, for instance, the subjects of such proposed amendments included regulation of campaign finance, term limits for members of Congress, the constitutional rights of corporations, and flag desecration.

Few of these resolutions get serious consideration, and very few win the two-thirds majorities needed for Congress to propose an amendment. As Table 6-2 shows, Congress has proposed only nine amendments that had the effect of over-riding Supreme Court decisions. Some of these amendments were directly aimed at recent decisions. The Twenty-Sixth Amendment, for instance, was proposed and ratified less than seven months after the Court ruled that Congress lacked the power to lower the voting age to eighteen in elections to state offices. This amendment prohibited the federal and state governments from establishing a minimum age

Table 6-2 Constitutional Amendments Proposed by Congress That Would Override Supreme Court Decisions

Amendment	Subject	Proposed	Ratified	Decisions overturned
11	Lawsuits against states	1794	1795	*Chisholm v. Georgia* (1793)
13	Abolition of slavery	1865	1865	*Scott v. Sandford* (1857)
14	Race and citizenship	1866	1868	*Scott v. Sandford* (1857)
16	Federal income tax	1909	1913	*Pollock v. Farmers' Loan & Trust Co.* (1895)
19	Voting by women	1919	1920	*Minor v. Happersett* (1875)
—	Child labor	1926	Not ratified	*Hammer v. Dagenhart* (1918); *Bailey v. Drexel Furniture* (1922)
24	Poll tax for voting in federal elections	1962	1964	*Breedlove v. Suttles* (1937); *Butler v. Thompson* (1951)
26	Voting age in state elections	1971	1971	*Oregon v. Mitchell* (1970)
—	Sex discrimination (Equal Rights Amendment)	1972	Not ratified	*Goesaert v. Cleary* (1948); *Hoyt v. Florida* (1961); earlier decisions

for voting that is higher than eighteen. Other amendments were not such direct responses to specific decisions but would have had the effect of overriding one or more decisions.

Of these nine amendments, only seven were ratified by the states. The child labor amendment that would have given Congress power to regulate the employment of people under eighteen and the Equal Rights Amendment (ERA) that would have established a more rigorous standard for scrutiny of laws that treat women and men differently each fell short of the requirement that three-quarters of the states ratify amendments. A recent effort to revive the ERA based on belated state ratifications appears to have little chance of success.

Often, a constitutional amendment is not needed to limit or even negate the effects of a decision interpreting the Constitution. When the Court upholds some government practice that was challenged under the Constitution, Congress can prohibit that practice by statute so long as doing so is within its power to legislate. If the Court upholds a provision of a federal statute that Congress no longer supports, it can simply revoke that provision. Congress undertook a variant of that action in a 2017 tax statute. In 2012 the Court ruled that Congress had the power under the Constitution to require that certain individuals purchase health insurance. The 2017 statute included a provision that reduced to zero the penalty for not purchasing the required insurance.[50]

When the Court holds that a federal statute is unconstitutional, Congress sometimes writes a new statute in an effort to meet the Court's objection to the old one and thereby to reinstate the same policy or something similar to it. Congress can also enact such a statute to protect other government practices that the Court has struck down.

Congress frequently considers taking this kind of action after the Court invalidates a statute, and a significant proportion of the time it actually does act.[51] Two examples concern First Amendment decisions involving military matters. In *Snyder v. Phelps* (2011), the Court ruled that the father of a Marine could not sue the members of a church who demonstrated near his son's funeral while proclaiming highly critical messages about the family. Congress responded the next year with a statute that limited demonstrations at military funerals. And after the Court ruled in *United States v. Alvarez* (2012) that a statute imposing criminal penalties for falsely claiming to have a military honor violated the First Amendment, Congress passed a narrower statute that criminalized such false claims if they were made "with intent to obtain money, property, or other tangible benefit."[52]

When Congress enacts such a statute, the Court often hears a case to determine whether the new statute avoids the constitutional problem it was designed to overcome. Sometimes the Court takes a proactive approach when it strikes down a statute, suggesting how Congress might revise the statute to avoid the constitutional problem that the Court identified. When the Court struck down a federal statute that made state governments subject to lawsuits for copyright infringement in *Allen v. Cooper* (2020), Justice Kagan's opinion for the Court outlined the form that a new statute with the same purpose should take in order to win the Court's approval.

Affecting the Implementation of Decisions

Congress can enact statutes to influence the implementation of Supreme Court decisions by other institutions. Its most important tool is money. Congress may provide funds to carry out a decision or choose not to provide them. It can also affect responses to Court decisions by state and local governments through its control over federal grants to them. Congressional use of this latter power in the Civil Rights Act of 1964 was the key step that brought about belated compliance with *Brown v. Board of Education* in the South.

When a Supreme Court decision requires Congress itself to comply with the decision, Congress generally does so. The legislative veto is a partial exception. In *Immigration and Naturalization Service v. Chadha* (1983), the Court indicated that any statute allowing Congress as a whole, one house, or a committee to veto proposed actions by executive branch agencies violates the Constitution. After the decision, Congress eliminated legislative veto provisions from several statutes. But it has maintained others and adopted more than 1,000 new legislative veto provisions—most of them requiring that specific congressional committees approve action by administrative agencies. Since *Chadha*, Congress does not use its veto power formally. Rather, veto provisions lead to informal accommodations between agencies and committees, accommodations that administrators accept as preferable to more stringent controls by Congress. As a result, the *Chadha* decision, which had appeared to be highly consequential, has had a limited effect.[53]

Attacks on Justices and the Court

When members of Congress are unhappy with the Supreme Court's policies, they can attack the Court or the justices directly. The easiest way to do so is verbally, and members of Congress sometimes criticize the Court in harsh terms. In the past two decades both Republican and Democratic members have issued strong criticisms of specific rulings and broader patterns of decisions, with Democratic criticism growing as the Court has become more conservative.

Senator Sheldon Whitehouse of Rhode Island has been a frequent critic of the current Court. In 2019 he authored an amicus brief for four other Democratic senators in which he argued that what he saw as the Court's undue support for the positions of conservative groups was damaging its legitimacy and could lead to public demands that the Court be "restructured."[54] In 2020 Senate Minority Leader Charles Schumer spoke to a rally outside the Court while the justices were hearing a case involving state restrictions on abortion clinics. Addressing President Trump's appointees Neil Gorsuch and Brett Kavanaugh, Schumer said that "you will not know what hit you if you go forward with these awful decisions."[55]

More concretely, Congress can take several types of formal action against the Court or its members.[56] One type is reduction of the Court's jurisdiction. The Constitution allows Congress to alter the Court's appellate jurisdiction and the jurisdiction of other federal courts through legislation, though it is uncertain what limits there are on that power.

▶ **Photo 6-2** Charles Schumer of New York, Minority Leader of the Senate. Schumer's verbal attack on two justices in 2020 was an example of the criticism that presidents and members of Congress sometimes direct at the Court.

Members of Congress often propose to limit jurisdiction in order to keep the Court from addressing a particular issue or to blunt the impact of its decisions. In a few instances, those proposals have been successful. In 1868 Congress withdrew the Court's power to hear appeals in habeas corpus actions in order to prevent the Court from deciding a pending challenge to the post-Civil War Reconstruction legislation. The Court upheld the congressional action in *Ex parte McCardle* (1869). In 1932 Congress withdrew the federal courts' power to hear certain kinds of cases in labor law, partly in reaction to Supreme Court decisions that were perceived as antagonistic to labor unions.[57]

After the Court ruled in *Rasul v. Bush* (2004) that prisoners at the Guantánamo Bay Naval Station had the right to seek release through habeas corpus petitions, Congress enacted statutes in 2005 and 2006 to prohibit all federal courts from hearing habeas cases brought by those prisoners. In *Boumediene v. Bush* (2008), the Court struck down the 2006 statute and ruled out use of the 2005 statute on the basis of the constitutional provision on habeas corpus. In doing so, it highlighted one limit on congressional power over federal court jurisdiction.

Members of Congress have proposed other types of actions against the Court with some frequency. One example is constitutional amendments to limit the justices' terms, which have attracted increased interest in recent years but have not yet received serious consideration in Congress. There have also been occasional threats to impeach justices whose decisions displease members of Congress or to use the budget power by limiting Court resources or refusing to increase the justices' salaries. (The Constitution prohibits Congress from reducing justices' salaries.) In 2019 the House passed a broad bill that included a provision making the Supreme Court subject to a code of conduct for federal judges, which reflected some Democrats' belief that conservative justices had violated ethical norms.[58] The House vote followed party lines, and the Republican-led Senate did not consider the bill.

At another level, members of Congress occasionally support bills to increase the number of justices in order to shift its ideological center of gravity. The most serious of these efforts was the "Court-packing" plan initiated by President Franklin Roosevelt in 1937. Since 2017, some Democrats have talked about increasing the Court's size after a Democratic president is next elected.

Proposals to attack the Court in these and other ways have been more common in some eras than in others. The activism of the Court in support of civil liberties since the 1950s has led to high rates of anti-Court proposals during several periods in this era. The early twenty-first century is one of those periods. Despite the Court's relative conservatism in this period, until recently most of the proposals to take action against the Court continued to come from congressional conservatives.[59]

In light of the range of congressional powers over the Court and the frequency with which members of Congress threaten to use them, it is striking how little Congress has actually employed its powers during the past century. Of the many actions that members of Congress contemplated using against the conservative Court in the early part of the twentieth century, culminating in the 1937 Court-packing plan, almost none were adopted.[60] The same is true of the attacks on the Court for its civil libertarian decisions since the 1950s. Why has Congress been so hesitant to use its powers, even at times when most members are unhappy about the Court's direction?

Several factors help explain this hesitancy.[61] First, there are always some members of Congress who agree with the Court's policies and lead its defense. The mechanisms available to block legislation give defenders of the Court tools to prevent the enactment of measures they oppose. Second, serious forms of attack against the Court, such as impeachment and reducing its jurisdiction, seem illegitimate to many people, even members of Congress who strongly disagree with the Court's decisions. Finally, when threatened with serious attack, the Court occasionally retreats to reduce the impetus for congressional action. For these reasons, the congressional bark at the Supreme Court has been a good deal worse than its bite.

The President

Like members of Congress, presidents frequently comment on the Supreme Court, and they sometimes attack its decisions. In 2010, for instance, President Obama used his State of the Union address to criticize *Citizens United v. Federal Election Commission* (2010), a week-old decision in which the Court narrowed congressional power to regulate the funding of election campaigns. Nine years later, President Trump criticized *Department of Commerce v. New York* (2019), which held that the Commerce Department had acted improperly in deciding to add a question on citizenship to the 2020 Census. Trump said that the Court had created a "totally ridiculous" situation.[62] In 2020, he criticized what he saw as a series of bad decisions by the Court.[63]

Presidents can also try to influence congressional responses to the Court's decisions by proposing action or taking a position on proposals initiated by others. Presidents frequently ask Congress to act in response to a decision, and occasionally Congress takes the requested action.[64] One successful effort came in response to *Ledbetter v. Goodyear Tire & Rubber Co.* (2007), which set a tight time limit on lawsuits for discrimination in pay under the Civil Rights Act of 1964. As a presidential candidate in 2008, Barack Obama championed an effort to override the decision by amending the Civil Rights Act. Within two weeks of his 2009 inauguration, he signed an override bill that Congress had speedily enacted. In 2019 President Trump announced his support for a constitutional amendment to overturn the Supreme Court's decisions that struck down laws against flag desecration. A year later Trump told governors that he hoped their states would enact new anti-flag-burning laws, saying that "we have a different court" from the one that had struck down such laws in 1989 and 1990.[65]

Using Executive Power

Presidents can use their powers as chief executive to shape the implementation and impact of Supreme Court decisions, acting themselves or through Cabinet departments. President Obama did so in several instances, and President Trump has also been active in responding to decisions.

A sample of the two presidents' responses to decisions underlines the range of actions they can take. In response to a 2007 Court decision upholding a Labor Department regulation that exempted certain home health care workers from the minimum wage law, the department under Obama changed the regulation in 2013 to eliminate that exemption.[66] In the same year, after the Court's ambiguous decision on affirmative action in college admissions in *Fisher v. University of Texas* (2013), the Justice and Education Departments sent a letter to college presidents encouraging the continuation of affirmative action programs.[67]

One response to the Court by the Trump administration came four years after a 2015 decision that allowed "disparate impact" lawsuits for discrimination under the Fair Housing Act of 1968. In 2019 the Department of Housing and Urban Development proposed a rule that would make such lawsuits more difficult for plaintiffs to win.[68] In contrast, a few weeks after *Lucia v. SEC* (2018) held that the method for appointing administrative law judges in the Securities and Exchange Commission was unconstitutional, President Trump issued an executive order building on that decision by requiring that all administrative law judges be appointed by agency heads rather than through a competitive hiring process.[69]

In *Burwell v. Hobby Lobby Stores* (2014), the Court ruled that certain corporations with religious objections must be exempted from a requirement to provide contraceptive coverage to their employees in insurance plans under the Affordable Care Act. In 2017 President Trump issued an executive order asking three Cabinet departments to consider expanding this exemption. The next year, the three departments adopted rules that exempted a wider range of employers that have religious or moral objections to contraceptive coverage. These rules were challenged on multiple grounds, but the Supreme Court upheld them in *Little Sisters of the Poor v. Pennsylvania* (2020).

In an era of wide ideological differences between the Republican and Democratic parties, a new president from one party can be expected to modify or reverse many actions taken by a predecessor from the other party. The Trump administration's proposed rules on contraceptive coverage represented a substantial change from those of the Obama administration. Another example involves labor–management relations. Reacting to Supreme Court decisions that let companies require employees to take legal grievances against them to arbitration rather than going to court, President Obama issued an executive order in 2014 that prohibited companies with substantial federal contracts from requiring arbitration for discrimination claims under the Civil Rights Act of 1964. Three years later President Trump revoked that order.[70]

Like Congress, presidents sometimes help the Court with implementation of its decisions. Three presidents did so after *Brown v. Board of Education*. In 1957, when a combination of state interference and mob action prevented court-ordered desegregation of the schools in Little Rock, President Dwight Eisenhower deployed federal troops in support of desegregation. President John Kennedy took similar action, using troops to enforce desegregation at the University of Alabama and the University of Mississippi. Most important, Lyndon Johnson's administration vigorously used both litigation and control over federal funds to break down segregated school systems in the South.

Compliance with Decisions

Occasionally, a Supreme Court decision requires compliance by the president, either as a party in the case or, more often, as head of the executive branch. Some presidents and commentators have argued that the president need not obey an order of the Supreme Court, on the ground that the Court is a co-equal body rather than a legal superior. Whether or not that argument is valid, presidents would seem sufficiently powerful to disobey the Court with impunity.

In reality, their position is not that strong. The president's political power is based largely on the ability to obtain support from other policy makers. In turn, this ability depends in part on perceptions of the president's legitimacy. Because disobedience of the Court would threaten this legitimacy, presidents feel some pressure to comply with the Court's decisions.

This conclusion is supported by presidential responses to two highly visible Court orders. In *Youngstown Sheet and Tube Co. v. Sawyer* (1952), the Court ruled that President Harry Truman had acted illegally during the Korean War when he seized steel mills to keep them operating if a threatened strike took place. The Court ordered an end to the seizure, and Truman immediately complied.

Even more striking is *United States v. Nixon* (1974). During the investigation of the Watergate scandal, President Richard Nixon withheld recordings of certain conversations in his offices that were sought by special prosecutor Leon Jaworski. In July 1974 the Supreme Court ruled unanimously that Nixon must yield the tapes.

In oral argument before the Court, the president's lawyer had indicated that Nixon might not comply with an adverse decision. But he did comply. At the least, this compliance speeded Nixon's departure from office. The content of the tapes provided strong evidence of presidential misdeeds, and opposition to impeachment evaporated. Fifteen days after the Court's ruling, Nixon announced his resignation.

In light of that result, why did Nixon comply with the Court order? He apparently did not realize how damaging the evidence in the tapes was. Perhaps more important, noncompliance would have fatally damaged his remaining legitimacy. For many members of Congress, noncompliance in itself would have constituted an impeachable offense, one on which there would be no dispute about the evidence. Under the circumstances, compliance may have been the better of two unattractive choices.

State Officials

State and local governments have no direct power over the Supreme Court as an institution. But like Congress and the president, state legislatures, governors, and their local counterparts have means to shape the impact of the Court's decisions. They can try to limit the effects of decisions that restrict practices they favor, they can act to take advantage of decisions that approve such practices, and they can respond in other ways.

Like Congress, state and local governments sometimes respond to a decision that invalidates one type of law by writing a new law in an effort to meet the Court's constitutional objection to the old ones. After *McDonald v. Chicago* (2010), in which the Court held that the right of individuals to own and use guns applied to the states, some local governments adopted new gun regulations in forms that they hoped the Court would accept. Lower federal courts have decided a number of cases in which these new laws were challenged, upholding some and invalidating others.

Most of the time, the Court's decision striking down a state law leaves no room for a new statute to achieve the same objective as the original one. In that situation, legislatures often leave those statutes on the books. According to a count in 2016, at least forty states retained statutes prohibiting desecration of the U.S. flag despite the Supreme Court's 1989 and 1990 decisions striking down such laws.[71] And at least five states have retained provisions in their constitutions that require a belief in God to hold public office despite the Supreme Court's invalidation of such laws in 1961.[72] This kind of inaction may simply reflect inertia or the difficulty of amending state constitutions. But sometimes it is a deliberate choice by legislators who disagree with the Court's decision or who think that their constituents disagree.

When a state statute that does not conform to a Supreme Court ruling is likely to be challenged in the future, legislators have more reason to change it. In *Miller v. Alabama* (2012), the Court ruled that states could not require life sentences without the possibility of parole for any crimes that were committed by juveniles. At the time, many states had such statutes for at least some forms of murder. After *Miller*, courts in a few states struck down these statutes. In the great majority of other states with mandatory life sentences for juveniles, legislatures enacted new statutes eliminating that provision. Many states went even further, ruling out life sentences for juveniles altogether.[73]

In *Loving v. Virginia* (1967), the Court struck down Virginia's prohibition of interracial marriage, along with similar laws in fifteen other states. Several of those states repealed their prohibitions within a few years of the decision, and the others followed later. But some states retained provisions that required people to designate their race on applications for marriage licenses. In 2019 a federal district judge struck down the Virginia law as unconstitutional.[74]

Brown v. Board of Education effectively struck down state laws that mandated racial segregation of schools. In the South, not only were these laws maintained, but state governments often took active steps to block school desegregation. Governors in Arkansas, Mississippi, and Alabama used their highly visible opposition to desegregation as a means to enhance their popularity with white voters. Some governors and legislatures have played a similar role in opposing the Court's limitations on religious observances in public schools.

Some Supreme Court decisions require states to do more than repeal laws. *Gideon v. Wainwright* (1963) and later decisions mandate that indigent criminal defendants be provided with legal counsel. The Court's decisions spurred state and local governments to increase their commitment to provide attorneys for indigent defendants. This commitment has been reflected in much higher levels of funding, and low-income defendants are certainly in a better position than they were prior to 1963. But funding of counsel has often been inadequate, and that inadequacy has increased as fiscal pressures on governments have grown. These pressures may help to explain why defendants frequently are charged money for the services of public defenders.[75]

When the Court allows state governments to do something that was formerly prohibited, states can decide whether to use their new freedom. In *South Dakota v. Wayfair, Inc.* (2018), the Court overruled its 1967 and 1992 decisions that had prohibited a state from collecting sales tax from businesses with no physical presence in the state. With a good deal of revenue from internet sales at stake, a year later nearly every state with a sales tax had acted to take advantage of the *Wayfair* decision.[76] Another 2018 decision, *Murphy v. National Collegiate Athletic Association*, struck down a federal law that indirectly prohibited nearly every state from legalizing gambling on sports. Over the next year most state legislatures considered bills to legalize sports gambling, and twenty states enacted these bills in the two years after the Court's decision.[77]

A more complex situation arose after the Court's decision in *Shelby County v. Holder* (2013). The decision effectively nullified the requirement in the Voting

▶ **Photo 6-3** A teller at a Delaware racetrack displaying a bet on a baseball game. Delaware was the first of many states to take advantage of the Supreme Court's decision overturning a federal law that prevented nearly all states from allowing gambling on sports.

Rights Act that certain state and local governments get clearance from the federal government before they change their election laws. In response, legislators in some southern states that were released from preclearance enacted new laws such as requirements that people show certain kinds of identification in order to vote.[78] These laws could still be challenged in court, but the outcome of those challenges was uncertain, and the laws might operate for a period of time even if they were ultimately held to be illegal. Federal courts did rule that some of the new laws violated the Voting Rights Act, including a set of registration and voting rules that North Carolina adopted shortly after the *Shelby County* decision.[79]

Two Case Studies of Responses by the Other Branches

When the Supreme Court rules on important policies of the legislative and executive branches, its decisions may become part of a long interaction between the Court and the other branches. That has been true of the Court's decisions on abortion and the death penalty.

Abortion

The Supreme Court's decision in *Roe v. Wade* (1973) mandated a general legalization of abortion prior to the time of viability for a fetus, which the Court's opinion defined as occurring approximately between the twenty-fourth and twenty-eighth weeks of pregnancy. In the first decade after *Roe*, opponents of the decision made efforts to enact a constitutional amendment overturning the decision. Taking a different approach, some members of Congress sought to remove the jurisdiction of the Supreme Court and other federal courts over this field so that they could not invalidate state and federal restrictions on abortion. Both initiatives were unsuccessful, and they have not been revived since then.

When *Roe* was decided, all but four states had statutes that put quite substantial limits on abortion, and most states allowed abortions only under very limited circumstances or not at all. After *Roe* most states eliminated those broad prohibitions, but some left them on their books without enforcing them. And across the country, a wide range of new laws was enacted to regulate or prohibit abortion under certain circumstances. Governors played important roles in some states as supporters or opponents of these laws, and they have continued to do so since then.

Many of the new laws were challenged in federal court, and the Supreme Court heard several cases on this legislation. The Court struck down a number of laws that substantially limited access to abortion. But it upheld other laws that a majority of the justices saw as consistent with *Roe*. One important example was restrictions on federal and state Medicaid funding of abortions.

The Court largely reaffirmed *Roe* in *Planned Parenthood v. Casey* (1992). But that decision gave states more freedom with a new rule that a regulation of abortion prior to viability would be unconstitutional if it had the intent or effect of putting an "undue burden" on women's choice to have an abortion. After *Casey*, states continued to enact laws that limited abortion, and restrictive legislation accelerated after 2010 because of Republican successes in legislative and gubernatorial elections. Bills on subjects such as physical and procedural requirements for abortion clinics and mandated waiting periods before abortions were performed were widely introduced in state legislatures, and many of these bills were enacted.[80]

In the first two decades after *Casey*, the Court decided few cases involving these new state laws. Then, in *Whole Woman's Health v. Hellerstedt* (2016), the Court struck down two Texas regulations of abortion clinics on the ground that they were inconsistent with the *Casey* rules. But state legislatures continued to enact restrictive legislation, in part because of the prospect of a change in the Court's membership that would lead it to overturn *Roe*.

Indeed, the appointment of Justice Brett Kavanaugh in 2018 was widely expected to shift the Court's position in favor of restrictions on abortion. In 2019 six state legislatures adopted general prohibitions of abortion after an early point in a pregnancy—in Alabama, from the beginning of pregnancy. In 2020 the Court's decision in *June Medical Services v. Russo* reaffirmed the 2016 decision in *Hellerstedt*. But in providing the fifth vote to strike down a Louisiana regulation of clinics, Chief Justice Roberts wrote an opinion that seemed to indicate he would be more favorable to some other kinds of regulations of abortion. In any event, the interplay between the Court and state governments is certain to continue.

Capital Punishment

In *Furman v. Georgia* (1972), the Supreme Court overturned three death sentences in cases from Georgia and Texas. The decision was ambiguous, primarily because each member of the five-justice majority wrote a separate opinion, but it clearly invalidated all the existing death penalty laws in the states. In response, state legislators who favored capital punishment sought to enact new statutes that would meet the Court's constitutional objections to the existing laws. Indeed, by 1975 thirty-one states had written new laws that were designed to avoid arbitrary use of capital punishment, the concern of the pivotal justices in *Furman*.[81]

In *Gregg v. Georgia* (1976), the Court held that the death penalty was not inherently unconstitutional. It struck down laws that made the death penalty mandatory for certain offenses but upheld other laws with rules on eligibility for the death penalty that were aimed at avoiding arbitrariness. The states whose laws had been struck down then had models they could follow in writing new statutes.

Defendants who were sentenced to death continued to challenge state laws on constitutional grounds. The Court has struck down provisions of capital punishment statutes in more than a dozen cases since 1977, and some of those decisions affected large numbers of states.

When the Court's invalidation of a statutory provision makes it impossible to maintain the death penalty without a new statute, state legislatures usually respond by adopting such a statute. In 2016, for instance, the Court struck down the Florida death penalty law because it gave too much power over fact-finding to the trial judge. The Florida legislature then moved to meet the Court's objection, enacting a new death penalty statute within two months of the Court's decision.[82]

In contrast, when capital punishment can still be used without a new statute, legislatures sometimes leave an offending provision on the books. After *Roper v. Simmons* (2005) ruled out the death penalty for offenses committed by a person who was under age eighteen, most states that had allowed death sentences for juveniles adopted new statutes that exempted juveniles. But other states did not do so, and their lack of action would not create any difficulties so long as no defendant was sentenced to death in violation of the *Roper* ruling.

The Court's decisions on capital punishment sometimes leave considerable leeway to state governments. *Atkins v. Virginia* (2002), which ruled out capital punishment for people with intellectual disabilities, left it to the states to determine the standards for identifying intellectual disabilities. Legislators in some states sought to minimize the effects of *Atkins* by making it very difficult for defendants to demonstrate the existence of these disabilities.[83] But the Court can rein in legislatures by clarifying its position, as it did on issues relating to *Atkins* in 2014, 2017, and 2019.[84]

On the whole, the Court is in a good position to achieve compliance with its death penalty decisions from state legislators and other policy makers because any death sentence that clearly violates the Court's rules is almost certain to be reversed on appeal or in a habeas corpus proceeding. In that respect, the Court's decisions on capital punishment have been more successful than its rulings on many other issues.

IMPACT ON SOCIETY

The broadest effects of Supreme Court decisions are on American society. Those effects are quite difficult to ascertain, but they merit examination because of their importance.

A General View

Supreme Court decisions can shape society in a variety of ways. Some effects are relatively direct, while others are broader and more diffuse.

The direct effects of decisions begin with what the Court allows or disallows. When someone challenges the legality of a government practice, the Court decides whether or not that practice can continue. When people outside of government have conflicts about their rights under the law, the Court decides whose rights prevail. Decisions of both types become resources for the favored side to use. How much they use these resources depends in part on their own interest and ability to use them and in part on the actions of other people within and outside of government.

A good example of direct effects is *Obergefell v. Hodges* (2015). By ruling out state prohibitions of same-sex marriage, the Court made such marriages possible in states in which they had not been allowed. Because many people are interested in making use of that right, the result has been a large number of marriages that would not have taken place otherwise. But the Court's impact is uncertain: if it had ruled that the Constitution does not require legalization of same-sex marriages, we do not know how many states would have legalized same-sex marriage on their own in the years after 2015.

The Court's decisions on economic issues are likely to have strong direct effects, at least when the beneficiaries of those decisions have the knowledge and resources to use their legal rights. When the Court gives an advantage to plaintiffs or defendants in lawsuits for infringement of patents, the businesses on the favored side are equipped to employ that advantage in bringing cases or defending against them. The same is true of businesses that are favored by decisions in antitrust or tax law and of employers and labor unions in labor law. For instance, the Court's decisions allowing businesses to require that employees and consumers take their disputes with a business to arbitration rather than going to court have brought about substantial increases in the use of these requirements. By one estimate, about 60 million U.S. employees were subject to mandatory arbitration in 2016.[85]

Election law is another area in which beneficiaries readily make use of favorable decisions. The decisions that gave state governments more freedom to impose requirements for voting have been seized upon by legislators who view certain requirements as good policy or as advantageous to their political party. Similarly, governors and majority parties in state legislatures can be expected to take full advantage of the Court's 2019 ruling that partisan gerrymandering cannot be challenged in federal courts when they redraw district lines after the 2020 Census.[86]

Candidates, parties, and contributors have taken advantage of the Court's rulings that prohibit most government restrictions on the funding of political campaigns. It appears that these rulings have had a substantial effect on patterns of campaign spending. There is also some evidence that changes in campaign spending resulting from the Court's decisions have made state legislatures more Republican and more conservative than they would have been otherwise.[87]

The Court's decisions can have a broader impact that follows from their direct effects and sometimes from their role as symbols. One relatively simple example is *Quill Corp. v. Heitkamp* (1992). In that decision, the Court reaffirmed its position that under the interstate commerce clause of the Constitution, states could not require merchants to collect tax from consumers in states where the merchants lacked a physical presence. The decision almost surely was one source of the enormous growth of online retailers such as Amazon because it gave them a competitive advantage over ordinary retailers: their total prices could be lower, all else being equal, and few consumers voluntarily paid the sales tax they owed.[88] But tax rules were hardly the only reason why people increasingly purchased products online.

The Court overruled *Quill* in *South Dakota v. Wayfair* (2018), and state legislatures rushed to apply sales taxes to internet sales. But e-commerce had become well established by then, and it continues to have powerful attractions to consumers. As a result, the loss of the price advantage that *Quill* had reaffirmed may not have much effect on consumers' choices between stores and online retailers.

Similar to *Quill* in some respects was the Court's decision in *Sony Corporation v. Universal City Studios* (1984), which held that recording television programs for future watching and selling devices that allowed people to do so did not violate copyright law. The decision facilitated the development of a range of digital devices and online services.[89]

A more complicated example is the impact of the Warren Court's expansions of the rights of criminal defendants on the incidence of crime. Some commentators have viewed those expansions as reducing the deterrent impact of the law and thus increasing the crime rate. While a link between the scope of defendants' rights and crime prevention may exist, that link is quite uncertain. Because procedural rights often have less effect on the behavior of defendants and law enforcement personnel than might be expected, there is some reason to think that rights expansions have only limited impact on the effectiveness of the criminal justice system. But scholars who probe that impact have reached conflicting conclusions.[90] More fundamentally, people's decisions whether to commit crimes are affected by a variety of factors, not just their perceptions of the likelihood that they will be convicted and punished. But this does not rule out the possibility that expansions of procedural rights have some effect on the crime rate.

In thinking about limits on the Court's impact, we should keep two things in mind. First, the factors that limit the Court's effects are not unique to the judiciary. It is true that the other branches of government have considerably greater power to shape society. But they too represent only one influence on phenomena such as the crime rate, the status of women, and the functioning of the economy.

Second, despite these limits, the Court can make a great deal of difference. Its ruling on same-sex marriage affected many people in a direct and significant way. Its decisions on voting and election rules have helped to determine the results of elections. Over more than a century, its rulings in antitrust law have shaped the structure of industries. It is easy to exaggerate the Court's impact, and people who disapprove of the Court's decisions often do so. But it would be equally mistaken to dismiss the Court as an unimportant policy maker.

Three Areas of Court Activity

The Court's impact on society and the forces that shape its impact can be probed by looking at three areas of the Court's activity as a policy maker. In different ways, these areas illustrate the complexity of the relationship between Supreme Court decisions and social reality.

Labor–Management Relations

The Supreme Court has long played a role in shaping government policy on the bargaining relationship between employers on one side and employees and labor unions on the other side. Some of the Court's decisions in this field are based on the Constitution. But the bulk of its business involves interpretation of statutes, especially the National Labor Relations Act of 1935 and amendments to that act.

The most important development in labor–management relations in the current era is the decline in the membership of labor unions. In 1970, by one count, about 25 percent of all employed workers were union members. That proportion dropped to 20 percent in 1980, 14 percent in 1990, and 10 percent in 2019. The decline has been especially sharp in the private sector, in which only 6 percent of workers belonged to unions in 2019. In contrast, 34 percent of government workers were union members.[91]

The reasons for the decline in union membership are a subject of debate, but it seems clear that a variety of factors have been responsible.[92] Developments outside government such as changes in the economy and in employers' attitudes toward unions have played a part. So have policies adopted by Congress and state legislatures.

Undoubtedly, Supreme Court decisions have had a more limited impact on union membership than these other factors. But by shaping the legal positions of employers and unions, the Court reinforced other sources of the decline. The Court since the 1970s has been less favorable to unions than it had been in earlier decades, and some of its decisions have weakened unions' ability to organize workers and to negotiate with employers.[93]

The history of one decision illustrates both the Court's impact and the more fundamental effects of other forces. In *National Labor Relations Board v. Mackay Radio & Telegraph Company* (1938), the Court indicated that federal law allowed employers to hire new employees as permanent replacements for striking workers. For many years after 1938, companies made little use of the decision. But they increasingly did so beginning in the 1980s. President Reagan's 1981 decision to hire replacements for striking air traffic controllers who were federal employees was perhaps the most important trigger for this change. But a reduced willingness of employers to accept the role of unions, based in part on a weakening of ties between companies and the localities in which they operated, created a key precondition for use of *Mackay* as a tool.

One recent decision may have a substantial impact on the public sector, where unions remain relatively strong. In *Janus v. AFSCME* (2018), the Court overruled a 1977 decision and held that the First Amendment prohibits agreements under which government employees who do not belong to a union are required to pay a fee to the union for representing them in collective bargaining. These agreements were mandated by statute in twenty-two states.[94] Early evidence about the effects of *Janus* on public employee unions is mixed, in part because state governments differ in the ways they are implementing the decision.[95] Here too, the Court's rulings will interact with other forces to shape relations between labor and management.

Abortion

The Supreme Court's 1973 decision in *Roe v. Wade* has been at the heart of the debate over government policy on abortion, with people on one side of the debate praising it and those on the other side denouncing it. These reactions to *Roe* reflect a belief that it is the dominant basis for the status of abortion in the United States. The discussion of abortion policy earlier in this chapter suggests a more complicated picture, in that the other branches of government have continued to shape abortion policy in significant ways since *Roe*. We would expect broader forces in society to exert considerable impact as well.

A good starting point in thinking about the extent of the Court's impact and the limits on that impact is the number of legal abortions over time, for which the best estimates are shown in Figure 6-1. As we would expect, Figure 6.1 shows a very substantial increase in the rate of legal abortions after *Roe* was decided. But two other patterns are less consistent with the idea that *Roe* has been the dominant factor in the state of abortion.

The first pattern is the increase in legal abortions between 1969 and 1972, an even sharper increase than the one that occurred after *Roe*. That increase reflected changes in state laws before and during that period, as some states relaxed their general prohibitions of abortion and a few eliminated most restrictions. If the Court had never handed down *Roe*, it is impossible to know how state laws would have evolved and how abortion rates would have changed. But the number of legal abortions probably would have continued to rise because of further changes in state laws and increasing abortion rates in the states that allowed abortion.

The second pattern is the decline in the number of legal abortions in the past three decades. Between 1990 and 2017, the most recent year for which data are available, the number of legal abortions declined by nearly half. The per capita rate

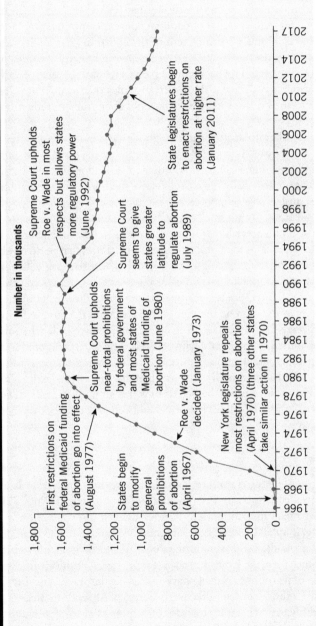

Figure 6-1 Estimated Numbers of Legal Abortions and Related Government Policy Actions, 1966–2017

Number in thousands

Supreme Court upholds Roe v. Wade in most respects but allows states more regulatory power (June 1992)

First restrictions on federal Medicaid funding of abortion go into effect (August 1977)

Supreme Court seems to give states greater latitude to regulate abortion (July 1989)

Supreme Court upholds near-total prohibitions by federal government and most states of Medicaid funding of abortion (June 1980)

States begin to modify general prohibitions of abortion (April 1967)

Roe v. Wade decided (January 1973)

State legislatures begin to enact restrictions on abortion at higher rate (January 2011)

New York legislature repeals most restrictions on abortion (April 1970) (three other states take similar action in 1970)

Sources: Estimated numbers of abortions for 1966–1972 are taken from Gerald N. Rosenberg, *The Hollow Hope: Can Courts Bring About Social Change?* 2nd ed. (Chicago: University of Chicago Press, 2008), 180; for 1973–1994, Lawrence B. Finer and Stanley K. Henshaw, "Abortion Incidence and Services in the United States in 2000," *Perspectives on Sexual and Reproductive Health* 35 (January–February 2003): 8; for 1995–2014, Rachel K. Jones and Jenna Jerman, "Abortion Incidence and Service Availability in the United States, 2014," *Perspectives on Sexual and Reproductive Health* 49 (March 2017): 20; and for 2015–2017, Rachel K. Jones, Elizabeth Witwer, and Jenna Jerman, "Abortion Incidence and Service Availability in the United States, 2017," Guttmacher Institute, September 2019, 13. In these sources, numbers for some years are interpolated from numbers for earlier and later years.

of abortions for women between the ages of fifteen and forty-four dropped by more than one-half between 1981 and 2017. In 2017 that rate was about 20 percent lower than it was in 1973.[96]

One source of this decline is policies of the other branches of government. For instance, comparisons of states indicate that restrictions on Medicaid funding of abortion and requirements of parental consent or notification before girls under eighteen can obtain abortions reduce the abortion rate.[97] The widespread policy of performing no abortions in government-run medical facilities probably has considerable impact. The substantial growth in state legislation restricting abortion in various ways since 2011, especially rules that lead to the closures of clinics that perform abortions, may have brought about further reductions in the numbers of abortions.

Conditions other than government policy also have contributed to this decline.[98] The number of abortions largely depends on the number of unintended pregnancies and on women's choices whether to seek abortions. Thus, increased use of contraception, especially the most effective methods of contraception, probably has made considerable difference. Another factor is the availability of facilities that perform abortions. Only a small minority of privately owned hospitals perform abortions. Most urban areas have clinics that perform abortions, but many rural areas lack such clinics. And the number of medical facilities that perform abortions has declined substantially in the past two decades. These patterns reflect the personal beliefs of medical personnel as well as restrictive laws and pressures against providing abortions. But there is some uncertainty about the impact of the decline in the availability of abortion on the numbers of abortions that are performed.

If the Supreme Court helped bring about the increase in legal abortions, it may have contributed to the later decline as well. The Court accepted some policies restricting abortion, including limits on Medicaid funding. And if *Roe* served as a symbol that helped to mobilize the pro-life movement, the justices in the *Roe* majority may have inadvertently helped to spur the adoption of restrictive legislation.[99] That possibility underlines the broad and complex impact that the Court's decisions can have.

Racial Equality

In debates about the Supreme Court's impact, no issue receives as much attention as racial equality. The Warren Court of the 1950s and 1960s did a great deal to combat racial discrimination. It ruled against discrimination in education and voting, it upheld federal antidiscrimination laws that were challenged on constitutional grounds, and it sought to protect the civil rights movement from legal attacks. Since then, the Court has taken a more mixed position on issues in this field, and some of its rulings arguably have worked against racial equality. To what extent have the Court's decisions affected the status of African Americans?

This is a difficult and complex question, so nothing like a definitive answer can be offered. But it is possible to reach some tentative judgments. To start with, the

Court's impact should be judged by a realistic standard. No single court is likely to have a dramatic impact on the status of a group in society, because the other branches of government and forces outside government can have more direct and more powerful effects. The question is how much of a difference the Court made within those limits.

The Court played its most active role in school desegregation, most dramatically in *Brown v. Board of Education*. *Brown* brought about considerable desegregation of public schools in the border states, but help from Congress and the president was required to make *Brown* effective in the South. In a later era, Court decisions in the 1990s that allowed school districts to end court-ordered programs to remedy segregation were an important cause of the growth in racial segregation of public schools since that time.[100]

The Court played a limited role in securing the right to vote by African Americans in the South. One reason was the justices' hesitancy about overturning legal barriers to voting. Another was the Court's lack of power to overcome barriers other than formal legal rules, barriers that came from both government and nongovernmental action. The Court did uphold key provisions of the Voting Rights Act of 1965 in *South Carolina v. Katzenbach* (1966). In turn, that statute was the key step that opened up access to the vote. However, the Court's ruling in *Shelby County v. Holder* (2013) effectively eliminated the requirement that changes in election laws in southern states be preapproved by the federal government. As a result, the impact of the Voting Rights Act on practices that limit voting by African Americans has been reduced.

Constitutional protections against racial discrimination apply to the private sector only in limited ways. For that reason, policies to address housing and employment discrimination had to come primarily from the other branches. However, the Court has been active in interpreting Title VII of the Civil Rights Act of 1964, the most important law prohibiting employment discrimination. There is some evidence that Title VII has improved the economic status of African Americans, and the Court's early Title VII decisions on issues such as affirmative action and employment policies that have a disparate impact on racial groups probably enhanced the law's effects to some degree.[101]

Perhaps the Court played an indirect role in furthering racial equality by contributing in a small way to the growth and success of the mass civil rights movement in the South. Its decisions created hope for change and established rights to be vindicated by political action. One legal scholar has argued that *Brown v. Board of Education* "provided supporters of racial equality with a powerful rhetorical and moral weapon that helped to catalyze the nation toward the goal of racial equality."[102]

Indeed, the series of civil rights laws adopted from 1957 on may owe something to the Court. In education and voting, the Court took the first significant government action against discrimination in the twentieth century. By doing so, the Court helped to create expectations that Congress and the executive branch were pressed to fulfill. In a proclamation commemorating the sixtieth anniversary of *Brown* in 2014, President Obama acknowledged its limitations but concluded that "*Brown's* moral guidance was translated into the enforcement measures of the Civil Rights Act and the Voting Rights Act."[103]

Clearly, the Supreme Court's decisions have had some effects on the status of African Americans. Its rulings from the 1950s to the 1990s helped determine levels of desegregation in public schools over time, and its upholding of the Voting Rights Act allowed that law to attack barriers to the right to vote. The Court's impact as a catalyst for developments elsewhere in government society is very difficult to ascertain, but that role may have been significant. Thus the Court can be seen as one source of the state of racial equality in the United States, though certainly not the most important one.

CONCLUSION: THE COURT, PUBLIC POLICY, AND SOCIETY

It is now possible to reach some tentative conclusions about the role of the Supreme Court as a public policy maker. There are fundamental limits on that role, but the Court is still quite important.

The most obvious limit is that the Court decides relatively few public policy questions. The Court can be only a minor participant in fields such as foreign policy, in which it seldom addresses major issues. Even in its areas of specialization, the Court intervenes only in limited ways. To take two examples, it makes decisions on a small sample of the issues that affect freedom of expression and the rights of criminal defendants.

The Court does address major issues of public policy with some frequency, and some of its decisions mandate significant changes in policy. The impact of these decisions, however, is mediated by the actions of other institutions and individuals. A ruling that public schools must eliminate organized prayer does not guarantee that those observances will disappear. Congress has reversed several of the Court's interpretations of civil rights laws. And the impact of the Court's decisions on issues such as abortion depends on the actions of people who play a variety of roles in and out of government.

These limitations must be balanced against the Court's strengths. Certainly, a great many Supreme Court decisions have significant effects. The Court influences business practices and the balance of power between labor and management. It affects the state of civil liberties through its rulings on an array of constitutional issues. Its decisions on capital punishment are literally a matter of life and death for some people.

The Court's impact is exemplified by its decisions about the political process in the last few decades. Its decision in *Bush v. Gore* (2000) resolved a presidential election. Its rulings about the drawing of legislative districts affect the ability of Republicans and Democrats to win seats. The limitations it has imposed on regulation of campaign finance in a series of decisions have helped to transform the funding of political campaigns.

The Court also shapes political and social change. Its partial opposition to government regulation of private business in an earlier era was ultimately overcome, but the Court slowed a fundamental change in the role of government. Although *Roe v. Wade* did not have as much impact as most people think, it has been the focus of a major national debate and struggle for more than four decades. The Court's decisions have not brought about racial equality, even in conjunction with other forces, but they helped to spur changes in race relations.

As the examples of abortion and civil rights suggest, the Court is perhaps most important in creating conditions for action by others. Its decisions help to put issues on the national agenda so that other policy makers and the general public consider them. The Court is not highly effective in enforcing rights, but it often legitimates efforts to achieve rights. By doing so, it provides an impetus for people to take legal and political action. Its decisions affect the positions of interest groups and social movements, strengthening some and weakening others.

The Supreme Court, then, is neither all-powerful nor inconsequential. Rather, it is one of many institutions that shape American society in significant ways. That is a more limited role than some have claimed for the Court. But the role that the Court does play is an extraordinary one for a single small body that possesses little tangible power. In this sense, the Supreme Court is a remarkable institution.

NOTES

1. Gerald N. Rosenberg, *The Hollow Hope: Can Courts Bring About Social Change?* 2nd ed. (Chicago: University of Chicago Press, 2008); Matthew E. K. Hall, *The Nature of Supreme Court Power* (New York: Cambridge University Press, 2011); Michael McCann, "How the Supreme Court Matters in American Politics: New Institutionalist Perspectives," in *The Supreme Court in American Politics: New Institutionalist Interpretations*, ed. Howard Gillman and Cornell Clayton (Lawrence: University Press of Kansas, 1999), 63–97. See also Thomas M. Keck, *Judicial Politics in Polarized Times* (Chicago: University of Chicago Press, 2014), chap. 5.

2. The case was *Knick v. Township of Scott* (3rd Cir. 2019).

3. *Archer and White Sales, Inc. v. Henry Schein, Inc.* (5th Cir. 2019).

4. See Jason Iuliano and Ya Sheng Lin, "Supreme Court Repeaters," *Vanderbilt Law Review* 69 (October 2016): 1349–1386.

5. *Moore v. Texas* (2017, 2019).

6. Brian Hallenbeck, "Mohegan Case That Led to U.S. Supreme Court Decision Is Settled on Its Merits," *The Day* (New London, Conn.), April 29, 2019.

7. Grace Toohey, "After 55 Years in Prison, Baton Rouge Man Key to Supreme Court Ruling Again Denied Freedom," *The Advocate* (Baton Rouge), April 11, 2019.

8. *James v. City of Boise* (Idaho Sup. Ct. 2015, U.S. Sup. Ct. 2016).

9. *District of Columbia v. Heller* (2008). The Court extended that right to the state level in *McDonald v. City of Chicago* (2010).

10. *Silvester v. Becerra* (2018).

11. *Snider v. City of Cape Girardeau* (8th Cir. 2014).
12. One example involves the Department of Education; see Erica L. Green, "Secretary Eases Church-State Separation in Education," *New York Times*, March 12, 2019, A14. The relevant decision was *Trinity Lutheran Church v. Comer* (2017).
13. U.S. Commission on Civil Rights, *Targeted Fines and Fees Against Communities of Color: Civil Rights and Constitutional Implications* (2017); Matthew Shaer, "The New Debtors' Prison," *New York Times Magazine*, January 13, 2019, 34–41. The first in this series of decisions was *Bearden v. Georgia* (1983).
14. *West Alabama Women's Center v. Williamson*, 900 F.3d 1310, 1330 (11th Cir. 2018).
15. *Cole v. Carson* (5th Cir. 2019).
16. See Richard M. Re, "Narrowing Supreme Court Precedent from Below," *Georgetown Law Journal* 104 (April 2016): 961–965.
17. See Lauren Maisel Goldsmith and James R. Dillon, "The Hallowed Hope: The School Prayer Cases and Social Change," *Saint Louis University Law Journal* 59 (Winter 2015): 440–452.
18. *CNH Industrial N.V. v. Reese*, 200 L. Ed. 2d 1, 7 (2018).
19. Seth W. Stoughton, "Policing Facts," *Tulane Law Review* 88 (May 2014): 876–882.
20. Ethan D. Boldt and Michael C. Gizzi, "The Implementation of Supreme Court Precedent: The Impact of *Arizona v. Gant* on Police Searches," *Journal of Law and Courts* 6 (Fall 2018): 355–378.
21. Joseph Crystal, "How Police Reinforce Misconduct," *New York Times*, August 15, 2016, A19.
22. Harrell R. Rodgers Jr. and Charles S. Bullock III, *Law and Social Change: Civil Rights Laws and Their Consequences* (New York: McGraw-Hill, 1972), 75.
23. The decision was *Cooper v. Aaron* (1958).
24. *Green v. School Board* (1968); *Alexander v. Holmes County Board of Education* (1969).
25. *Brady v. Maryland*, 373 U.S. 83, 87 (1963).
26. Adam M. Gershowitz, "The Challenge of Convincing Ethical Prosecutors That Their Profession Has a *Brady* Problem," *Ohio State Journal of Criminal Law* 16 (Spring 2019): 310–311.
27. Radley Balko, "The Jaw-Dropping Police/Prosecutor Scandal in Orange County, Calif.," *Washington Post*, July 13, 2015; "Justice Gone Wrong in New Orleans," *Washington Post*, October 20, 2015, A22; Michael Wines, "Lawyer Cites 45 Cases of Prosecutor Misconduct," *New York Times*, January 18, 2018, A18.
28. See David Keenan, Deborah Jane Cooper, David Lebowitz, and Tamar Larar, "The Myth of Prosecutorial Accountability after *Connick v. Thompson*: Why Existing Professional Responsibility Measures Cannot Protect Against Prosecutorial Misconduct," *Yale Law Journal Online* 121 (2011): 203–265.
29. Evan Sernoffsky, "S.F. Prosecutor Who Allegedly Hid Evidence in Four Cases Fired," *San Francisco Chronicle*, December 8, 2017, D1; Pamela Colloff, "Jail Time May Be the Least of Ken Anderson's Problems," *Texas Monthly*, November 14, 2013; Jan Ransom and Ashley Southall, "If Prosecutors Go Bad, a New Commission Could Rein Them In," *New York Times*, April 6, 2019, A17.
30. See Shawn Musgrave, "Scant Discipline Follows Prosecutors' Impropriety in Massachusetts," *WGBH News*, March 6, 2017, https://www.wgbh.org/news/2017/03/06/local-news/scant-discipline-follows-prosecutors-impropriety-massachusetts.
31. *United States v. Bagley* (1985); *Turner v. United States* (2017).
32. Beth Schwartzapfel, "Videos Withheld, Leading Suspects to Accept Prison," *New York Times*, August 8, 2017, A1.
33. *Costanza v. Caldwell*, 167 So. 3d 619, 622 (La. Sup. Ct. 2015).

34. *Conde Vidal v. Garcia-Padilla* (D.P.R. 2016).

35. Alan Blinder, "Alabama Judge Orders a Halt to Gay Marriages," *New York Times*, January 7, 2016, A12.

36. *In re: Conde-Dival*, 818 F.3d 765, 766 (1st Cir. 2016).

37. Alan Blinder and Tamar Lewin, "Clerk Chooses Jail Over Deal on Gay Unions," *New York Times*, September 4, 2015, A1.

38. Campbell Robertson, "Chief Justice in Alabama Is Suspended a Second Time," *New York Times*, October 1, 2016, A9.

39. Matt Stevens, "State Must Pay Legal Fees in Clerk Case," *New York Times*, July 22, 2017, A12.

40. Kim Chandler, "Getting Married in Alabama? Changes Coming to the Process That You Need to Know," *Montgomery Advertiser*, August 21, 2019.

41. *Pidgeon v. Turner* (Texas Sup. Ct. 2017).

42. Examples include *Dvash-Banks v. Pompeo* (C.D. Calif. 2019) and *Henderson v. Box* (7th Cir. 2020).

43. Hall, *The Nature of Supreme Court Power*.

44. Matthew R. Christiansen and William N. Eskridge Jr., "Congressional Overrides of Supreme Court Statutory Interpretation Decisions, 1967–2011," *Texas Law Review* 92 (2014): 1317–1541.

45. Bethany Blackstone and Greg Goelzhauser, "Congressional Responses to the Supreme Court's Constitutional and Statutory Decisions," *Justice System Journal* 40 (2019): 101. See James Buatti and Richard L. Hasen, "Conscious Congressional Overriding of the Supreme Court, Gridlock, and Partisan Politics," *Texas Law Review* 93 (2015): 263–288.

46. *Midland Funding, LLC v. Johnson*, 197 L. Ed. 2d 790, 805 (2017).

47. *Obduskey v. McCarthy & Holthus LLP*, 203 L. Ed. 2d 390, 401 (2019). See Douglas Rice, "Placing the Ball in Congress' Court: Supreme Court Requests for Congressional Action," *American Politics Research* 47 (2019): 803–831.

48. Richard E. Custin, "Congress Grants Military Members Partial Victory, but Feres Doctrine Survives," *The Hill*, December 20, 2019. The decision was *Feres v. United States* (1950).

49. Deborah A. Widiss, "Shadow Precedents and the Separation of Powers: Statutory Interpretation of Congressional Overrides," *Notre Dame Law Review* 84 (January 2009): 511–583; Deborah Widiss, "Undermining Congressional Overrides: The Hydra Problem in Statutory Interpretation," *Texas Law Review* 90 (March 2012): 859–942.

50. *National Federation of Independent Business v. Sebelius* (2012).

51. Blackstone and Goelzhauser, "Congressional Responses to the Supreme Court's Constitutional and Statutory Decisions," 101.

52. Stolen Valor Act of 2013, 18 U.S.C. § 704(b).

53. Louis Fisher, *The Law of the Executive Branch: Presidential Power* (New York: Oxford University Press, 2014), 205–207; Hall, *The Nature of Supreme Court Power*, 105–108.

54. *New York State Rifle & Pistol Association v. City of New York*, 18-280, Amicus Brief of Senator Sheldon Whitehouse et al., 18.

55. Adam Liptak, "Roberts Condemns Schumer's Remarks," *New York Times*, March 5, 2020, A19.

56. This discussion draws much from the catalog and analyses of congressional action against the Court in Tom S. Clark, *The Limits of Judicial Independence* (New York: Cambridge University Press, 2011), chap. 2.

57. George I. Lovell, *Legislative Deferrals: Statutory Ambiguity, Judicial Power, and American Democracy* (New York: Cambridge University Press, 2003), 162.

58. Tony Mauro and Marcia Coyle, "Justices Would Get Ethics Code Under New Democrat Bill," *National Law Journal*, January 7, 2019.

59. Clark, *The Limits of Judicial Independence*, 49–60. See Stephen M. Engel, *American Politicians Confront the Court: Opposition Politics and Changing Responses to Judicial Power* (New York: Cambridge University Press, 2011), chap. 7.

60. William G. Ross, *A Muted Fury: Populists, Progressives, and Labor Unions Confront the Courts, 1890–1937* (Princeton, N.J.: Princeton University Press, 1994); Jeff Shesol, *Supreme Power: Franklin Roosevelt vs. the Supreme Court* (New York: W. W. Norton, 2010).

61. See Charles Gardner Geyh, *When Courts and Congress Collide: The Struggle for Control of America's Judicial System* (Ann Arbor: University of Michigan Press, 2006).

62. John Wagner and Deanna Paul, "Trump Asks Lawyers if Census Can Be Delayed, Calls Supreme Court Decision 'Totally Ridiculous,'" *Washington Post*, June 27, 2019.

63. Adam Liptak and Michael D. Shear, "In Blow to Trump, Justices' Decision Backs 'Dreamers,'" *New York Times*, June 19, 2020, A1.

64. Paul M. Collins, Jr., and Matthew Eshbaugh-Sosa, *The President and the Supreme Court: Going Public on Judicial Decisions from Washington to Trump* (New York: Cambridge University Press, 2020), 116–123.

65. Chandelis Duster, "Trump Calls for Supreme Court to Reconsider Flag Burning Laws," *CNN*, June 1, 2020.

66. U.S. Department of Labor, "Application of the Fair Labor Standards Act to Domestic Service," *Federal Register* 78 (October 1, 2013): 60454–60557. The decision was *Long Island Care at Home, Ltd. v. Coke* (2007).

67. The letter and related materials are available at http://www2.ed.gov/about/offices/list/ocr/letters/colleague-201309.html.

68. Department of Housing and Urban Development, "HUD's Implementation of the Fair Housing Act's Disparate Impact Standard," *Federal Register* 84 (August 19, 2019): 42854–42863. The decision was *Texas Department of Housing and Community Affairs v. Inclusive Communities Project* (2015).

69. Executive Order 13843, "Excepting Administrative Law Judges from the Competitive Service," *Federal Register* 83 (July 13, 2018): 32755–32758.

70. Executive Order 13673, "Fair Pay and Safe Workplaces," *Federal Register* 79 (August 5, 2014): 45309–45315; Executive Order 13782, "Revocation of Federal Contracting Executive Orders," *Federal Register* 82 (March 30, 2017): 15607.

71. David Mercer, "States' Flag-Burning Laws Unconstitutional, but Persist," *Columbus Dispatch*, July 31, 2016, A3.

72. *Torcaso v. Watkins* (1961). See Holly Meyer, "Atheists Want Law Removed That Bars Them from Office," *Nashville Tennessean*, March 19, 2015.

73. Josh Rovner, *Juvenile Life Without Parole: An Overview* (Washington, D.C.: The Sentencing Project, 2019).

74. Theresa Waldrop, "Virginia Law Requiring Couples to Disclose Race Is Unconstitutional, Judge Says," *CNN*, October 14, 2019.

75. Helen A. Anderson, "Penalizing Poverty: Making Criminal Defendants Pay for Their Court-Appointed Counsel through Recoupment and Contribution," *University of Michigan Journal of Law Reform* 42 (Winter 2009): 323–380; Mark Walker, "In S.D., Right to an Attorney Comes with a Price," *Sioux Falls Argus Leader*, March 8, 2016.

76. Gail Cole, "Online Sales Taxes: Will Every State Tax Out-of-State Sellers by End of 2019?" *CPA Practice Advisor*, July 2, 2019, https://www.cpapracticeadvisor.com/sales-tax-compliance/article/21087042/online-sales-taxes-will-every-state-tax-outofstate-sellers-by-end-of-2019.

77. "Legislative Tracker: Sports Betting," *Legal Sports Report*, May 19, 2020, https://www.legalsportsreport.com/sportsbetting-bill-tracker/.

78. Michael Cooper, "After Ruling, States Rush to Enact Voting Laws," *New York Times*, July 6, 2013, A9.

79. *North Carolina State Conference of the NAACP v. McCrory* (4th Cir. 2016).

80. Anne Ryman and Matt Wynn, "Anti-Abortion Wave Swelled for Decade," *USA Today*, June 21, 2019, 1A, 3A.

81. Lee Epstein and Joseph F. Kobylka, *The Supreme Court and Legal Change: Abortion and the Death Penalty* (Chapel Hill: University of North Carolina Press, 1992), 87.

82. Lizette Alvarez, "Florida Senate Backs Bill Making It Harder for Juries to Sentence Someone to Die," *New York Times*, March 4, 2016, A10. The decision was *Hurst v. Florida* (2016).

83. Carol S. Steiker and Jordan M. Steiker, *Courting Death: The Supreme Court and Capital Punishment* (Cambridge, Mass.: Harvard University Press, 2016), 227–228.

84. *Hall v. Florida* (2014); *Moore v. Texas* (2017, 2019).

85. Alexander J. S. Colvin, *The Growing Use of Mandatory Arbitration* (Washington, D.C.: Economic Policy Institute, 2018), 5. The most recent of these decisions was *Epic Systems Corporation v. Lewis* (2018).

86. The decision was *Rucho v. Common Cause* (2019).

87. Tilman Klumpp, Hugo M. Mialon, and Michael A. Williams, "The Business of American Democracy: *Citizens United*, Independent Spending, and Elections," *Journal of Law & Economics* 59 (February 2016): 1–44; Wendy L. Hansen and Michael S. Rocca, "The Impact of *Citizens United* on Large Corporations and Their Employees," *Political Research Quarterly* 72 (June 2019): 403–419; Anna Harvey, "Is Campaign Spending a Cause or an Effect? Reexamining the Empirical Foundations of *Buckley v. Valeo* (1976)," *Supreme Court Economic Review* 27 (2019): 67–110; Anna Harvey and Taylor Mattia, "Does Money Have a Conservative Bias? Estimating the Causal Impact of *Citizens United* on State Legislative Preferences," *Public Choice*, published ahead of print, October 9, 2019.

88. Austan Goolsbee, "In a World Without Borders: The Impact of Taxes on Internet Commerce," *Quarterly Journal of Economics* 115 (May 2000): 561–576; William F. Fox, "Inability to Collect Sales Tax on Remote Sales Still Harms the Economy," *State Tax Notes*, November 6, 2017, 575–581.

89. Robert S. Schwartz, "It's the 30th Anniversary of the Supreme Court Monumental Decision About Betamax," *Slate*, January 17, 2014.

90. George C. Thomas III and Richard A. Leo, "The Effects of *Miranda v. Arizona*: 'Embedded' in Our National Culture?" *Crime and Justice: A Review of Research* 29 (2002): 203–266; Paul G. Cassell and Richard Fowles, "Still Handcuffing the Cops? A Review of Fifty Years of Empirical Evidence of *Miranda*'s Harmful Effects on Law Enforcement," *Boston University Law Review* 97 (May 2017): 685–848.

91. "Union Members—2019," U.S. Bureau of Labor Statistics, January 22, 2020, 1, https://www.bls.gov/news.release/union2.nr0.htm.

92. Jake Rosenfeld, *What Unions No Longer Do* (Cambridge: Mass.: Harvard University Press, 2014), chap. 1; Nelson Lichtenstein, *State of the Union: A Century of American Labor* (Princeton, N.J.: Princeton University Press, 2002), chaps. 4, 6.

93. See James J. Brudney, "Reflections on Group Action and the Law of the Workplace," *Texas Law Review* 74 (June 1996): 1572–1580; and Julius G. Getman, *The Supreme Court on Unions: Why Labor Law Is Failing American Workers* (Ithaca, N.Y.: Cornell University Press, 2016), chaps. 1–3.

94. The earlier decision was *Abood v. Detroit Board of Education* (1977). The number of states with these statutes is from Steven Greenhouse, *Beaten Down, Worked Up: The Past, Present, and Future of American Labor* (New York: Alfred A. Knopf, 2019), 195.

95. Daniel DiSalvo and Michael Hartney, "Teachers Unions in the Post-Janus World," *Education Next* 20 (Fall 2020).

96. Guttmacher Institute, "Induced Abortion in the United States," September 2019, 1.

97. Michael J. New, "Analyzing the Effect of Anti-Abortion U.S. State Legislation in the Post-Casey Era," *State Politics & Policy Quarterly* 11 (March 2011): 28–47.

98. See Elizabeth Nash and Joerg Dreweke, "The U.S. Abortion Rate Continues to Drop: Once Again, State Abortion Restrictions Are Not the Main Driver," *Guttmacher Policy Review* 22 (2019): 41–45.

99. The differing views about the role of *Roe* in mobilization of the pro-life movement are discussed in Linda Greenhouse and Reva B. Siegel, "Before (and After) *Roe v. Wade*: New Questions about Backlash," *Yale Law Journal* 120 (June 2011): 100–159.

100. The growth in segregation is discussed in Erica Frankenberg, Jongyeon Ee, Jennifer B. Ayscue, and Gary Orfield, "Harming Our Common Future: America's Segregated Schools 65 Years after *Brown*," The Civil Rights Project, University of California at Los Angeles, 2019, https://www.civilrightsproject.ucla.edu/research/k-12-education/integration-and-diversity/harming-our-common-future-americas-segregated-schools-65-years-after-brown.

101. On the effects of Title VII, see Gavin Wright, "The Regional Economic Impact of the Civil Rights Act of 1964," *Boston University Law Review* 95 (May 2015): 764–778; and Joni Hersch and Jennifer Bennett Shinall, "Fifty Years Later: The Legacy of the Civil Rights Act of 1964," *Journal of Policy Analysis and Management* 34 (Spring 2015): 431–436. The key decision on affirmative action was *United Steelworkers v. Weber* (1979); the key decision on disparate impact was *Griggs v. Duke Power Company* (1971).

102. Justin Driver, *The Schoolhouse Gate: Public Education, the Supreme Court, and the Battle for the American Mind* (New York: Pantheon, 2018), 312.

103. Office of the Press Secretary, The White House, "Presidential Proclamation—60th Anniversary of *Brown v. Board of Education*," May 15, 2014, https://obamawhitehouse.archives.gov/the-press-office/2014/05/15/presidential-proclamation-60th-anniversary-brown-v-board-education.

GLOSSARY OF LEGAL TERMS

Affirm: In an appellate court, to reach a decision that agrees with the outcome for the parties to the case in the lower court whose decision is being reviewed.

Amicus curiae: "Friend of the court." A person, private group or institution, or government agency that is not a party to a case but that participates in the case at the invitation of the court or, far more often, on its own initiative. That participation is usually in the form of a brief, but amici in the Supreme Court (most often, the federal government) sometimes participate in oral argument.

Appeal: In general, a case brought to a higher court for review. In the Supreme Court, a small number of cases are designated as appeals under federal law. These cases fall under the Court's mandatory jurisdiction, so the Court must reach some kind of decision on the merits.

Appellant: The party that appeals a lower-court decision to a higher court. In the Supreme Court, the parties to cases are designated as appellants and appellees in appeals, cases that the Court is required to hear.

Appellee: A party to an appeal that wishes to have the lower-court decision upheld and that responds when the case is appealed. (See *Appellant*.)

Brief: A document submitted to a court, usually by attorneys, that argues in support of one of the parties to a case. The Supreme Court receives briefs at the stage in which it decides whether to hear a case and at the stage in which it actually decides cases on the merits.

Certiorari, writ of: A writ issued by the Supreme Court to call up the record of a case from a lower court for a hearing and decision on the merits. The overwhelming majority of cases that come to the Court are brought to it as petitions for writs of certiorari. In turn, the Court denies the overwhelming majority of petitions for certiorari.

Civil cases: All legal cases other than criminal cases.

Class action: A lawsuit brought by one person or group on behalf of all people who are in similar situations.

Concurring opinion: An opinion by a member of a court that agrees with the outcome for the parties in the court's decision but that offers its own perspective on the case. A "regular" concurring opinion agrees with the court's opinion as well as the outcome; a "special" concurring opinion disagrees with the court's opinion and offers a different rationale for reaching the same outcome.

Decision on the merits: A court's decision that addresses the legal issue or issues in a case. In the Supreme Court, after the Court agrees to hear a case, it then reaches a decision on the merits.

Dicta: See *Obiter dictum*.

Discretionary jurisdiction: Jurisdiction that a court may accept or reject in particular cases. The Supreme Court has discretionary jurisdiction over the great majority of cases that come to it, cases in which it decides whether or not to issue a writ of certiorari and then reach a decision on the merits.

Dissenting opinion: An opinion by a member of a court that disagrees with the outcome for the parties in the court's decision.

Habeas corpus: "You have the body." A writ issued by a court to inquire whether a person is lawfully imprisoned or detained. Habeas corpus actions are a means by which someone convicted of a crime, whose appeals of that conviction were unsuccessful, can bring a second challenge to the legality of the conviction in a civil case.

Holding: In a majority opinion, the rule of law necessary to decide the case. That rule is binding as precedent in future cases, though a court sometimes decides to overrule a precedent it had established in an earlier case.

In forma pauperis: "In the manner of a pauper." In the Supreme Court, cases brought in forma pauperis by indigent persons are exempt from the Court's usual fees and from some formal requirements. These petitions for hearings are called paupers' petitions or unpaid petitions.

Judicial review: Review of legislation or other government action to determine whether it is consistent with the federal or state constitution. Actions that are found to be inconsistent with a constitutional provision can be struck down as invalid. The Supreme Court reviews government action only under the federal Constitution, not state constitutions.

Jurisdiction: The power of a court to hear a case in question.

Litigants: The parties to a court case.

Majority opinion: An opinion in a case that is subscribed to by a majority of the judges who participated in the decision. Also known as the opinion of the court.

Mandamus: "We command." An order issued by a court that directs a lower court or other authority to perform a particular act.

Mandatory jurisdiction: Jurisdiction that a court must accept. Cases falling under a court's mandatory jurisdiction must be decided officially on their merits, although a court may avoid giving them full consideration.

Merits decision: See *Decision on the merits*.

Moot: A moot case is one that has become hypothetical so that a court cannot decide it.

Obiter dictum: (Also called *dictum* [sing.] or *dicta* [pl.].) A statement in a court opinion that (in contrast with the holding) is not necessary to resolve the case before the court. Dicta are not binding in future cases.

Original jurisdiction: Jurisdiction as a trial court. The Supreme Court has original jurisdiction over a few types of cases.

Paupers' petitions: See *In forma pauperis*.

Per curiam: "By the court." An opinion of an appellate court that is not signed by a specific judge. Per curiam opinions are sometimes quite brief.

Petitioner: One who files a petition with a court seeking action or relief, such as a writ of certiorari. Parties whose cases have been accepted by the Court through a grant of certiorari continue to be referred to as petitioners when their case is decided on the merits.

Remand: To send back. When a case is remanded, it is sent back by a higher court to the court from which it came for further action.

Respondent: The party in opposition to a petitioner. See *Petitioner*.

Reverse: In an appellate court, to reach a decision that disagrees with the outcome for the parties in the lower court whose decision is being reviewed. In the Supreme Court, according to the Court's Style Manual, reversal means that the Court thinks the lower court's decision was "absolutely wrong." See *Vacate*.

Standing: The requirement that the party who files a lawsuit have a legal stake in the outcome.

Stare decisis: "Let the decision stand." The doctrine that principles of law established in earlier judicial decisions should be accepted as authoritative in later cases whenever they are relevant to those cases.

Statute: A law enacted by a legislature.

Stay: To halt or suspend action by a court or by the executive branch. The Supreme Court sometimes issues a stay to prevent a lower court's order from going into effect or remaining in effect.

Vacate: To make void or annul. In the Supreme Court, according to the Court's Style Manual, vacating a lower-court decision means that the Court thinks this decision was "less than absolutely wrong." See *Reverse*.

SELECTED BIBLIOGRAPHY

General

Cushman, Clare. *Courtwatchers: Eyewitness Accounts in Supreme Court History*. Lanham, Md.: Rowman & Littlefield, 2011.

Epstein, Lee, Jeffrey A. Segal, Harold J. Spaeth, and Thomas G. Walker. *The Supreme Court Compendium: Data, Decisions, and Developments*. 6th ed. Washington, D.C.: CQ Press, 2016.

Savage, David G. *Guide to the U.S. Supreme Court*. 5th ed. Washington, D.C.: CQ Press, 2011.

Chapter 1

Davis, Richard, ed. *Covering the United States Supreme Court in the Digital Age*. New York: Cambridge University Press, 2014.

Gibson, James L., and Gregory A. Caldeira. *Citizens, Courts, and Confirmations: Positivity Bias and the Judgments of the American People*. Princeton, N.J.: Princeton University Press, 2009.

Hume, Robert J. *Ethics and Accountability on the U.S. Supreme Court: An Analysis of Recusal Practices*. Albany: State University of New York Press, 2017.

Peppers, Todd C., and Clare Cushman, eds. *Of Courtiers and Kings: More Stories of Supreme Court Law Clerks and Their Justices*. Charlottesville: University of Virginia Press, 2015.

Solberg, Rorie Spill, and Eric N. Waltenburg. *The Media, the Court, and the Misrepresentation: The New Myth of the Court*. New York: Routledge, 2014.

Zilis, Michael A. *The Limits of Legitimacy: Dissenting Opinions, Media Coverage, and Public Responses to Supreme Court Decisions*. Ann Arbor: University of Michigan Press, 2015.

Chapter 2

Abraham, Henry J. *Justices, Presidents, and Senators: A History of the U.S. Supreme Court Appointments from Washington to Bush II*. 5th ed. Lanham, Md.: Rowman & Littlefield, 2008.

Davis, Richard. *Supreme Democracy: The End of Elitism in Supreme Court Nominations*. New York: Oxford University Press, 2017.

Hulse, Carl. *Confirmation Bias: Inside Washington's War Over the Supreme Court, from Scalia's Death to Justice Kavanaugh*. New York: HarperCollins, 2019.

Kalman, Laura. *The Long Reach of the Sixties: LBJ, Nixon, and the Making of the Contemporary Supreme Court*. New York: Oxford University Press, 2017.

Marcus, Ruth. *Supreme Ambition: Brett Kavanaugh and the Conservative Takeover*. New York: Simon & Schuster, 2019.

Nemacheck, Christine L. *Strategic Selection: Presidential Nomination of Supreme Court Justices from Herbert Hoover through George W. Bush.* Charlottesville: University of Virginia Press, 2007.

Yalof, David Alistair. *Pursuit of Justices: Presidential Politics and the Selection of Supreme Court Nominees.* Chicago: University of Chicago Press, 1999.

Chapter 3

Baird, Vanessa A. *Answering the Call of the Court: How Justices and Litigants Set the Supreme Court Agenda.* Charlottesville: University of Virginia Press, 2007.

Bennett, Daniel. *Defining Faith: The Politics of the Christian Conservative Legal Movement.* Lawrence: University Press of Kansas, 2017.

Black, Ryan C., and Ryan J. Owens. *The Solicitor General and the United States Supreme Court: Executive Branch Influence and Judicial Decisions.* New York: Cambridge University Press, 2012.

Cole, David. *Engines of Liberty: The Power of Citizen Activists to Make Constitutional Law.* New York: Basic Books, 2016.

Collins, Paul M., Jr. *Friends of the Supreme Court: Interest Groups and Judicial Decision Making.* New York: Oxford University Press, 2008.

McGuire, Kevin T. *The Supreme Court Bar: Legal Elites in the Washington Community.* Charlottesville: University of Virginia Press, 1993.

Pacelle, Richard L., Jr. *Between Law and Politics: The Solicitor General and the Structuring of Civil Rights, Gender, and Reproductive Rights Litigation.* College Station: Texas A&M Press, 2003.

Chapter 4

Bailey, Michael A., and Forrest Maltzman. *The Constrained Court: Law, Politics, and the Decisions Justices Make.* Princeton, N.J.: Princeton University Press, 2011.

Black, Ryan C., Ryan J. Owens, Justin Wedeking, and Patrick C. Wohlfarth. *U.S. Supreme Court Opinions and Their Audiences.* New York: Cambridge University Press, 2016.

Black, Ryan C., Ryan J. Owens, Justice Wedeking, and Patrick C. Wolhfarth. *The Conscientious Justice: How Supreme Court Justices' Personalities Influence the Law, the High Court, and the Constitution.* New York: Cambridge University Press, 2020.

Brenner, Saul, and Joseph M. Whitmeyer. *Strategy on the United States Supreme Court.* New York: Cambridge University Press, 2009.

Danelski, David J., and Artemus Ward, eds. *The Chief Justice: Appointment and Influence.* Ann Arbor: University of Michigan Press, 2016.

Epstein, Lee, and Jack Knight. *The Choices Justices Make.* Washington, D.C.: CQ Press, 1998.

Hall, Matthew E. K. *What Justices Want: Goals and Personality on the United States Supreme Court.* New York: Cambridge University Press, 2018.

Harvey, Anna. *A Mere Machine: The Supreme Court, Congress, and American Democracy.* New Haven, Conn.: Yale University Press, 2013.

Hitt, Matthew P. *Inconsistency and Indecision in the United States Supreme Court*. Ann Arbor: University of Michigan Press, 2019.

Maltzman, Forrest, James F. Spriggs II, and Paul J. Wahlbeck. *Crafting Law on the Supreme Court: The Collegial Game*. New York: Cambridge University Press, 2000.

Pacelle, Richard L., Jr., Brett W. Curry, and Bryan W. Marshall. *Decision Making by the Modern Supreme Court*. New York: Cambridge University Press, 2011.

Segal, Jeffrey A., and Harold J. Spaeth. *The Supreme Court and the Attitudinal Model Revisited*. New York: Cambridge University Press, 2002.

Chapter 5

Adler, Jonathan H., ed. *Business and the Roberts Court*. New York: Oxford University Press, 2016.

Clark, Tom S. *The Supreme Court: An Analytic History of Constitutional Decision Making*. New York: Cambridge University Press, 2019.

Fletcher, Kimberley L. *The Collision of Political and Legal Time: Foreign Affairs and the Supreme Court's Transformation of Executive Authority*. Philadelphia: Temple University Press, 2018.

Kahn, Ronald, and Ken I. Kersch, eds. *The Supreme Court and American Political Development*. Lawrence: University Press of Kansas, 2006.

McCloskey, Robert G., and Sanford Levinson. *The American Supreme Court*. 6th ed. Chicago: University of Chicago Press, 2016.

Pacelle, Richard L., Jr. *The Supreme Court in a System of Separation of Powers: The Nation's Balance Wheel*. New York: Routledge, 2015.

Pacelle, Richard L., Jr. *The Transformation of the Supreme Court's Agenda: From the New Deal to the Reagan Administration*. Boulder, Colo.: Westview Press, 1991.

Rudenstine, David. *The Age of Deference: The Supreme Court, National Security, and the Constitutional Order*. New York: Oxford University Press, 2016.

Whittington, Keith E., *Repugnant Laws: Judicial Review of Acts of Congress from the Founding to the Present*. Lawrence: University Press of Kansas, 2019.

Winkler, Adam, *We the Corporations: How American Businesses Won Their Civil Rights*. New York: W. W. Norton, 2018.

Chapter 6

Canon, Bradley C., and Charles A. Johnson. *Judicial Policies: Implementation and Impact*. 2nd ed. Washington, D.C.: CQ Press, 1999.

Collins, Paul M., Jr., and Matthew Eshbaugh-Sosa. *The President and the Supreme Court: Going Public on Judicial Decisions from Washington to Trump*. New York: Cambridge University Press, 2020.

Hall, Matthew E. K. *The Nature of Supreme Court Power*. New York: Cambridge University Press, 2011.

Miller, Mark C. *The View of the Courts from the Hill: Interactions between Congress and the Federal Judiciary.* Charlottesville: University of Virginia Press, 2009.

Pickerill, J. Mitchell. *Constitutional Deliberation in Congress: The Impact of Judicial Review in a Separated System.* Durham, N.C.: Duke University Press, 2004.

Rosenberg, Gerald N. *The Hollow Hope: Can Courts Bring About Social Change?* 2nd ed. Chicago: University of Chicago Press, 2008.

Sweet, Martin J. *Merely Judgment: Ignoring, Evading, and Trumping the Supreme Court.* Charlottesville: University of Virginia Press, 2010.

SOURCES ON THE WEB

There are many sources on the Supreme Court on the World Wide Web. Some of the most useful websites are listed here. Access to each of these websites is available without charge. As is true of websites in general, the content of these sites changes over time, and websites sometimes disappear altogether. However, all of the listed sites have been maintained for many years.

Supreme Court of the United States (https://www.supremecourt.gov). This is the Supreme Court's official website. The site includes the Court's rules and the calendar for oral arguments in the current term. The website also includes the docket sheets for each case that comes to the Court, sheets that list all the briefs filed and the actions taken by the Court in a case. For cases filed since 2017, the docket sheets include links to every document filed in a case as well. The site provides transcripts and audio of oral arguments, the Court's opinions dating back to 1991, and other information about the Court and its cases.

SCOTUSblog (https://www.scotusblog.com). Along with the Supreme Court's own website, SCOTUSblog stands out as a very extensive source of material about the Court. Postings provide a great deal of information and analysis on cases that the Court has accepted and decided since the 2007 term and some information on other cases filed in the Court. The site includes links to briefs, oral arguments, and decisions. Also included are statistics on the Court's work and news and commentary on the Court. Material on each case accepted by the Court is pulled together under "merits cases," organized by term.

FindLaw (https://caselaw.findlaw.com/court/us-supreme-court). This website provides a searchable database of opinions in the Supreme Court decisions since its founding.

Legal Information Institute (https://www.law.cornell.edu/supremecourt/text). The law school at Cornell University maintains this website, which includes collections of Supreme Court decisions and other kinds of information about the Court such as previews of cases that the Court will hear.

Oyez (https://www.oyez.org). This site provides several types of information about cases and decisions in the Supreme Court. The most distinctive feature is a collection of audio recordings of oral arguments and announcements of decisions in the Court. The site also provides biographical information about current and past justices.

The Constitution of the United States of America: Analysis and Interpretation (https://constitution.congress.gov). This publication, also known as the *Constitution Annotated*, is compiled by the Congressional Research Service of the Library of Congress. It provides a highly detailed summary of the Supreme Court's interpretations of each provision of the Constitution, along with citations of the relevant cases and links to the opinions in those cases. Also included are lists of federal, state, and local laws that the Court has declared unconstitutional and Supreme Court decisions that have been overruled by subsequent decisions.

CASE INDEX

Case titles normally are followed by case citations. These begin with the volume of the reporter in which the case appears, for example, 374 in the first case listed below. This is followed by the abbreviated name of the reporter; "U.S." is the United States Reports, the official reporter of Supreme Court decisions. The last part of the citation is the page on which the case begins (203 in the first case below). There is a delay of several years before cases are published in the United States Reports, so recent Supreme Court decisions are cited to unofficial reporters. In this book, the Lawyers' Edition (L. Ed. 2d) is the unofficial reporter used for that purpose. Lower court decisions have their own reporters, including the Federal Reports (F.3d) for the federal courts of appeals and various regional reporters for decisions of state supreme courts. For lower courts, the year of the decision is preceded by a designation of the specific court—the circuit for the federal courts of appeals, the district for the federal district courts, and the state for state supreme courts. Cases that have not yet been decided and thus do not have citations are denoted as "pending."

INDEX

background, 13, 39, 52, 56, 57, 59, 85
as commentator, 58, 59, 75, 103,
113–115, 141, 142
as justice, 118, 126, 131, 132, 142, 207
as solicitor general, 85
Kahn, Ronald, 239
Kalman, Laura, 67, 68, 237
Karlen, Pamela S., 108
Kastellec, Jonathan P., 67
Katzmann, Robert A., 155
Kavanaugh, Brett
activities outside Court, 21
appointment to Court, 11, 12, 16,
27, 30–37, 39, 48, 49, 59, 69,
136, 216
background, 13, 39, 53, 54, 57, 58
as justice, 17, 69, 70, 97, 117, 131, 132,
151, 208
Kay, Stanley, 23
Keck, Thomas M., 226
Kearney, Joseph D., 106
Keefe, Patrick Radden, 25
Keenan, David, 227
Keith, Linda Camp, 188
Kennedy, Anthony
activities outside Court, 33
appointment to Court, 38
background, 39, 55
as commentator, 91, 99, 113
as justice, 16, 140, 143, 144, 186
retirement, 35, 62, 63, 135
Kennedy, John
response to Court decisions, 212
role in Frankfurter retirement, 62
selection of justices, 186
Kennedy, Justin, 62
Kersch, Ken I., 239
Khun, James, 158
Kimberly, Michael, 107
Klein, David E., 156
Klumpp, Tilman, 230
Knight, Jack, 156, 238
Kobylka, Joseph F., 230
Kopan, Tal, 157
Korean War, 212
Kristol, Bill, 154, 157
Kritzer, Herbert M., 155
Krog, Ryan, 158

Kromphardt, Christopher D., 24
Krystal, Becky, 25

Labor, Department of, 54
Labor, organized. *See also*
Labor-management issues
as Court concern, 162
in litigation, 70, 79
in selection of justices, 33, 45
Labor-management issues
Court policies, 169, 170, 177, 180
implementation and impact of Court
policies, 172, 207, 209, 211, 212,
218, 220, 221, 225
Lachman, Samantha, 157
Lamb, Brian, 66, 154
Landler, Mark, 66
Lanier, Drew Noble, 187
Larsen, Allison Orr, 82, 105, 106, 154, 155
Lat, David, 24, 25
Law clerks
post-Court careers, 13, 30, 62, 74
roles and impact on Court, 13, 18, 22,
81, 91–93, 99, 115, 119, 139, 143
selection, 12, 57
Law reviews, influence on Court, 146
Lawyers. *See also* American Bar Association
admission to practice before Court, 77
roles and impact on Court, 69, 72–77,
81–83, 99, 101, 114, 146, 152, 194.
See also Oral argument;
Solicitor General
in selection of justices, 32, 53, 62
Lax, Jeffrey R., 158
Lazarus, Richard J., 108, 158
Lebowitz, David, 227
Legislative veto, 208
Lempert, Daniel, 107
Leo, Richard A., 230
Leo, Leonard, 32
Lerer, Tamar, 227
Leuchtenburg, William E., 189
Levinson, Sanford, 25, 239
Lewin, Tamar, 228
Lichtenstein, Nelson, 230
Lin, Ya Sheng, 226
Lincoln, Abraham, Court's review of
actions, 171

CPSIA information can be obtained
at www.ICGtesting.com
Printed in the USA
BVHW031231220722
642380BV00003B/4